EMPLOYEE ENGAGEMENT AND HR INITIATIVES

Edited by

Prof. B. N. Mishra

Prof. S. K. Tripathy

Department of PMIR

Utkal University, Vanivihar

Bhubaneswar-751 004

Himalaya Publishing House

MUMBAI • NEW DELHI • NAGPUR • BENGALURU • HYDERABAD • CHENNAI • PUNE • LUCKNOW • AHMEDABAD • ERNAKULAM • BHUBANESWAR • INDORE • KOLKATA • GUWAHATI

First Edition : 2011

Published by : Mrs. Meena Pandey for **Himalaya Publishing House Pvt. Ltd.**, "Ramdoot", Dr. Bhalerao Marg, Girgaon, **Mumbai - 400 004.** Phone: 022-23860170/23863863, Fax: 022-23877178 **E-mail: himpub@vsnl.com; Website: www.himpub.com**

Branch Offices :

New Delhi : "Pooja Apartments", 4-B, Murari Lal Street, Ansari Road, Darya Ganj, New Delhi - 110 002. Phone: 011-23270392, 23278631; Fax: 011-23256286

Nagpur : Kundanlal Chandak Industrial Estate, Ghat Road, Nagpur - 440 018. Phone: 0712-2738731, 3296733; Telefax: 0712-2721215

Bengaluru : No. 16/1 (Old 12/1), 1st Floor, Next to Hotel Highlands, Madhava Nagar, Race Course Road, Bengaluru - 560 001. Phone: 080-32919385; Telefax: 080-22286611

Hyderabad : No. 3-4-184, Lingampally, Besides Raghavendra Swamy Matham, Kachiguda, Hyderabad - 500 027. Phone: 040-27560041, 27550139; Mobile: 09848130433

Chennai : No. 85/50, Bazullah Road, T. Nagar, Chennai - 600 017. Phone: 044-28144004/28144005

Pune : First Floor, "Laksha" Apartment, No. 527, Mehunpura, Shaniwarpeth (Near Prabhat Theatre), Pune - 411 030. Phone: 020-24496323/24496333

Lucknow : Jai Baba Bhavan, Church Road, Near Manas Complex and Dr. Awasthi Clinic, Aliganj, Lucknow - 226 024. Phone: 0522-2339329, 4068914; Mobile: 09305302158, 09415349385, 09389593752

Ahmedabad : 114, "SHAIL", 1st Floor, Opp. Madhu Sudan House, C.G. Road, Navrang Pura, Ahmedabad - 380 009. Phone: 079-26560126; Mobile: 09327324149, 09377088847

Ernakulam : 39/104 A, Lakshmi Apartment, Karikkamuri Cross Rd., Ernakulam, Cochin - 622011, Kerala. Phone: 0484-2378012, 2378016; Mobile: 09344199799

Bhubaneswar : 5 Station Square, Bhubaneswar - 751 001 (Odisha). Phone: 0674-2532129, Mobile: 09861046007

Indore : Kesardeep Avenue Extension, 73, Narayan Bagh, Flat No. 302, IIIrd Floor, Near Humpty Dumpty School, Indore - 452 007 (M.P.). Mobile: 09301386468

Kolkata : 108/4, Beliaghata Main Road, Near ID Hospital, Opp. SBI Bank, Kolkata - 700 010, Phone: 033-32449649, Mobile: 09910440956

Guwahati : House No. 15, Behind Pragjyotish College, Near Sharma Printing Press, P.O. Bharalumukh, Guwahati - 781009, (Assam). Mobile: 09883055590, 09883055536

DTP by : HPH, Editorial Office, Bhandup (Megha)

Printed by : M/s. Aditya Offset Process (I) Pvt. Ltd., Hyderabad on behalf of HPH Mumbai

☞ From Editors' Desk ....

Employee Engagement is relatively a new concept which has been developed from researches on involvement, empowerment, motivation, commitment, etc. It refers to positive feelings of employees about their jobs and the organisations, and also the motivation, commitment and effort they put into their work. It is a real time effort by the organisation to effectively use the services of human resource to achieve its objectives, generating positive behaviour among employees in a competitive environment. The contractual relationship between employee and employer limiting the motivation to "how much I get" has been shifted to "how much we gain" due to effective strategies for employee engagement. It is no more a concept limited to employee retention but the organisational attempt to engage their employees by creating the situation where employees become emotionally and intellectually committed to the organisation, where they not only speak positive about the organisation, but also develop the desire to continue with it and put extra efforts for its success. Engaged employees identify themselves with the organisation and care for its success willingly contributing their discretionary efforts.

Employee Engagement has three related components cognitive, emotional and behavioural. Cognitive component includes employees' beliefs about the organisation, its leadership and working environment. Emotional aspect is related to employees' feelings towards the organisation and the leadership which contributes to develop positive attitude towards them. The behavioural component refers to the value added component for the organisation and consists of discretionary efforts engaged employees bring to their work in the form of extra time and energy devoted to the task.

Employee Engagement initiative directly influences the organisational result and also is influenced by the growth of the organisation, its leadership and the value addition experienced by the employees. It is a totality concept which is influenced by the questions like how do employees accept the organisation, do they find opportunity for growth in it, what are the incentives available to them, who are the people to work with, whether everything is transparent here and is there any scope for using the brain independently. If the answers are positive they feel to accept the organisation as their own and contribute more than expected for its success.

Realising the above, companies are developing strategies for employee engagement to generate the willingness among employees to contribute towards companies' success through commitment, loyalty and belongingness. These strategies include creating positive work culture, transparent communication system, better work relationship, effective incentive, opportunities for growth, freedom at work and effective leadership. The objective is to help the engaged employee to enjoy the work and be involved in the process and own the organisation.

The papers in this edited volume, "Employee Engagement and HR Initiatives" highlight on organisational initiatives towards employee engagement. Academicians and scholars have contributed article based on their research findings. Reputed executives have shared their experiences on how they do it in their organisations. Because the area is new, we found it relevant to publish the book that will contribute towards further research while helping the practitioners to work more on it getting new ideas from different sources. This is an attempt to bring the best out of theory and practice on the issues and challenges relating to employee engagement. We expect this volume to be of great help for all of them who are concerned with the subject.

We are thankful to all the contributors of articles published in this volume because it is for them this academic endeavor has been successful. We also thank Himalaya Publishing House Pvt. Ltd for taking the pain to publish the volume. The Department of PM&IR of Utkal University is determined to pursue its efforts to promote this kind of academic activities through industry academia interface with the cooperation of its well wishers, promoters, collaborators, alumni and students.

Dr. B.N. Mishra
Dr. S.K. Tripathy

About the Contributors

Prof. Dr. Guru Charan Patro, Former Professor and Head, Dept of IR & PM and currently Director School of Management, Centurian University of Technology and Management, Paralakhemundi, Gajapati, Odisha.

Er. Sonali S. Sahoo, a Student of Dept of Business Administration, Utkal University.

Prof. Dr. P.K. Mohanty, Former Director (Curriculum), Biju Pattanaik University of Technology and Currently Professor, Department of Business Administration, Utkal University.

Ms. Binita Panda, Asst. Prof. Department of Business Management, C.V. Raman College of Engineering, Bhubaneswar.

Ms. Leena P. Singh, Asst. Prof. Department of Business Management, C.V. Raman College of Engineering, Bhubaneswar.

Prof. Dr. Swaroop Chandra Sahoo, Former Professor, Department of Business Administration, Utkal University and Currently Advisor, Department of Business Management, C.V. Raman College of Engineering, Bhubaneswar.

Mr. Sukanta Mishra, Research Scholar, Commerce and Management, North Orissa University, and Currently working at M.D.'s Secretariat, Rourkela Steel Plant, Rourkela.
(e-mail: sukantmishra.phd.nou@gmail. com)

Dr. Chandan Kumar Sahoo, Associate Professor, School of Management, National Institute of Technology, Rourkela, Odisha. (e-mail: cks_pd@yahoo.co.in)

Mr. Sitaram Das, Lecturer, Department of Business Administration, North Orissa University, Baripada, Odisha. (e-mail: bhanu_narayan@rediffmail.com)

Mr. Sushovit Mishra, Management Trainee, EXIDE Industries Ltd. Jameshedpur.
(e-mail: shushovit.mishra@gmail.com)

Mr. Rudra Narayan Mishra, Head, HR/IR-Legal, Tata Steel, Jameshedpur. (e-mail:rudramishra1@gmail.com)

Ms. Signdha Mohapatra, Asst. Prof., Srusty Academy of Management, Bhubaneswar.

Mr. Bijaya Kumar Sundaray, Associate Professor, Regional College of Management, Chandrasekharpur, Bhubaneswar-23, Odisha. (e-mail: bijaya_callme@yahoo.com)

Prof. Dr. Santosh Kumar Tripathy, Professor, P.G. Department of Personnel Management and Industrial Relation, Utkal University, Bhubaneswar-4. (e-mail: skt_sm@yahoo.com)

Dr.(Mrs.) Padmalita Routray, Lecturer, Dept. of Business Management, Fakir Mohan University, Balasore, Odisha. (e-mail: proutray2007@rediffmail.com)

Dr.(Mrs.) Kalyani Mohanty, Reder, P.G. Department of Personnel Management and Industrial Relation, Utkal University, Bhubaneswar-4. (e-mail: mkalyani58@yahoo.co.in)

Ms. Kalpana Sahoo, Faculty, Asian School of Business Management, Chandaka, Bhubaneswar-12, Odisha. (e-mail: klpnshoo@gmail.com)

Mr. Nihar Ranjan Agasti, Faculty, Asian School of Business Management, Chandaka, Bhubaneswar-12, Odisha. (e-mail: niharagasti@gmail.com)

Dr. Sujit Kumar Acharya, Lecturer, Business Administration, Directorate of Distance and Continuing Education, Utkal University, Vanivihar, Bhubaneswar-7. (e-mail: sujit_acharya@hotmail.com)

Ms. Vandana Mohanty, Lecturer, Rajdhani College of Engineering and Management, Bhubaneswar-10. (e-mail: vandanamohanty7@gmail.com)

Mr. Chinmay Kumar Podder, Executive Director, Nilachal Ispat Nigam Ltd., IDCO Tower, Bhubaneswar, Odisha and Fellow, NIPM, ISTD and AIMA.

Ms. Tapati Nandy, Faculty, Institute of Business and Computer Science, SOA University, Bhubaneswar. (e-mail: tapati.nandy@gmail.com)

Ms. Barnishikha Das, Online Faculty, American Hospitality Academy, USA. (e-mail:barnishikha @veloxian.com)

Prof. Ramchandra Mahapatra, Faculty, Institute of Business and Computer Science, SOA University, Bhubaneswar. (e-mail: mahapatra.ramchandra@gmail.com)

Ms. Sasmita Nayak, Asst. Prof., Academy of Management Studies, Krupajala Groups of Institutions, Bhubaneswar. (e-mail:sasmitanayak_2006@yahoo.com)

Dr. Mahendra Kumar Mohanty, Manager (Computer), Regional Office, Food Corporation of India, Bhubaneswar. (e-mail:mkmohanty@gmail.com)

Ms. Lopamudra, Asst. Prof.(HR), Academy of management Studies, Krupajala Groups of Institutions, Bhubaneswar. (e-mail:imlopa11@yahoo.com)

Ms. Susri Sangita Mohanty, Asst. Prof. Rajdhani College of Engineering and Management, Bhubaneswar-10. (e-mail:zlalit@yahoo.com)

Ms. Swati Mishra, Lecturer(HR), United School of Business Management, Bhubaneswar, (e-mail: swatimishra0674@gmail.com)

Ms. Lopamudra Hati, Lecturer(HR), United School of Business Management, Bhubaneswar, (e-mail:lopamudra_hati@yahoo.com)

Dr. (Mrs.) Pratima Sarangi, Principal, Innovation Business School, Khurda, Odisha.

Mr. Sanat Kumar Patnaik, Faculty. Rajdhani College of Engineering and Management, Bhubaneswar-10.

Ms. Subhasree Kar, Asst. Prof., Sambhram Academy of Management Studies, Bangalore. (e-mail: karsubhasreeyahoo.com)

Prof. (Dr.) Rayaguru Kumar Shri Mangesh Dash, Institute of Management and Information Science, Vivekananda Marg, Bhubaneswar-2. (e-mail:mangeshds@yahoo.co.in)

Prof. (Dr.) Biranchi Narayan Mishra, Professor, P.G. Department of Personnel Management and Industrial Relation, Utkal University, Bhubaneswar-4. (e-mail: bnmpmir@yahoo.co.in)

Ms. Tripti Jha, Executive (HR-P&A), Jindal Steel and Power Ltd., Anugul , Odisha.

Mr. Sitanshu Sekhar Das, Lecturer, Affinity Business School,Bhubaneswar. (e-mail:sitanshusekhar. hrm@gmail.com)

Ms. Namita Rath, Asst. Prof., Academy of Management Studies, Krupajala Groups of Institutions, Bhubaneswar. (e-mail:rath_namita@rediffmail.com)

Ms. Sujata Rath, Asst. Prof., Academy of Management Studies, Krupajala Groups of Institutions, Bhubaneswar. (sujatarath_1973@yahoo.co.in)

Prof. Ajit Kumar Sahoo, Dean, DRIEMS Business School, Tangi, Cuttack (e-mail:tuku.ajit@gmail.com)

Mr. Chandrakanta Sahoo, Lecturer, Bhubaneswar Institute of Management and Information Technology, Bhubaneswar-10.

Prof. (Dr.) Subash Chandra Parida, Professor, Department of IR & PM, Berhampur University, Berhampur, Odisha. (e-mail:subash.parida@gmail.com)

Miss. Priyadarshini Hota, Research Scholar, Department of IR & PM, Berhampur University, Berhampur, Odisha.

Mrs. Snigdhamayee Chudhury, Lecturer(HR), Bhavan Centre for Communication and Management, Bhubaneswar. (e-mail: manshita_2005@rediffmail.com)

Mr. Siddharth ShankarKanungo, Lecturer, Bhavan Centre for Communication and Management, Bhubaneswar. (e-mail:sid1982@gmail.com)

CONTENTS

1 Real Time Employee Engagement: Concept and Strategies

Prof. (Dr) Guru Charan Patro

ABSTRACT

The paper highlights the concept of real time engagement as a human resource utilization strategy which assumed importance in the context of the imperatives of global competition. First the issues underlying the nature of individual employees in relation to work/job; the group processes and dynamics; and organization conditions are highl:ghted. It is attempted to briefly highlight the three pronged strategies focusing on individual employee, the groups and the organization. However, the paper takes the assumption that it is ultimately the organization's responsibility to use the potential of individuals and dovetail the energy of groups towards achievement of organizational objectives. The HR practices, team building processes, organizational culture, knowledge management and communication systems and other strategies are discussed as possible action plans for real time employee engagement.

CONCEPT

Employee Engagement is a real time exercise by the organization to effectively use the services of its human resource in relation to its objectives, resources, and competitive environment. Earlier it was conceived as a contractual relationship between employee and employer explaining the terms and conditions of employment. With the onset of globalization, many organizations, in their endeavor to cope with the challenges of change and competition, found redundancy in human resource structure and systems. They first went for HR rightsizing. It was followed by strengthening the practices of HR utilization. It is in this second phase of HR utilization that the real time employee engagement assumed strategic importance.

The seminal principles of real time employee engagement are as follows:

- Real time employee engagement rests on a tripod of individual, group and organization centric activities with ultimate responsibility being laid on the organization.
- The organization is responsible for finding work for the individual employee, for unleashing the potential of the groups and for making the organizational expectations known to the human resource.

- Individual's work need to be dovetailed into group efforts contributing to achievement of organizational objectives. This is the responsibility of the organization. Any failure located at individual and group levels are to be conceived as caused by the organization.
- Work shall be 'meaningful' to the individual, 'involving' for the group and 'profitable' for the organization. In this process it shall be an ideal 'win-win' situation for all.
- As the reality is farther from the ideal, organization has to continuously develop strategies for real time employee engagement.

Characteristics of Work

- Work is a remunerative activity which is performed at the behest of the organization. So any self serving activity is not 'work'.
- Individuals consider work as burden even though remunerative and hence try to do the minimum and if possible, avoid it. Work alienation resulting out of work avoidance is a serious malady, which need to be addressed by the organization.
- Work entrusted to and performed by groups run the risk of suffering from the possibility of "Everybody's responsibility is no body's responsibility". Therefore, work assignments, measurements and rewards are largely done at individual level.
- Any 'average' organization doesn't know what "a fair day's work" is. This is a truth as on today, though it was F.W.Taylor whose propagation of scientific management started a century back with this assumption.
- Work is shrouded in the cloak of 'job', whose roles; responsibilities; risks; and offers are defined and described by the organization formally. Even then, job contours are often blurred because of lack of perceptual clarity; the need for job overlapping; and organization's failure at real time job designing.
- For successful completion of work/job; material, human, capital, and technology resources get more prominence than two equally important resources namely 'time' and 'place (space)'.
- Work and work tools and processes tend to expand into 'time' and 'space' there by leading to wastage of all the resources.
- Work engagement in a work period takes off slowly, reaches a peak or crescendo and then falls down until an end spurt at the end of the work period. Therefore, it is not expected that one can work with same level of efficiency over a period of time.
- The organization hence has to go for real time employee engagement. This imperative is now realized as never before.

Characteristics of 'Individual' as an Employee

- Individual, as an employee, relates one's work to the organizational functioning through the job. Job sets the identity of an employee in the organization and Job description sets the boundaries of a job.
- Individual, as an employee, is caught in a quagmire of 'triple allegiance'- to oneself (including family); to the formal and informal groups; and to the organization.

- It is situational dynamics, which determines the potency of these three influencing forces. However, the ultimate decision to develop a 'zone of indifference' or to be fully swayed away by any one of these forces is taken by the individual basing on one's own perception of the laws of the situation.
- Individual, as an employee, tends to limit work performance and stifle potential either on one's own or at the behest of the group or because of experience in the organization.
- Individual, as an employee, expects work/job to be rewarding and satisfying, which in turn may shape one's commitment level to the organization.

Characteristics of Group Processes in Organizations

- Groups in organizations manifest in two ways namely, formal and informal.
- Formal workgroups are designed as work in organizations requires efforts of many people in a work area leading to job overlapping. Work groups interweave into departments. Inter-department relations along with hierarchy culminate into total organization.
- Informal groups spontaneously emerge out of formal systems to satisfy inter-personal interests and social needs of belongingness of its members. These groups are highly normative and are valued by the members.
- The formal systems cannot escape from the informal group processes even though the later could be inimical to the former. So, organizations attempt to integrate these two through teams, small group activities, quality circles, kaizen groups. In this way, team is the most positive expression of group process.
- Unions, as employee associations, have got recognition as a force to be reckoned with. These bodies shape the destiny of organizations by raising disputes and by collective bargaining process.

Characteristics of organization as employee engager:

- Organization pursues socially approved objectives for which resources are allocated to it. It also sets job designs at micro level to make employees engage in real time work that ultimately contributes to achieving the organizational goals.
- HR as a resource pulsates with life. Its engagement at the optimal level is impossible as it can resist, and stifle optimization of other resources. Organization finds a challenge here.
- Organization tends to feel that employees restrict their productivity and hence expenses on employees as a bargainable cost can be reduced. Employees and their unions, on the other hand nourish a notion that, profit maximization and competitive advantages as organizational goals are pursued at the cost of the employees' interests. This mutual mistrust is a challenge for organization in real time employee engagement
- Organization seldom gives credence to the informal group process. Even in organizing the formal workgroups and teams, it loses sight of real time problems. This failure to integrate the individual employee through a healthy group process is a challenge in employee engagement.

STRATEGIES FOR REAL TIME EMPLOYEE ENGAGEMENT

The concepts underlying real time employee engagement shape the strategies. The real time employee engagement strategies are individual, group and organization focused. Though these strategies are discussed separately; yet, they should not be construed as independent of one another. All are authored by the organization, only the target differs.

Individual Focused

Placement is an extended function of selection, where the right person is placed in the right job. In selection itself the best fit between the job and the prospective employee is attempted to be determined. In the placement phase, the job-person matching is taken at the real time level taking into account the human engineering, ergonomics and attitudinal aspects of employee behavior. It generates inputs for training and job design decisions. In India the system of 'probation' and 'confirmation' addresses to the issue of placement. But, currently this is almost a half-hearted HR strategy not having discernible impact on employee engagement even though it is the first step.

Induction (employee on-boarding & orientation) is the first step in micro HRD. Organizational policies, systems and practices are explained to the new employees who after learning those formally try to shape their skill and mindset to the requirements of the job and organization. It is a kind of acculturation process which integrates the new employee with the organization. Informal induction is imperative in any human organization. But, it could be highly negative if the new employee is fed with negative peer opinions. Therefore, formal induction shall be strong enough to influence the impressions of the new employee. Further, induction shall be at both organizational as well as social levels; because, work life and social life are equally new to the new employee. Induction can have an important and long lasting impact on the positive attitude of employee which would help in real time employee engagement.

The performance management systems (PMS) cut across a myriad of strategies like performance appraisal, competency mapping, and performance feedback with forward linkages to career planning and training. The PMS identifies both the strengths (competencies) and weaknesses (may be attitudes) of the job holder, in a non- threatening way and recognizes the potential of the employee to overcome the weaknesses. It gives appropriate feedback through a formal system of communication followed by counseling and mentoring to stimulate the employee towards better performance. It resorts to a developmental approach through training thereby substituting the traditional punitive approach of performance appraisal. Under PMS, real time employee engagement is much better.

Employee Compensation and Reward Systems motivate employees to engage themselves with committed zeal. The compensation systems take into account the time, effort and degree of difficulty involved in a job/work to structure wage and salaries in consultation with Unions. The incentives and other rewards take into account real time performance measures and score cards. As monetary rewards are not conceived as sole motivators of behavior, non-monetary rewards are also extended. Currently, systems are developed for group and team rewards.

Grievance handling and Disciplinary actions are mutually complimentary twin strategies for employee engagement. Richard P. Calhoon, integrating these strategies observes that, "Grievance is as much a control of the employee on the employer as discipline is the control of the employer on the employee".

Despite best efforts of an organization, and intentions of its human resource, the grievances and acts of indiscipline become obvious in organizations. Both are addressed at individual level.

Grievance is a complaint nourished by an employee against the decision of the employer. It may be justified or unjustified; expressed or latent; and is a potential industrial dispute. Grievance heard is half redressed. Therefore formal channels of grievance redressal do have an advantage. Open door policy of grievance redressal works in small organizations having small number of people and decisions centers. Model grievance procedure adopting a time bound step ladder system was suggested by the Indian Labour Conference in 1958 as a part of the Code of Discipline, which is in vogue in organizations. The Industrial Disputes Amendment Act of 1982 has prescribed for the formation of Grievance Redressal machinery in every industry employing more than 100 workers. But this Act is yet to come into effect as the rules are yet to be framed. Grievance handling shall be timely as the employee nourishes it for a specific period of time and any redressal beyond the time may not have the desired effect. A grievance need not always be redressed in favor of the employee. But the organization gets an opportunity to explain its stand on the grievance. This in itself gives a relief to the aggrieved employee.

Acts of indiscipline occur when the behavior of the employee is not in consonance with the organization's prescriptions. 'Hot stove rule' meaning; instant, constant, consistent, non-discriminatory responses to the acts of indiscipline is a governing principle. 'Principle of natural justice' meaning no one shall be condemned without being heard is another cardinal principle. Establishing the onus, intensity and outcome of acts of indiscipline lie with the accuser, i.e., the organization. The Industrial Employment (standing orders) Act 1946 and various judicial pronouncements have set out a well laid disciplinary procedure. The disciplinary procedure starts with the listing out of minor and major misconducts, which as per the law shall be clearly, widely circulated to one and all in an organization. The procedure also lays down the minor and major punishments. The process of enquiring into an event of indiscipline, establishing the truth by following the principles of natural justice, determining the adequacy of punishment are all laid down procedures.

Group Focused

Team building exercises are meant for harnessing and channelizing group energy into a reckonable force contributing to the effectiveness of the organization.If not harnessed, it can lead to disastrous consequences through informal group processes or unions. After the Hawthorne Studies identified the group processes in organizations and group dynamics theorists like Kurt Lewin, Bales further refined the understanding of groups; the group integration assumed strategic importance. Team building, small group activities in the form of Quality circles became popular methods of dovetailing group energy for organizational success. Embedded groups provided the much cherished comfort zone to the individuals as much as the propelling force to the organizational performance.

Team is an organized and purposeful association of likeminded people, who using their individual skills, aptitudes and efficiencies, contribute to the total effectiveness of the formal work group with which they are associated by virtue of being members of the organization, so that put together all can contribute to the ultimate success of the organization. Teams exist to achieve a shared goal. Members are interdependent regarding a common goal and they are bounded and remain relatively stable over time. Members have and assume the authority to manage their own work and internal processes.

Teams do not stand contrary to the division of labor and functional specialization principles of organization structuring process. Rather they work with these principles in conjunction with the imperatives of willing collaboration, cooperation, and coordination. Teams are group activities but not merely groups and collectivity of individuals. They are purposeful formal organization of small groups which endeavor for achieving commonly set out objectives in a distinct spirit of *'espirit de corps'*. It doesn't entail coercion of any type; rather it rests on the foundation of cohesion.

Significance of Teams

- Incubator of new IDEAS (Intelligently Developed Effective Action Plan)
- Performer of multi-disciplinary tasks
- Builder of Relationships.
- Relieving individual weakness with collective strengths.
- Promoter of learníng better practices and excellent performance.
- Strengthener of formal communication by beating the grapevine.
- Producer of better quality (output) at cost effective (input) levels.
- Reducer of change resistance by way of group adoption.
- Derivers of strength from competition driven challenge

B.W.Tuckman's 4 stages of team formation namely, Forming, Storming, Norming, Performing; Theodore Newcomb's proximity and propinquity principles; C.J.G. Gersick's inertia and activation phases of team formation ; Orsburn, Moran, White and Zenger's five stages model of team building namely; start-up, State of Confusion, Leader-Centered Teamwork, Tightly formed teams, and skill directed teams; M.Shaw's determinants of Team Cohesiveness comprising team homogeneity, team maturity, team size, team communication, team goals, perception of threat and competition, and team leadership; L.Hoffman's team roles such as Task-Oriented Roles; Relations-Oriented Roles and Self-Oriented Roles are some of the important theoretical constructs which give the inputs for developing team strategies.

Team building in fact, is the best group strategy for real time employee engagement as the control comes from the group and not from the organization. As employees cherish their image in the group, the acceptance of group norms becomes more willful.

Quality Circles (QC)

The spoils of Hiroshima and Nagasaki bombardment moved two quality experts of U.S.A namely Edward Deming and Joseph Juran who came to Japan to rebuild it on the quality philosophy. It is a known fact that Japan emerged as the quality leader in the World. Quality Circle is a typical Japanese Experiment which started in 1962 and its success made it a worth emulating strategy by organizations all over the world. India imported the idea of QC through Mr. S.R.Udpa of Bharat

Heavy Electricals in 1982 and since then industrial organizations have adopted them as strong strategies of problem solving through employee empowerment

QC is a group of 10-12 members drawn from the same work area who voluntarily come forward to discuss, deliberate, and suggest measures for the day to day problems faced by them. There will be a leader and a deputy leader in every QC nominated by the QC members. A management representative, not a participant in the QC, will act as a facilitator. The non members of QC though do not take active part, yet they are important because in the ultimate implementation of the QC suggestions their role is of paramount importance.

QC Techniques are Brain Storming exercises, Pareto Analysis, Fish-bone Analysis (Ishikawa Diagram), Financial Analysis, Statistical Presentations, and Management presentation. By applying these techniques, QC has addressed to many basic work related problems with creative and cost-effective solutions.

QC functions well due to the novelty of the concept, its participatory nature and practicality. But, once the initial euphoria dies down, QC participation becomes lukewarm. QC needs management support for its success as its recommendations need to be accepted by the management. This distances the Unions from QC, who play foul games for dissipation of QC.

QC provides scope for real time workplace problems to come to surface through the voluntary group process. It not only designs scientific methods of understanding causes and effects of those problems but also gives the opportunity to think of solutions of those problems. This could be one of the best examples of grass root level participation leading to real time employee engagement.

Organization Focused

Organizational Climate and Culture: Every organization possesses a typical climate and exudes a culture of its own. Climate prevails and culture pervades and permeates. Both appear synonymous as the indicators are almost same. But, in reality climate is itself indicative of culture of an organization. Both develop a pattern over years there by providing an image and identity to the organization. People learn and shape their behavior and response patterns keeping in view the organizational climate and culture. Work culture, is a people centered but organizationally relevant culture that determines the work values and performance efficiency of people.

Organizations are mechanistic in structure and organic in spirit. Organizational Climate largely emerges from the mechanistic product/service processes, technological, structural and contextual variables and reflects the perceptions of the people. Climate becomes visible and felt in terms of the nature of work activities, working conditions, employee lingua franca, and in segments of sub-climate. The synergy of these sub-climates ultimately indicates the organizational climate which endures test of time. Some events like industrial strife, accidents, absenteeism, and attrition may vitiate the climate, but an organization with strong climate can overcome them. Promoters of durable climate are corporate vision, mission and policies; managerial actions; public image, employee characteristics; union and industrial relations scenario.

Like air, culture is everywhere, but invisibly felt. The organic spirit of organization makes every organization culture specific. Culture is a set of shared values, beliefs, morals, customs, assumptions, traditions, ideologies, language, norms, legends, stories, anecdotes, arts & artifacts held by any entity namely society, organization, group and individual, which influence their activities and behavior.

Culture is built around heroes, symbols and values. It is transmitted from one generation to the other and leaves an indelible mark of uniqueness for an organization. Organizations on the strength of their culture get institutionalized as perpetual and immortal entities. People of all hues namely the corporate leaders, professional managers, shop floor level supervisors, skilled workers and others, are culture builders, transmitters and followers. Share holders, Customers, collaborators, competitors and other stake holders also shape their responses by observing the culture of an organization.

Organizational culture is reflected in the perception of people about managerial intentions and actions in terms of addressing to issues like equity, promoting team work, resolving conflict, encouraging risk taking abilities, unit integration, goal- directed orientation etc.

Organization exudes a dominant culture reflecting its core values. It also subsumes a set of subcultures typically department, shop floor, and even people specific. Corporate world is replete with instances of CEO influenced strong and weak organizational Cultures. The stages of cultural assimilation are pre-arrival stage, confrontation and encounter stage and metamorphosis stage.

Organizational culture can stimulate optimization of organizational resources by inculcating in people habits of reducing waste, ensuring quality, achieving cost-effectiveness and customer delight as performance goals. All these are achieved by subjective handling of resources. Thus, culture can condition the usage of subjectivity for objective purposes.

High levels of morale and job satisfaction through innovative, effective decision-making and executing excellence can be promoted by organizational culture leading to organizational citizenship behavior which exudes high levels of real time employee engagement.

Work culture is a sub set of organizational culture. It is conditioned by the personal values of individual employees, impacting forces of group norms and the organizational approach towards the human resource. A real time employee engagement cultivates a positive work culture in the minds of the employees by a judicious combination of soft and synergic approaches. (Jai B.P.Sinha)

QWL & Workplace Democracy: QWL movement has transcended from mundane working conditions and welfare measures to workplace democracy. The strategies of employee empowerment, creating and using autonomous work teams, descending participation i.e. workers' participation in work, are some of the QWL thoughts reflecting workplace democracy. Set into a three-tier process of representative democracy (participative management); interest-group democracy (collective-bargaining); work- linked democracy (QWL); the edifice of industrial democracy is considered to be resting on the last one i.e. QWL, which has been hither to neglected. (Eric Tryst, Fred Emery & Einar Thorsrud). Employee empowerment strategies obviously help in real time employee engagement.

Equity & Organizational Justice: Equity and more precisely inequity is a pervasive concern of any organization and its people. It emanates not only from the imperative economic differentials found in organizations; but also from the psychological fairness one relatively derives vis-à-vis others. Largest Good of the largest number of people, if is the concise idea of Aristotelian Social Justice; getting one's due is the motto of equity. Sense of inequity arises in the psyche of a person, when one compares the outcome of one's own efforts with the perceived outcome of other's efforts.

In organizations, employers and employees indulge in an exchange and perceptually seek a balance between what they offer and get. The employee gives knowledge, skill, time, physical services, experience, training etc. in lieu of employment, pay and working conditions extended by the employer. HRM is an instrument for balancing this exchange through dispensation of organizational justice. Organizational justice is composed of Distributive and Corrective justice. Distributive justice mechanisms of HRM distributes results among the employees such as pay, incentives, perks and benefits, career progression etc. as per ones due determined by praxis of performance appraisal, organizational positions, seniority, merit etc. With best of mechanisms also, it is not true that there could be no aberrations in distributive justice.

Corrective Justice intervenes here when feelings of inequity and cognitive dissonance appear loudly. The HRM processes devise intrinsically built warning systems & intervening systems to correct the aberrations. Grievance methods, suggestion schemes, dispute prevention and settlement mechanisms, amending the decisions on appeal are some of the corrective justice tools.

The third dimension of organizational justice, conceived in recent years, is the participative justice. HRM envisages for participation of the effected employees in the dispensation of justice. Transparency in decision making, employee involvement in decision implementation, and employee share in decision results are contemplated as methods of participative justice. All these facilitate the real time employee engagement.

Organizational justice has been an allusive goal. No organization has achieved it completely. The best effort is towards developing internal systems to ward off external interventions of judicature; and to keep the information open for the employees to know what and why of things happening in the organization. Knowledge itself empowers and helps in real time engagement. Knowledge management & Communication plays a significant role in this regard.

KNOWLEDGE MANAGEMENT AND COMMUNICATION

Knowledge capital is currently conceived as the most powerful instrument for having any kind of competitive edge. Innovation and creativity are expected from human resource now as never before. The potential and capabilities of human resource as 'knowledge workers' have been long recognized by Peter F.Drucker. Knowledge as 'the revolutionary wealth' (Alvin & Heidi Toffler) has made it a singularly pursuable goal for corporates and countries. The information technology has opened up unprecedented opportunities to generate, transmit, store, retrieve and utilize knowledge. But the main source as well as target of knowledge is the human resource. Knowledge can be theoretical and practical. Taking cue from the apt adage that, "theory is advanced by practice and practice is disciplined by theory", the intricate relationship between these two can be established. The real time employee engagement generates the practical knowledge, which if could be compiled and stored would be a rich warehouse of knowledge capital.

Organizational Communication systems are crucial to knowledge management. Information flow is central to any communication, be it at rudimentary inter-personal level or at organizational and currently global levels. Information technology has no doubt revolutionized the communication systems, but it has not substituted the human element. Communication is of, by, and for the people.

Organizational communication endeavors to in-reach the bottom of pyramid levels with its vision, mission, policy and goal statements while out-reaching markets, competitors and collaborators across the board. Thus, it acts as a nervous system working for sensitizing, activating the whole human and non-human aspects of the organization towards achievement of the organization's competitiveness, growth and development. Real time employee engagement is nearly impossible without the communication systems integrating the micro with the macro.

ENDNOTE

These strategies are only illustrative. Each organization can conceive distinct strategies for real time employee engagement, provided it realizes the potency of the employees as the repositories of path-breaking ideas. One thing is but sure that the whole gamut of real time employee engagement is a kind of self discovery for the organization.

❖❖❖

2 Correlates of Employee Engagement – A Study in CESU

Sonali S. Sahoo & P. K. Mohanty

ABSTRACT

This study makes an attempt to determine the engagement levels of the employees of the corporate office of the Central Electricity Utility of Orissa (CESU) and to find out the inter relationships among the variables used in the study. Data have been collected on a 5-point scale from 67 respondents. The average age of the sample is 37.37 years. Results indicate that the difference in opinions of the respondents on the basis of age, gender and position did not show any significant relationship. However there is a significant relationship between the views of the sample on the basis of the department. The study revealed that there is a strong correlation between organization engagement and organization commitment, organization engagement and rewards and recognition, organization engagement and perceived organization support and organization commitment and job engagement.

INTRODUCTION

Employee Engagement refers to positive feelings held by the employees about their jobs and also the motivation and efforts they put into work. It leads to positive employee behavior that leads to organizational success. The term was coined by Gallup research group and it has direct relationship with productivity, profitability, employee retention, safety and customer satisfaction (Buckingham & Coffman, 1999; Coffman & Gonzalez Molina, 2001).

Lockwood (2005) defines engagement as the state by which individuals are emotionally and intellectually committed to the organization or group, as measured by the three primary behaviors:

- Speaking positively about the organization to co-workers and referring it to potential employees and customers.
- Having an intense desire to be a member of the organization, despite having opportunities to work elsewhere.
- Exerting extra effort and exhibiting behaviors that contributes to business success.

Employee engagement means a person who is fully involved in, and enthusiastic about his or her work. Engaged employee's cares about the future of the company and are willing to invest the discretionary effort to see that the organization succeeds (Seijts and Crim, 2006). Kanrad (2006) states that employee engagement has three related components: a cognitive, an emotional and a behavioral aspect. The cognitive aspect of employee engagement encompasses employee's beliefs about the organization, its leaders and working conditions. The emotional aspect concerns how employees feel about each of those three factors and whether they have positive or negative attitude towards the organization and its leaders. The behavioral aspect of employee engagement is the value added component for the organization and consists of the discretionary effort engaged employees bring to their work in the form of extra time, brain power and energy devoted to the task and the firm.

OBJECTIVES

The present paper is based on the survey in corporate office of CESU at Bhubaneswar. The main objectives of this paper are to determine the engagement levels of each person in the study, the gender-age-department-position wise variations in engagement levels and the interrelationship among the variables.

THE ORGANIZATION

The Orissa Electricity Regulatory Commission (OERC) vide its order dated 31.03.1999 (passed in case no. 2/99, under the provisions of The Orissa Electricity Reforms Act, 1995) had issued license to Central Electricity Supply Company of Orissa Ltd. (CESCO) to carry out the business of distribution & retail supply as its licensed activity. The OERC revoked the license of CESCO with effect from 01.04.2005 and on 18.04.2005, it appointed Chief Executive Officer And Administrator (CEO&A) to discharge the licensed activity of Central Zone Electricity Distribution And Supply Utility (CZEDSU). Later vide order dated 08.09.2006,the OERC in exercise of power U/s 22 of the Electricity Act,2003 has formulated a scheme named "Central Electricity Supply Utility" of Orissa (CESU) (Operation And Management) Scheme,2006 for operation and management of the utility. Accordingly, all assets, liabilities, rights, proceedings and manpower as well as the license for distribution and supply of electricity held by CESCO has been developed and vested on CESU and it has been authorized to carry out the business of distribution of electricity in accordance with license conditions in respect of areas assigned to CESCO under revoked license has to abide by the directions of OERC from time to time.

METHODOLOGY

In the corporate office of CESU, there are 145 employees at present. Questionnaires have been administered to 90 employees up to the rank of General Manager, out of which 67 Questionnaires have been returned back during three days. Care has been taken to ensure the representations from all departments. The variables used for study have been picked from Kahn's (1990) and Maslach et al's(2001) model .Their opinions were ascertained on a five point Likert type of scale; Strongly Agree-5, Agree-4, Undecided-3, Disagree-2, Strongly Disagree-1. Few negative questions have been put to ensure correctness, for which the scoring pattern has been reversed.

The variables included in the study are job characteristics (JC), rewards and recognition (RR), perceived organizational support (POS), perceived supervisor support (PSS), employee engagement

(EE), job engagement (JE), organizational commitment (OC), organization citizenship behavior directed at individuals (OCBI) and organization citizenship behavior directed at organization (OCBO). The data collected have been processed using SPSS (version 16.0).

MEASURES

1. **Job Characteristics** were measured by four items with each corresponding to core job characteristics i.e. autonomy, skill variety and feedback from others.
2. **Perceived Organizational Support** was measured by seven items corresponding to the concern for employees, caring for their opinions and well being, extending help when needed, forgiving in case of honest mistakes and emphasizing goals and values.
3. **Organization Engagement** was measured by six items corresponding to the level of involvement in the job, intrinsic desired satisfaction, available opportunities for enriching cultural life and a high sense of identification with the organization.
4. **Job Engagement** was measured by five items corresponding to the involvement in the job, the time devoted, internalizing the purpose of the job etc.
5. **Rewards and Recognitions** were measured by five items corresponding to the recognition and appreciation for good work, challenging opportunities for performers, effecting promotions on time etc.
6. **Perceived Supervisor Support** was measured by four items corresponding to the concern for subordinates, caring for the wellbeing, extending help in the job when needed etc.
7. **Organizational Commitment** was measured six items corresponding to identification with the organization being forward to serve the organization, developing a sense of belongingness and developing a lifetime commitment etc.
8. **Organizational Citizenship Behavior** directed for individuals was measured by four items corresponding to helping colleagues in their problems, adjusting and accommodating others request for time off, assisting others etc.
9. **Organizational Citizenship Behavior** directed for organization was measured by four items corresponding to help in building organizational image, offering ideas for better functioning of the organization, protecting the organization from potential problems and defending it from criticism by others.

Organizational commitment differs from engagement in that it refers to a person's attitude and attachment towards their organization. Engagement is not an attitude; it is the degree to which an individual is attentive and absorbed in the performance of their roles. While OCB involves voluntary and informal behaviors that can help co-workers and the organization, the focus of engagement is one's formal role performance rather than extra role and voluntary behavior. Engagement has to do with how individuals employ themselves in the performance of their job.

Organizational Citizenship Behavior consists of employee behaviors that are beyond the call of duty. Examples include such gestures as constructive statements about the department, expression of personal interest in the work of others, suggestions for improvement, training new people, respect for the spirit as well as the letter of housekeeping rules, care for organizational property and punctuality and attendance well beyond standard or enforceable levels (Fry, 1982).

Organizational Commitment reflects the extent to which an individual identifies with an organization and is committed to its goals. It is an important work attitude because committed individuals are expected to display a willingness to work harder to achieve organizational goals and a greater desire to stay employed at an organization (Kreitner & Kinicki, 2006).

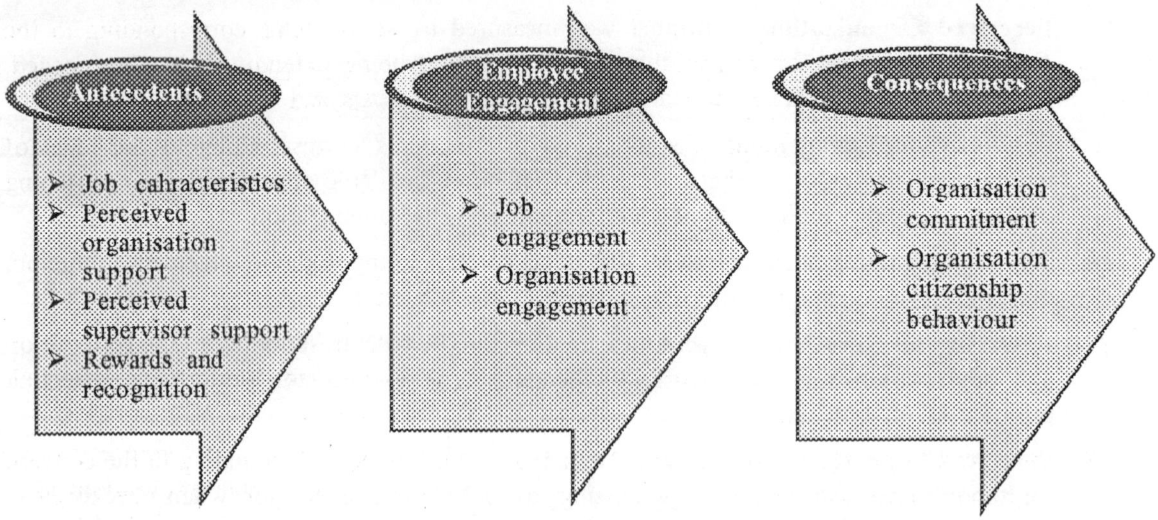

Fig. 2.1: A Model of Antecedents and Consequences of Employee Engagement

Source: Saks, Alan. M. (2006), antecedents and consequences of employee engagement, *Journal of Managerial Psychology*, vol. 21. No.7.

The above model clearly reveals that the antecedents lead to employee engagement, which in turn leads to consequences. But for this study, it is argued that organization commitment and citizenship behavior are very well linked to employee engagement and therefore are considered to be the correlates of employee engagement.

THE SAMPLE

The sample predominantly consists of 79% of male and 21% of female, 67% of executives and 33% of non-executives and about 42% are having experience between 5 - 10 years and 21% each are having experience of more than 20 years and less than 5 years respectively. The average age of the sample is 37.37 years. The department wise analysis of the sample reveals that maximum 25% belongs to Finance department, 13.43% to IT/ABT department, 12% to Construction/P & M and 10.44% each are from HR and Purchase department.

Levels of Engagement: Since there are 44 questions in the questionnaire, the possible minimum score is 44 and maximum score is 220.On the basis of the scores obtained, the sample is divided into three equal groups', i.e., low engagement, medium engagement and high engagement.

Table 2.1: Engagement Levels of the Respondents

Engagement Level	Score Range	No of Employees	Percentage of Employees
Low Engagement	44-99	1	1.5
Medium Engagement	100-159	20	29.85
High Engagement	160-220	46	68.65
Total	**44-220**	**67**	**100**

A majority of the sample, i.e., 68.65% belong to the category of high engagement levels.

Table 2.2: Variable wise Engagement Scores

Sl. No	Variables	Average Score	Minimum Score	Maximum Score
1	JC	15.16	4	20
2	POS	24.68	7	35
3	OE	21.79	6	30
4	JE	17.91	5	25
5	RR	18.07	5	25
6	PSS	13.92	4	20
7	OC	23.23	6	30
8	OCBI	15.83	4	20
9	OCBO	15.38	4	20

Though the average score against each variable is influenced by the number of questions asked (minimum and maximum score), the value is higher in case of Perceived Organizational Support (POS), Organizational Commitment (OC) and Organizational Engagement (OE) and lower in case of Perceived Supervisor Support (PSS), Job Characteristics (JC) and Organization Citizenship Behavior (OCBI and OCBO). The results are demonstrated in the following pie charts:

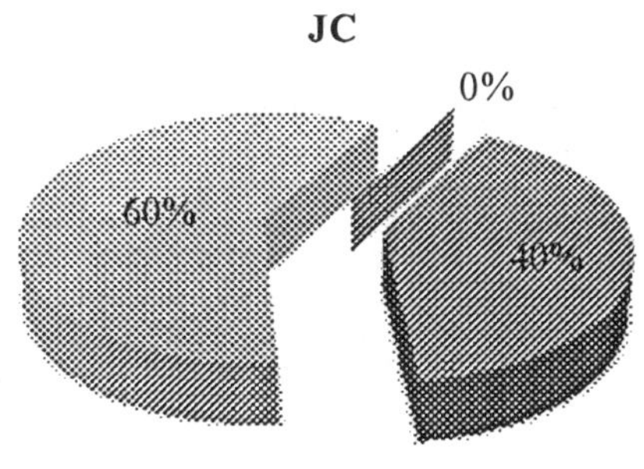

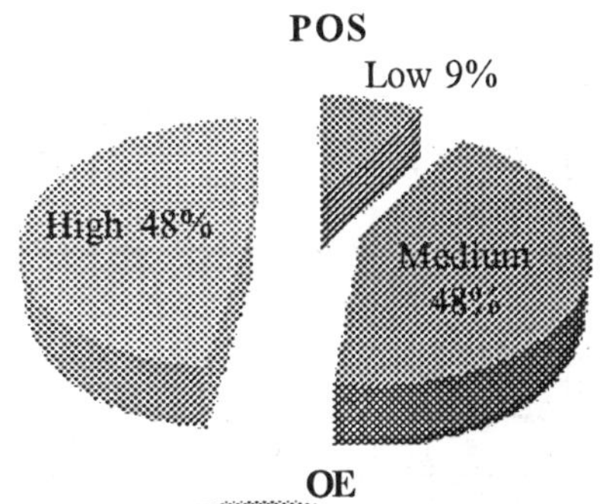

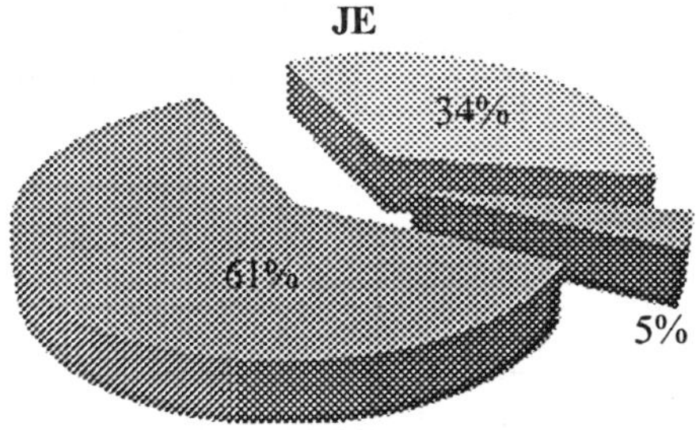

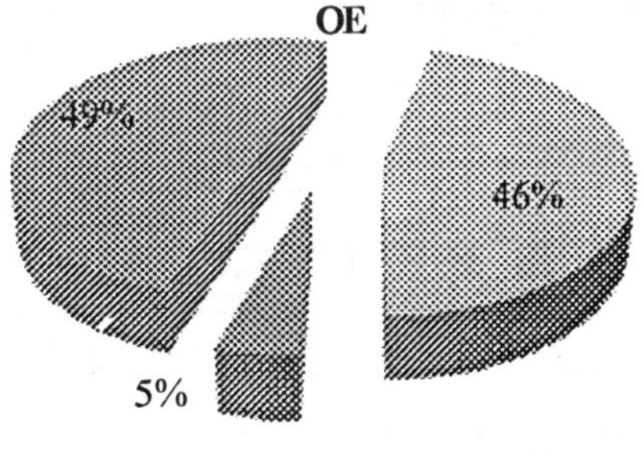

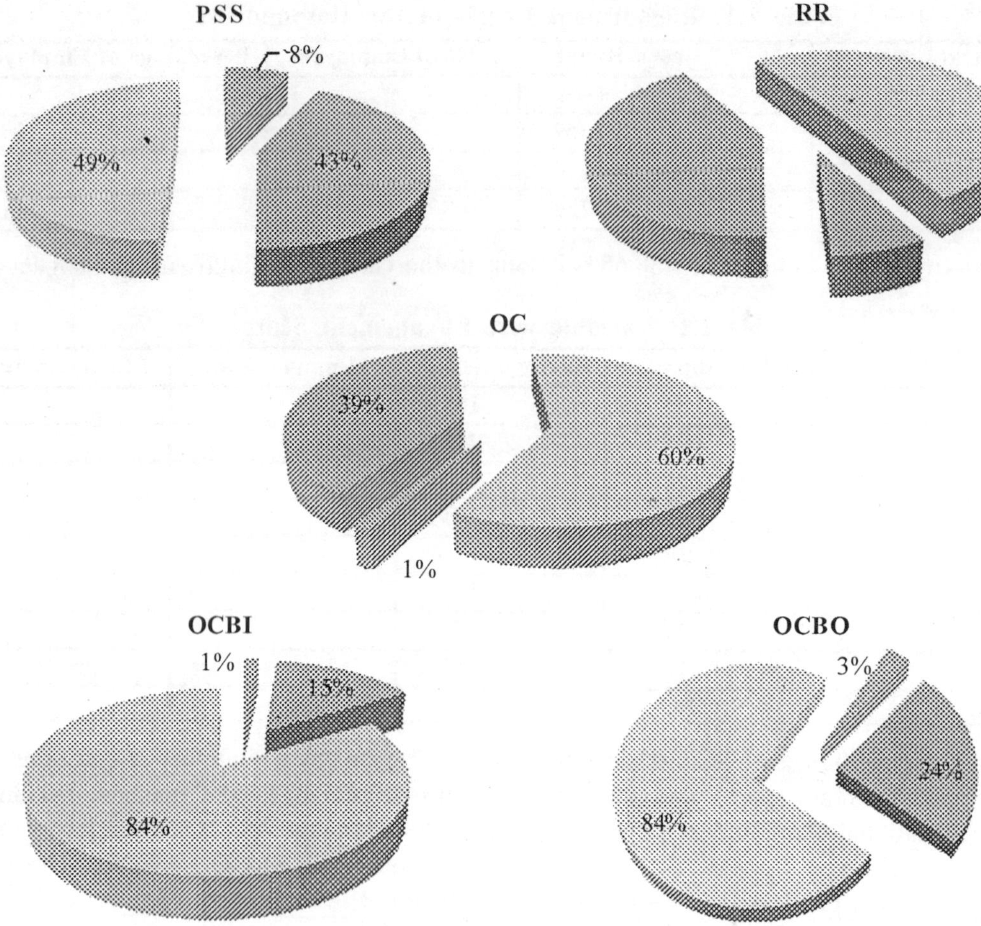

Fig. 2.2: Variable-wise Level of Engagement of the Sample

Table 2.3:Gender wise Analysis of Engagement Scores

	N	Mean	Std. Deviation	Std. Error	95% Confidence Interval for Mean		Minimum	Maximum
Gender					**Lower Bound**	**Upper Bound**		
Male	53	142.34	21.43	2.94	136.43	148.24	46.00	179.00
Female	14	144.07	14.18	3.79	135.87	152.26	116.00	171.00
Total	**67**	**142.70**	**20.05**	**2.45**	**137.80**	**147.59**	**46.00**	**179.00**

Table 2.4: One-way Analysis of Variance by Gender

	Sum of Squares	Df	Mean Square	F	Sig.
Between Groups	33.214	1	33.214	.081	.776
Within Groups	26510.815	65	407.859		
Total	**26544.030**	**66**			

The difference of opinions between male and female respondents is not statistically significant as revealed by the ANOVA test.

Table 2.5: Position-wise Analysis of Engagement Scores

	N	Mean	Std. Deviation	Std. Error	95% Confidence Interval for Mean		Minimum	Maximum
Position					**Lower Bound**	**Upper Bound**		
Executive	45	142.84	21.53534	3.21	136.37	149.31	46.00	179.00
Non-Executive	22	143.14	17.15601	3.74	135.33	150.95	106.00	171.00
Total	**67**	**142.70**	**20.05448**	**2.45**	**137.80**	**147.59**	**46.00**	**179.00**

Table 2.6: One-way Analysis of Variance by Position

	Sum of Squares	df	Mean Square	F	Sig.
Between Groups	251.547	2	125.774	.306	.737
Within Groups	26292.483	64	410.820		
Total	**26544.030**	**66**			

There is no significant relationship between the executives and non executives of CESU so far as the engagement levels are concerned.

Table 2.7: Experience wise Analysis of Engagement Scores

	N	Mean	Std. Deviation	Std. Error	95% Confidence Interval for Mean		Minimum	Maximum
Experience					**Lower Bound**	**Upper Bound**		
less than 5	14	140.79	13.12	3.50	133.20	148.36	116.00	163.00
5-10	28	139.36	26.33	4.97	129.14	149.57	46.00	179.00
10-15	6	155.17	11.75	4.79	142.83	167.50	132.00	163.00
15-20	5	147.60	18.24	8.15	124.94	170.25	127.00	175.00
More than 20	14	144.21	12.71	3.39	136.87	151.55	124.00	166.00
Total	**67**	**142.70**	**20.05**	**2.45**	**137.80**	**147.59**	**46.00**	**179.00**

Table 2.8: One-way Analysis of Variance by Experience

	Sum of Squares	df	Mean Square	F	Sig.
Between Groups	1448.854	4	362.213	.895	.473
Within Groups	25095.176	62	404.761		
Total	**26544.030**	**66**			

The one way ANOVA test of the engagement scores of different experience groups in the sample also did not reveal statistical significance.

Table 2.9: Department wise Analysis of Engagement Scores

	N	Mean	Std. Deviation	Std. Error	95% Confidence Interval for Mean		Minimum	Maximum
Department					**Lower Bound**	**Upper Bound**		
HR	7	153.57	13.06	4.93	141.49	165.65	133.00	171.00
Finance	17	144.18	17.30	4.19	135.27	153.07	99.00	175.00
Technical	5	130.00	14.50	6.48	111.98	148.01	106.00	141.00
Purchase	7	146.71	17.43	6.58	130.59	162.83	128.00	179.00
Commerce	6	153.17	8.03	3.28	144.73	161.59	143.00	163.00
Loss Reduction	3	145.33	25.10	14.49	82.96	207.70	124.00	173.00
Cons/P&M	8	141.12	8.52	3.01	133.99	148.25	128.00	155.00
Energy Audit	5	102.40	31.60	14.13	63.15	141.64	46.00	120.00
IT/ABT	9	151.33	9.36	3.12	144.13	158.53	134.00	166.00
Total	**67**	**142.70**	**20.05**	**2.45**	**137.80**	**147.59**	**46.00**	**179.00**

Table 2.10: One-way Analysis of Variance by Department

	Sum of Squares	Df	Mean Square	F	Sig.
Between Groups	11272.841	8	1409.105	5.352	.000
Within Groups	15271.188	58	263.296		
Total	**26544.030**	**66**			

RESULTS OF ANOVA

The ANOVA test of the opinions of the department wise classification of the sample reveals that the differences are significant. The respondents differed significantly in their opinions on the basis of their departments. Therefore the post Hoc test was applied to find out the significance of these differences in between the departments. Only one table showing the comparison between HR department and other departments is illustrated below.

Table 2.11: Post Hoc Test showing the comparison of HR Dept with other Departments

	(J) Dept	Mean Difference (I-J)	Std. Error	Sig.	95% Confidence Interval Lower Bound	95% Confidence Interval Upper Bound
HR	Finance	9.39496	7.28710	.202	-5.1918	23.9817
	Technical	23.57143*	9.50121	.016	4.5527	42.5902
	Purchase	6.85714	8.67338	.432	-10.5045	24.2188
	Commerce	.40476	9.02754	.964	-17.6658	18.4753
	Loss-redn	8.23810	11.19729	.465	-14.1757	30.6519
	Cons/PM	12.44643	8.39796	.144	-4.3639	29.2568
	EnrgyAudit	51.17143*	9.50121	.000	32.1527	70.1902
	IT/ABT	2.23810	8.17734	.785	-14.1306	18.6068

No significant difference was found between groups on the basis of gender, position and experience. But the difference of opinions between the respondents of different departments was found to be significant. Therefore it became relevant to apply Post Hoc test to analyze the significance of the differences.

Grouping variable	Impact on total score of Employee Engagement	Remarks
Sex	No significant difference between groups	p value of F-statistic 0.776
Position	No significant difference between groups	p value of F-statistic 0.737
Experience	No significant difference between groups	p value of F-statistic 0.473
Department	Significant difference found	p value of F-statistic 0.000

Results of Post Hoc (LSD) Test on Differences Between Different Departments

1. There is a significant difference between employee engagement of HR department and technical department (p value 0.016). Employee engagement is significantly more in case of HR department.

2. There is a significant difference between employee engagement of HR department and Energy Audit department (p value 0.000). Employee engagement is significantly more in case of HR department.

3. There is a significant difference between employee engagement of Finance department and Energy Audit department (p value 0.000). Employee engagement is significantly more in case of Finance department.

4. There is a significant difference between employee engagement of Technical department and Commerce department (p value 0.022). Employee engagement is significantly more in case of Commerce department.

5. There is a significant difference between employee engagement of Technical department and Energy Audit department (p value 0.009). Employee engagement is significantly more in case of Technical department.

6. There is a significant difference between employee engagement of Technical department and IT/ABT department (p value 0.022). Employee engagement is significantly more in case of IT/ABT department.

7. There is a significant difference between employee engagement of Purchase department and Energy Audit department (p value 0.000). Employee engagement is significantly more in case of Purchase department.

8. There is a significant difference between employee engagement of Commerce department and Energy Audit department (p value 0.000). Employee engagement is significantly more in case of Commerce department.

Table 2.12: Inter Correlation Matrix showing the relationship among the Variables

	JC	POS	OE	JE	RR	PSS	OC	OCBI	OCBO
JC	1	-.082	.418**	-.127	.525**	.265*	.335**	.073	.244*
POS	-.082	1	-.015	.077	-.265*	-.066	-.119	.022	-.053
OE	.418**	-.015	1	.463**	.807**	.697**	.809**	.533**	.618**

JE	-.127	.077	.463**	1	.262*	.413**	.351**	.436**	.394**
RR	.525**	-.265*	.807**	.262*	1	.636**	.760**	.497**	.582**
PSS	.265*	-.066	.697**	.413**	.636**	1	.674**	.491**	.554**
OC	.335**	-.119	.809**	.351**	.760**	.674**	1	.616**	.690**
OCBI	.073	.022	.533**	.436**	.497**	.491**	.616**	1	.706**
OCBO	.244*	-.053	.618**	.394**	.582**	.554**	.690**	.706**	1

**.Correlation is significant at the 0.01 level (2-tailed).

*.Correlation is significant at the 0.05 level (2-tailed).

The above table reveals that there is a strong correlation between organization engagement (OE) and organizational commitment (OC), between organization engagement and rewards and recognitions (RR), between organization engagement (OE) and perceived supervisor support (PSS), between organizational commitment (OC) and job engagement (JE).Negative Correlation exists between job characteristics (JC) and perceived organizational support (POS) (-0.82),between job characteristics (JC) and job engagement (JE) (-0.127),between perceived organizational support (POS) and rewards and recognitions (RR) (-0.265), between perceived organizational support (POS) and perceived supervisor support (PSS) (-0.066), and between perceived organization support (POS) and organizational commitment (OC) (-0.119).

CONCLUSION

The result of the study suggest that employee engagement is a meaningful construct that is worthy of future research. The results also have some practical implications. The managers need to understand the importance of social exchange for employee engagement. In particular, managers need to provide employees with resources and benefits that will oblige then to reciprocate in kind with high levels of engagement. They should understand that employee engagement is a long term and ongoing process that requires continued interactions overtime in order to generate obligations and a state of reciprocal interdependence. In addition, engagement needs to be viewed as a broad organizational and cultural strategy that involves all levels of the organization.

References

1. Buckingham, M. & Coffman, C. (1999), First break all the rules:What the world's greatest managers do differently, New York, Simon & Shuster.
2. Coffman, C. & Gonzalez-Molina, G. (2002), Follow this path:How the world's greatest organizations drive growth by unleasing human potential, New York, Warner Books<Inc.
3. Fry, L W, (1982), 'Technology-Structure Research: Three critical issues,' Academy of Management Journal.
4. Kahn,W.A., (1990) Psychological Conditions of personal engagement and disengagement at work, Academy of Management Journal, Vol.33.
5. Kreitner Robert & Kinicki Angelo, 'Organizational Behavior, (2008), Tata McGraw-Hill Publishing Company Ltd, New Delhi'.
6. Lockwood, N.R. (2005), Employee Engagement, SHRM Research Briefly Stated.
7. Maslach,C., Schaufelli,W.B. and Leiter, M.P. (2001), Job Burnout, Annual Review of Psychology, Vol.52.
8. Saks, Alan. M. (2006), Antecedents and consequences of employee engagement, Journal of Managerial Psychology, Vol. 21. No.7.

3

Employee Engagement (An Imperative for Organizational Success)

Sushovit Mishra
R. N. Misra

ABSTARCT

The research evidence across both public and private sectors supports the notion that staffs who are engaged, deliver higher productivity and organizational performance, which is visible through increased operating and net profit, improved customer focus, lower levels of absenteeism and higher retention. A successful employee engagement helps create a community at work place and not just a work force. When the employees are effectively and positively engaged with their organization they form the emotional connection with the company. Creation of "emotional ownership" is the key to keep employees motivated and engaged.

Woody Allen, comedian, screenwriter, and director, once said: "Eighty percent of success is showing up". If this was ever true, it certainly is not anymore. "Success today requires a good bit more than good attendance. Yet multiple studies in different countries and across industries show that the employees who are passionate about their jobs and the organizations in which they work are in the minority."

All over the world, the organizations are plagued by number of concerns such as rising cost, cut-throat competition, job insecurity and employees dissatisfaction due to several reasons. While attractive remuneration packages and perks are vital to retain employees, it may not necessarily motivate them to give their best to the organizations, if there is no sense of emotional engagement/ ownership towards the organization.

There is an old joke in which a CEO was asked - how many people work in his company and he responded, "about half of them'. Not so funny when you look at the following statistics and begin to realize how much time, energy and resources are wasted.

SURVEY REPORTS

At a time when the companies are focused on their growth path and looking to their work forces to achieve that growth, a new study of employees worldwide offers disturbing news i.e. just around 14% of the people are fully engaged on the job and willing to go the extra mile for their companies. A Gallop survey conducted in 2005 reveals that employees' disengagement cost about $300 billion dollars in an annual financial year to US economy. Another study conducted by Towers Perrins's HR Services Business in August, 2005 among more than 85,000 people working for large and mid-sized companies in 16 countries on four continents shows that there is a vast reserve of untapped 'employee performance potential' which can drive better financial results provided the companies can successfully tap into these reserves. Thus sustaining employees' engagement has become a great challenge.

The survey conducted by Towers Perrins shows that highly engaged workers believe that they can do and do contribute more directly to the business results than do the less engaged employees. For instance, 84% of the highly engaged employees believe that they can positively impact the quality of their company's product, compared with 31% of the disengaged. 72% of the highly engaged believe that they can positively affect customer service versus 27% of the disengaged. 68% of the highly engaged believe that they can positively engage cost in their job or unit versus 19% of the disengaged. Highly engaged employees are also far less likely to leave for another job than their less engaged peers. Worldwide, 59% of the highly engaged stay with their current employer compared with just 24% of the disengaged group.

WHAT CONSTITUTES EMPLOYEE ENGAGEMENT?

The engaged employees are not just committed, not just passionate or proud. They have "**line of sight**" on their own future and on the organization's mission and goals. They are '**enthused**' and 'in-gear' using their talents and discretionary efforts to make a difference in their employer's quest for sustainable business thrust.

A positive attitude is held by the employees towards the organization and its values. An engaged employee is aware of the business contexts and works with the colleagues to improve upon the performance within the job for the benefit of the organization. It requires a two way relationship between the employer and the employee. Thus, employee engagement is a combination of commitment to the organization and its values plus a willingness to help out the colleagues.

Ingredients of Employee Engagement

Definitions may vary but there is a broad agreement on the basics with regard to the qualities of an engaged employee. They are namely;

- A positive attitude towards and pride in the organization
- Belief in the organizations' product/ services
- A sense that the organization enables the employee to perform well
- A wish to behave collaboratively and be a good team player
- A willingness to go beyond the requirements of the job

- A desire to work to make things better
- An understanding of business context and 'bigger picture'
- Being respectful of, and helpful to, colleagues
- Keeping up to date with developments in the field.
- More innovative
- More committed to customer satisfaction
- Consistently go the extra mile

CATEGORIES OF EMPLOYEES

In an organization, there are basically three categories of employees depending upon their level of engagement.

Engaged Employees: Engaged employees are **'builders'**. They want to know the desired expectations for their role so that they can meet and exceed them. They are always curious about their company and their place in it. They perform consistently at high levels. They want to use their talents and strengths at work every day. They work with passion; they drive innovations and move their organization forward. They display outstanding level of commitment and loyalty to the work for the better benefits of the organization. They make efforts without distress meaning working harder and deriving satisfaction.

Not Engaged Employees: The 'not-engaged' employees are the **'task doers'**. They tend to focus on tasks rather than the goals and outcomes they are expected to accomplish. They want to be told what to do, so that they can do accordingly and say they have finished. They concentrate on accomplishing tasks vs. achieving an outcome. Employees who are not-engaged tend to feel that their contributions are being constantly overlooked, and their potential is not being tapped. They often feel this way because they do not have productive relationships with their managers or with their coworkers. Generally in an organization a higher percentage of employees fall into this category. They make efforts with distress (strain) i.e. working harder but with fatigue and anxiety.

Actively Disengaged Employees: The actively disengaged employees are the **'cave dwellers'**. They are **'consistently against virtually everything'**. They are not just unhappy at work; they are busy acting out their unhappiness. They sow seeds of negativity at every opportunity. Every day, actively disengaged workers undermine what their engaged coworkers accomplish. As workers increasingly rely on each other to generate products and services, the problems and tensions that are fostered by actively disengaged workers can cause great damage to an organisation's functioning. They are with least level of commitment and loyalty to the organization. They get distressed without effort and feel bad about it.

The Scary Statistics

The statistics on workforce engagement are shocking. According to the Gallop Management Journal's semi-annual Employee Engagement Index,

- 29% of employees are actively engaged in their jobs,
- 54% are not-engaged &
- 17% are actively disengaged.

DRIVERS OF EMPLOYEE ENGAGEMENT

- **Organizational Commitment:** A psychological attachment of an employee to an organization
- **Service Commitment:** The shared ethos of meeting customer needs
- **Job Satisfaction:** The date to day impact of work done and the immediate context within which it is set
- **Work and Career Commitment:** The importance an individual places on the actual work he does and the development of a career

Types of Employee Engagement

The 'engagement' has two components namely, rational engagement and emotional engagement. The "rational engagement" means the involvement, understanding and motivation of an employee in the job. The "emotional engagement" constitutes the attitudinal attachment of an employee to the company and the source of pride.

Emotional Engagement	Rational Engagement
" I am proud to tell others I work for my company beyond what is normally expected to help my company be successful	" I am willing to put in a great deal of effort
" The work I have to do is reasonable the success of my company	" I understand how my work group contributes to
" I am unlikely to look for a job in another company in the net 12 months	" I understand how my role is related to my company's overall goals, objectives and direction.
" I would recommend my company to a close friend as a good place to work	" My job provides me with a sense of personal accomplishment
" My company inspires me to do my best work	

GALLOP'S STUDY

The Gallop's Q12 format is very popular so far as conducting employee engagement survey is concerned. The said format primarily reveals the following twelve (12) aspects important to the employees:

1. Knowing what is expected
2. Having the right materials and equipment
3. Opportunity to 'Do What they do Best'

4. Recognition and praise
5. Caring for employee as a person
6. Encourages development
7. Employee opinion counts
8. Connection with mission of organization
9. Co-workers committed to quality work
10. Employee has a best friend at work
11. Someone talks with the employee about his progress
12. Opportunities to learn and grow.

WHY EMPLOYEES LEAVE AN ORGANIZATION?

- The jobs / work places do not live up to their expectations.
- Mismatch between jobs and the employees.
- Too little coaching / feedback.
- Too few growth and advancement opportunities
- Feelings devalued and unrecognized.
- Stress from over work and lack of work-like balance.
- Loss of trust and confidence in the senior leadership.

WHY DO THE COMPANIES PERFORM BADLY?

- Poor management
- Lack of growth and advancement opportunities
- Poor communication (top down)
- Pay inequalities and in-effective performance appraisal
- Lack of recognition
- Poor senior leadership
- Lack of training
- Excessive work load
- Lack of tools and resources
- Lack of team work

EMPLOYEE ENGAGEMENT COMPONENTS

1. *Career Support*

✓ "I have opportunities to develop further skills in my career"

✓ "There are clear performance criteria outlined for my job"

✓ "I receive feedback on my performance."

2. *Recognition of Competence*

✓ "I am given recognition for my contributions."

✓ "I have the authority to make decisions"

3. *Intra Departmental Relations*

✓ "I have good relationships with colleagues in my unit."

✓ "Turnover is NOT a problem in my unit."

✓ "There is strong leadership in my unit."

✓ "I have a best friend at work"

4. *Working Conditions*

✓ "My unit receives adequate resources."

✓ "I am satisfied with my salary."

5. *External Relations*

✓ "I have a good relationship with faculty."

6. *Job fit*

✓ "My work utilizes my full abilities."

✓ "I feel competent and fully able to handle my job."

✓ "My job and I are well matched."

7. *Role fit*

✓ "I like the identity my job gives me."

✓ "My job "fits" how I see myself."

8. *Social Support*

✓ "My immediate supervisor goes out of his/her way to do things to make my job easier."

✓ "It is easy to talk with my immediate supervisor."

✓ "My immediate supervisor can be relied on when things get tough at work."

9. *Job Satisfaction*

✓ "I enjoy working in my position."

✓ "I have the trust and confidence of my colleagues."

✓ "Compared to my peers of similar experience and skills, my salary compensation is fair."

10. *Work Engagement*

✓ "At my work, I feel bursting with energy."

✓ "I am enthusiastic about my job."

✓ "I get carried away when I am working."

✓ "My job inspires me."

✓ "I am proud of the work that I do."

Advantages of Engaged Employees

An organization's capacity to manage employee engagement is closely related to its ability to achieve high performance levels and superior business results. Some of the advantages of engaged employees are:

1. Engaged employees will stay with the company, be an advocate of the company and its products and services, and contribute to bottom line business success.
2. They will normally perform better and are more motivated
3. There is a significant link between employee engagement and profitability
4. They form an emotional connection with the company. This impacts their attitude towards and company's clients, and thereby improves customer satisfaction and service levels.
5. It builds passion, commitment and alignment with the organization's strategies and goals
6. Increases employees' trust in the organization
7. Creates a sense of loyalty in a competitive environment
8. Provides a high-energy working environment
9. Boosts business growth
10. Makes the employees effective brand ambassadors for the company.

RECOMMENDATIONS

☐ Start with engaged people; Hire well

- ✓ *First look inside*
- ✓ *Be clear and accurate*
- ✓ *Integrity first*

☐ Commit to Coaching and Feedback

- ✓ *Performance Management*
- ✓ *Hold leaders accountable*
- ✓ *Clear expectations*

☐ Commit to their Careers, not just your own

- ✓ *Overall career development*
- ✓ *Internal pathways*
- ✓ *Succession planning*
- ✓ *Training*

- ☐ Rewards and Recognition
  - ✓ *It's not only about the money*
  - ✓ *Formal and Informal*
  - ✓ *Genuine appreciation*
- ☐ Work/Life Balance
  - ✓ *Care*
  - ✓ *Flexibility when possible*
  - ✓ *Encourage positive relationships*
  - ✓ *Have some fun*
- ☐ Be Trustworthy
  - ✓ *Honor commitments*
  - ✓ *Trust them and their solutions*
  - ✓ *Detect their value*
  - ✓ *Give up control to gain control*
- ☐ Support Meaningful work
  - ✓ *Value connection*
  - ✓ *"Fit"*
- ☐ Make it Safe
  - ✓ *Let them express their uniqueness*
- ☐ Support their Availability
  - ✓ *Reasonable expectations*
  - ✓ *Appropriate resources*

CONCLUSION

The market competitiveness for the industries is compelling the Managers to retain high potential talents to be the best workers. A successful employee engagement strategy helps create a community at the work place and not just a work force. When employees are effectively and positively engaged with their organization, they form an emotional connection with the company. This affects their attitude towards both their colleagues and the company's clients and improves customer satisfaction and service levels. The major challenges for managers and HR leaders is now to convert the threats into opportunities effectively via best available resources in order to recruit, grow and develop as well as retain them in the organization. An enthusiastic team will be better equipped to succeed while the luster employees will drag the company down with them. It is the responsibility for all the company managements to enhance their ability to create an environment so as to inspire and lead the employees for achieving highest level of employee engagement so as to achieve the organizational goal.

4 The Real Essence and Key Drivers of Employee Engagement: An Evidence of Organizational Effort

Mr. Sukanta Mishra
Dr. Chandan Kumar Sahoo
Mr. Sitaram Das

ABSTRACT

A successful employee engagement strategy helps to create a committed community at the workplace and not just a workforce. Employee engagement is the level of commitment and involvement that an employee has towards the organization and its values. When employees are effectively and positively engaged with their organization, they form an emotional connection with the company. This affects their attitude towards both their colleagues and the company's clients and improves customer satisfaction and service levels. This article contributes to the existing literature of *"the real essence and key drivers of employee engagement : an evidence of organizational effort"* and will inspire employees to improve performance within the job for the benefit of the organization as well as achieving organizational goals, environment of new challenges & opportunities and improvement in customer satisfaction. This study will specifically emphasize the relationship between the management and employee and provide an opportunity of fair and equitable environment for effective improvement in service levels as well as organizational performance and customer satisfaction. At the end part of this paper the employee engagement initiatives taken by RSP (a unit of SAIL) will definitely support and evidence the existing literature in this field.

Keywords: Employee engagement, Commitment, Involvement, Antecedents, Organizational support

INTRODUCTION

Engagement at work was conceptualized by Kahn (1990) as the 'harnessing of organizational members' to their work roles. In engagement, people employ and express themselves physically, cognitively, and emotionally during role performances. The second related construct to engagement in organizational behavior is the notion of flow advanced by Csikszentmihalyi (1975, 1990). Csikzentmihalyi (1975) defines flow as the 'holistic sensation' that, people feel when they act with total involvement. Flow is the state in which there is little distinction between the self and environment. When individuals are in flow state little conscious control is necessary for their actions. Employee engagement is thus the level of commitment and involvement an employee has towards their organization and its values. An engaged employee is aware of business context, and works with colleagues to improve performance within the job for the benefit of the organization. The organization must work to develop and nurture engagement, which requires a two-way relationship between employer and employee. Thus employee engagement is a barometer that determines the association of a person with the organization.

Engagement is most closely associated with the existing construction of job involvement (Brown 1996) and flow (Csikszentmihalyi, 1990). Job involvement is defined as 'the degree to which the job situation is central to the person and his or her identity (Lawler & Hall, 1970). Kanungo (1982) maintained that job involvement is a cognitive or belief state of psychological identification. Job involvement is thought to depend on both need saliency and the potential of a job to satisfy these needs. Thus job involvement results form a cognitive judgment about the needs satisfying abilities of the job. Jobs in this view are tied to one's self image. Furthermore engagement entails the active use of emotions. Finally engagement may be thought of as an antecedent to job involvement in that individuals who experience deep engagement in their roles should come to identify with their jobs. When Kahn talked about employee engagement he has given important to all three aspects physically, cognitively and emotionally, whereas in job satisfaction importance has been more given to cognitive side.

Human resource (HR) practitioners believe that the engagement challenge has a lot to do with how employee feels about the work experience and how he or she is treated in the organization. It has a lot to do with emotions which are fundamentally related to drive bottom line success in a company. There will always be people who never give their best efforts no matter how hard (HR) and line managers try to engage them. But for the most part employees want to commit to companies because doing so satisfies a powerful and a basic need in connect with and contribute to something significant.

CONCEPTUAL FRAMEWORK

The concept of engagement can be traced back to Kahn (1990). Drawing from the earlier work of Goffman (1961), Kahn has developed the idea of employee engagement. Goffman here suggests that people's attachment to and detachment from their roles varies. Using a theatrical metaphor, Goffman argues that people act out momentary attachments and detachments in role performances. When an individual's behaviour shows a lack of separation between that person and his or her role, it indicates role embracement, and when an individual's behaviour reveals a resistance to a disdained role, it indicates role distance. On the basis of this distinction, Kahn (1990) has focused specifically on how people occupy their roles at work in varying degrees or how much people are psychologically present during particular moments of role performances at work. For Kahn (1990, p. 700), the self and the role "exist in some dynamic, negotiable relation in which a person drives personal energies into role behaviors (self-employment) and displays the self within the role (self-expression)". Kahn sets these varying degrees of psychological conditions of "overlap" between the self and the role at work on a continuum from personal engagement on one end to personal disengagement on the other. According to Kahn, when employees are engaged, "people employ and express themselves psychologically, cognitively and emotionally during role performances" (Kahn, 1990, p. 694). In his qualitative mapping of the general conditions of experience that influence degrees of personal engagement, he expressed that there are three psychological conditions associated with engagement or disengagement: meaningfulness; safety; and availability.

Consequently, workers were more engaged when they were in situations that offered them greater meaning and when they felt psychological safety and were more psychologically available. May *et al.* (1994) employed a quantitative test of Kahn's (1990) original findings. The results from the study reveal that all three psychological conditions exhibit significant positive relations with engagement. Although Kahn (1990) provided a definition of engagement, there are a number of definitions of the construct of engagement in the literature. However, these definitions often overlap with two pairs of better known and established constructs: organizational commitment and organizational citizenship (Robinson *et al.*, 2004) and job involvement and flow (May *et al.,* 1994). Moreover, recent studies have shown that the concept of engagement differs both theoretically and empirically from concepts such as job involvement and organizational commitment (Hallberg and Schaufeli, 2006).

Britt, Adler, and Bartone (2001) found that engagement in meaningful work can lead to perceived benefits from the work. Other research using a different measure of engagement (involvement and enthusiasm) has linked it to such variables as employee turnover, customer satisfaction-loyalty, safety, and to some degree, productivity and profitability criteria (Harter, Schmidt, & Hayes 2002). Thus, there are practical reasons that managers and researchers of organizations should be concerned with employees' engagement in work. Since then, engagement has been defined more completely as when employees feel positive emotions toward their work, find their work to be personally meaningful, consider their workload to be manageable, and have hope about the future of their work (Nelson & Simmons 2003). The findings of studies conducted to create measurement tools in this area have further refined its definition to include a three-dimensional concept of work engagement (May, Gilson, & Harter 2004). The three factors include a physical component, an emotional component, and a cognitive component. Most often it has been defined as emotional and intellectual commitment to the organization (Baumruk 2004; Richman 2006; Shaw 2005) or the amount of discretionary effort exhibited by employees in their jobs (Frank *et al.* 2004).

According to Maslach *et al.* (2001), engagement is characterized by energy, involvement, and efficacy, which are the direct opposite of the three burnout dimensions of exhaustion, cynicism, and inefficacy. Employee engagement predicts employee outcomes, organizational success, and financial performance (Bates 2004; Baumruk 2004; Harter *et al.* 2002; Richman 2006). However, it has also been reported that employee engagement is on the decline and there is a deepening disengagement among employees today (Bates 2004; Richman 2006). Most efforts to measure engagement have been at the level of the individual worker. These individual-level scores can be aggregated to measure engagement at the organizational or work group level as well.

IMPORTANCE OF EMPLOYEE ENGAGEMENT

An organization's capacity to manage employee engagement is closely related to its ability to achieve high performance levels and superior business results. A highly engaged employee will consistently deliver beyond expectations. Some of the advantages of engaged employees are:

- Engaged employees will stay with the company, be an advocate of the company and its products and services, and contribute to bottom line business success.

- They will normally perform better and are more motivated.
- There is a significant link between employee engagement and profitability.
- They form an emotional connection with the company. This impacts their attitude towards the company's clients, and thereby improves customer satisfaction and service levels.
- It builds passion, commitment and alignment with the organization's strategies and goals.
- Increases employees' trust in the organization.
- Creates a sense of loyalty in a competitive environment.
- Provides a high-energy working environment and boosts business growth.
- Makes the employees effective brand ambassadors for the company.

ANTECEDENTS OF EMPLOYEE ENGAGEMENT

Although there is little empirical research on the factors that predict employee engagement, it is possible to identify a number of potential antecedents from the different studies conducted.

Job Characteristics: This is based on Hackman and Oldham's (1980) job characteristics model and, the five core job characteristics (skill variety, task identity, task significance, autonomy, and feedback). Psychological meaningfulness can be achieved from task characteristics that provide challenging work, variety, allow the use of different skills, personal discretion, and the opportunity to make important contributions. Job enrichment was positively related to meaningfulness and meaningfulness mediated the relationship between job enrichment and engagement (May *et al.* 2004). Maslach *et al.* (2001) model also suggest the importance of job characteristics for employee engagement.

Intrinsic and Extrinsic Rewards: Extrinsic rewards are the tangible rewards mostly of a financial nature such as pay raises, bonuses, and benefits, given to employees. Intrinsic rewards are psychological rewards that employees get from doing meaningful work and performing it well. Extrinsic rewards though significant, play a dominant role in organizations where work is generally more routine and bureaucratic in nature. Furthermore, a sense of return on investments can come from external rewards and recognition in addition to meaningful work. Hence one might expect that employees' to be more engaged at work to the extent that they perceive a greater amount of rewards and recognition for their role performances.

Perceived Organizational and Supervisor Support: According to the organizational support theory (Eisenberger *et al.* 1986; Shore & Shore 1995) in order to determine the organization's readiness to reward increased work effort and to meet socio-emotional needs, employees develop global beliefs concerning the extent to which the organization values their contributions and cares about their well-being. Perceived organizational support (POS) is also valued as assurance that assistance will be available from the organization when it is needed to carry out one's job effectively and to deal with stressful situations (George et al. 1993). Supportive environments allow members to experiment and to try new things and even fail without fear of the consequences (Kahn 1990). In other words, when employees believe that their organization is concerned about them and cares about their well-being, they are likely to respond by attempting to fulfill their obligations to the organization by becoming more engaged. Further, because employees tend to view their supervisor's orientation toward them as indicative of the organization's support (Rhoades and Eisenberger 2002), POS is also likely to be an important predictor of employee engagement. In addition, first-line supervisors are believed to be especially important for building engagement and to be the root of employee disengagement (Bates 2004; Frank et al. 2004).

Distributive and Procedural Justice: There are two forms of organizational justice: distributive justice and procedural justice. Distributive justice deals with the ends achieved (what the decisions are) or the content of fairness, whereas procedural justice is related to the means used to achieve those ends (how decisions are made) or the process of fairness. It has been argued that distributive justice predicts satisfaction with the outcome (i.e., pay satisfaction), whereas procedural justice influences the evaluation of the organization and its authorities (i.e., trust in supervision and organizational commitment) (Cropanzano & Folger 1991; Sweeney and McFarlin 1993). A review of organizational justice research found that justice perceptions are related to organizational outcomes such as job satisfaction, organizational commitment, organizational citizenship behavior, withdrawal, and performance (Colquitt et al. 2001). When employees have high perceptions of justice in their organization, they are more likely to feel obliged to also be fair in how they perform their roles through greater levels of engagement. On the other hand, low perceptions of fairness are likely to cause employees to withdraw and disengage themselves from their work roles.

CONSEQUENCES OF EMPLOYEE ENGAGEMENT

The main reason behind the popularity of employee engagement is that it has positive consequences for organizations. Employee engagement leads to both individual outcomes (quality of people's work and their own experiences of doing that work), as well as organizational-level outcomes (the growth and productivity of organizations). The antecedents are expected to predict engagement and engagement predicts the outcomes, it is possible that engagement mediates the relationship between the antecedents and the consequences.

There are a number of reasons to expect engagement to be related to work outcomes. The experience of engagement has been described as a fulfilling, positive work-related experience and state of mind (Schaufeli and Bakker 2004; Sonnentag 2003) and has been found to be related to good health and positive work affect. These positive experiences and emotions are likely to result in positive work outcomes. As noted by Schaufeli and Bakker (2004), engaged employees likely have a greater attachment to their organization and a lower tendency to leave their organization.

Where there is a high degree of identification with work, the internalization of value judgments about the goodness or importance of the work serves as a psychological surrogate for the goodness or the importance of the individual performing the work. Hence, individuals who are more engaged are likely to be in more trusting and high-quality relationships with their employer and will, therefore, be more likely to report more positive attitudes and intentions toward the organization. Schaufeli and Bakker (2004) found that engagement was negatively related to turnover intention and mediated the relationship between job resources and turnover intention.

Three basic aspects of employee engagement according to the global studies are: the employees and their own unique psychological makeup and experience; the employers and their ability to create the conditions that promote employee engagement; and interaction between employees at all levels. Thus it is largely the organization's responsibility to create an environment and culture conducive to this partnership and a win-win equation. There is a general belief that a connection between employee engagement as an individual level construct and business results (Harter et al. 2002) and to be related to individuals' attitudes, intentions, and behaviors. According to the Gallup, the Consulting organization has identified three different types of people on the basis of degree of engagement as reflected in figure 1.

'Engaged' employees are builders. They want to know the desired expectations for their role so they can meet and exceed them. They perform at consistently high levels. They want to use their talents and strengths at work every day. They work with passion and they drive innovation and move their organization forward. 'Not-engaged' employees tend to concentrate on tasks rather than the goals and outcomes they are expected to accomplish. They want to be told what to do just so they can do it and say they have finished. They focus on accomplishing tasks vs. achieving an outcome. Employees who are not-engaged tend to feel their contributions are being overlooked, and their potential is not being tapped. The 'actively disengaged' employees are not just unhappy at work; they are busy acting out their unhappiness. They show seeds of negativity at every opportunity. Every day, actively disengaged workers undermine what their engaged coworkers accomplish. As workers increasingly rely on each other to generate products and services, the problems and tensions that are fostered by actively disengaged workers can cause great damage to an organization's functioning.

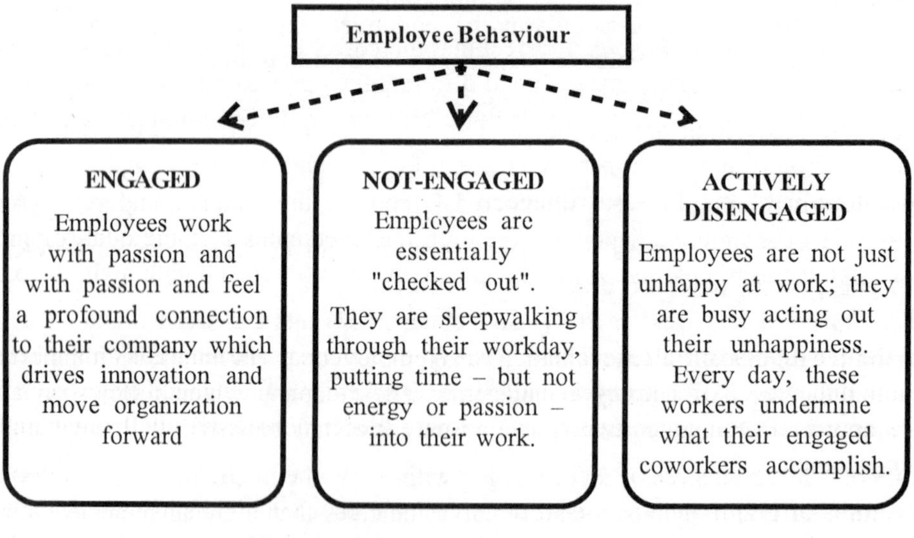

Fig. 4.1: Degree of Engagement

Source: Authors' own.

FACTORS LEADING TO EMPLOYEE ENGAGEMENT

The various factors which are influencing the degree of employee engagement are as follows (figure 2):

Career Development: Organizations with high levels of engagement provide employees with opportunities to develop their abilities, learn new skills, acquire new knowledge and realize their potential as per the career plans. Career development influences engagement for employees and retaining the most talented employees and providing opportunities for personal development.

Empowerment: Employees want to be involved in decisions that affect their work. The leaders of high engagement workplaces create a trustful and challenging environment, in which employees are encouraged to dissent from the prevailing orthodoxy and to input and innovate to move the organization forward. If the employee is given a say in the decision making and has the right to be heard by his boss then the engagement levels are likely to be high.

Equal Opportunities and Fair Treatment: Successful organizations show respect for each employee's qualities and contribution -regardless of their job level. The employee engagement levels would be high if their bosses (superiors) provide equal opportunities for growth and advancement to all the employees.

Pay and Benefits: The company should have a proper pay system so that the employees are motivated to work in the organization. In order to boost engagement levels the employees should also be provided with certain benefits and compensations.

Communication: Employees need to feel that the core values for which their companies stand are unambiguous and clear. The company should follow the open door policy. There should be both upward and downward communication with the use of appropriate communication channels in the organization.

Image: How much employees are prepared to endorse the products and services which their company provides its customers depends largely on their perceptions of the quality of those goods and services. High levels of employee engagement are inextricably linked with high levels of customer engagement.

Performance Appraisal: Fair evaluation of an employee's performance is an important criterion for determining the level of employee engagement. The company which follows an appropriate performance appraisal technique (which is transparent and not biased) will have high levels of employee engagement.

Health and Safety: Previous research works indicates that the engagement levels are low if the employee does not feel secure while working. Therefore every organization should adopt appropriate methods and systems for the health and safety of their employees.

Co-operation: If the entire organization works together by helping each other i.e. all the employees as well as the supervisors co-ordinate well then the employees will be engaged.

Family Wellbeing Measures: A person's family life influences his work life. When an employee realizes that the organization is considering his family's benefits also, he will have an emotional attachment with the organization which leads to engagement

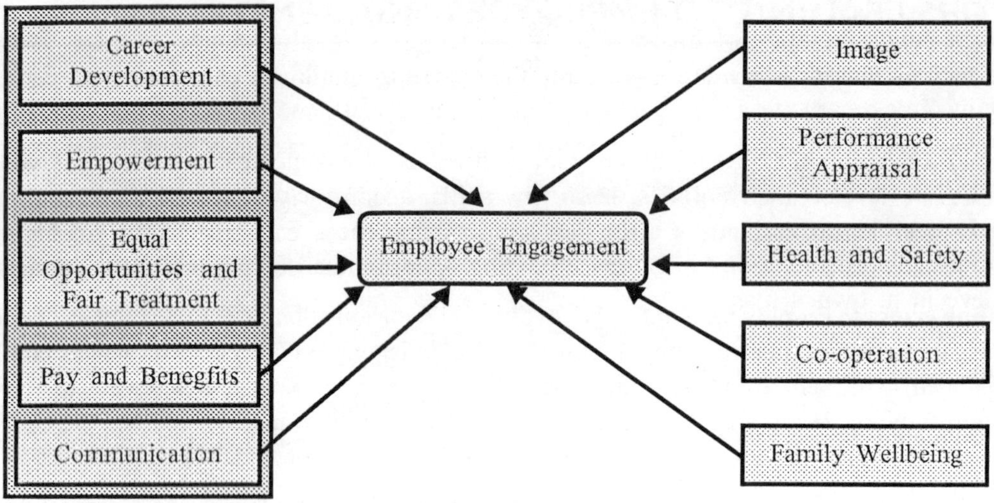

Fig. 4.2: Drivers of Employee Engagement

Source: Authors' own.

EMPLOYEE ENGAGEMENT EFFORTS: THE RSP EXPERIENCE

The organization where the study is undertaken is Rourkela Steel Plant (a unit of SAIL), Rourkela. SAIL is India's largest steel maker with a turnover of Rs. 43,935 crores and ranks among the leading steel producers in the world, having sufficient facilities for optimum utilization of its human resources. SAIL among the four 'Maharatnas' of the country, owns and operates eight manufacturing plants - five integrated steel plants at Bhilai, Durgapur, Rourkela, Bokaro, and Burnpur producing carbon steels and three plants at Salem, Durgapur and Bhadravati making Stainless and Alloy Steels. SAIL's Subsidiary at Chandrapur is a bulk producer of Ferro-alloys. RSP is one of the unique Steel Plants under the SAIL umbrella with a wide variety of special purpose steels, started during the mid 50's of the 20th century in collaboration with leading steel makers from the federal republic of Germany. Pandit Jawaharlal Nehru, India's first Prime Minister had described the public sector steel plants set up in the 1950s as the temples of modern India. It is a unique plant producing a wide variety of flat steel products, which serve various special purposes. The present study is about enhancing employee engagement and its impact on organizational performance. The efforts given by RSP towards fostering employee engagement are:

(a) Vision, Culture and Core Values: In an organization Mission/Vision leads to strategies. The long-term strategy leads to systems and structures. To have the right system and structure, culture should be good. The vision of RSP has been evolved with the reality in mind to achieve competitive advantage and takes into account the realities of the environment and articulates the core concern of the organization.

Organization culture refers to the traditions, attitudes, beliefs and practices followed in an organization by the constituent members. However, culture by itself cannot be observed. It can only be reflected in the observed behaviour of the employees - behaviour towards other employees, towards the customers, towards outsiders and most importantly, behaviour towards ones' job. RSP promoting a strong work culture in which the goals and values of the organization are aligned across all work sections. It builds a culture of trust, confidence, tolerance, low ambiguity, and mutual respect by keeping success stories alive will not only keep their existing employees engaged but also encourages the new incoming employees with this contagious spirit of work culture. Consistent with company's vision, goals and strategies, RSP given emphasis on core values (customer satisfaction, concern for people, consistent profitability, and commitment to excellence) for business success.

(b)Role of Top Management: Employee engagement requires active support and commitment from top executives through establishing clear mission, vision and values. Unless the people at the top believe in it, own it, pass it down to managers and employees, and enhance their leadership, employee engagement will never be more than just a corporate fad or another HR thing. Employee engagement does not need lip-service rather dedicated heart and action-oriented service from top management. Keeping in mind for active engagement of employees, strategic actions must be taken for the following:

- building long lasting relationships with customers.
- uphold highest ethical standards in conduct of business.
- create and nurture a culture that supports flexibility, learning and is proactive to change.
- charting a challenging career for employees with opportunities for advancement and rewards.
- the opportunity and responsibility to make a meaningful difference in employees life style.

(c) Employee Socialization: RSP executives are very careful in pooling out the potential talent of the new employee through effective recruitment. The manager has to ensure role-talent fit when placing an employee in a certain position. Once hiring decision is made the new employee should be given both general orientation which is related to the company mission, vision, values, policies and procedures and job-specific orientation such as his/her job duties, and responsibilities, goals and current priorities of the department to which the employee belongs in order to enable him/her to develop realistic job expectations and reduce role conflict that might arise in the future.

(d) Redeployment: The meaning of the term redeployment is to change the job / workplace of the employees in their service after necessary training / up gradation of skill to meet the requirement of the organization and individual's requirement. This process is continuously carried out in RSP to meet the changing needs of individual and organization. Redeployment in an organization helps individual employees in learning new skills and thereby breaks the monotony of doing the same job over the years. It helps them to get exposure to newer technology and also prevents job loss in the process of technological up gradation. For the organization also there are gains in redeployment in the form of improved productivity as because of employees' satisfaction and perceived engagement.

(e) Employee Involvement: Clear and consistent communication of what is expected by employees will pave the way for engaged workforce. Involve employees and always show respect their input. Share power with employees through participative decision making so that they would feel sense of belongingness thereby increasing their engagement in realizing it. Some key employee involvement strategies which are adopted by RSP towards proper engagement of the existing workforce are:

- Mass Contact Exercise which does not have a parallel in the corporate sector, where the Managing Director along with the Executive Director (Works) sits with nearly 500 employees on each Wednesday. The purpose is to identify the priorities of the organization through talking face-to-face and making presentations that spell out the achievements and shortcomings pointing out the areas where thrust is needed. Employees come forward with their commitment regarding what they would like to do individually and as members of their department to overcome the shortcomings and take the Rourkela Steel Plant forward.
- Performance Excellence Workshops is another programme where again the Managing Director along with the Executive Director (Works) sits with nearly 100 employees belonging to a specific department or function which also includes key members of support service departments. The workshop is highly interactive in nature where employees not only provide inputs about difficulties but also come out with concrete implementable suggestions involving their own actions.

(f) Training Initiatives: Competing through people's competence requires continual updating of knowledge and upgrading of skill of employees in tune with the changes in the internal and external environment. Training facilitates the development of employee's knowledge and skills which in turn help in attainment of organization's goals and objectives. Generally it is understood that when employees get to know more about their job, their confidence increases there by being able to work without much supervision from their immediate managers which in turn builds their self-efficacy, commitment, and job involvement. Accordingly, RSP has formulated training and development initiatives for its employees and the salient features of these initiatives are:

- development of base-line standard of competency for different positions,
- meeting organizational, occupational and individual training needs identified every year
- developing leadership skills to create proactive and dynamic organization.
- creating climate of continuous learning through knowledge management.
- providing re-training for redeployment and multi-skill training to support manpower rationalization.
- Evaluating effectiveness of training to continually enhance the quality of training in SAIL.

(g) Performance Management: For an objective assessment of the performance and potential of the employees and to distinguish between different levels of performance, the HR department of RSP takes proper steps towards effective performance management. Besides to motivate the employees for their better performance, HR department takes care of the aspiration of the employees towards promotion, career planning and succession planning. A comprehensive appraisal system for the employees has been developed to ensure an objective assessment of performance and potential of the employees and to integrate company's and individual goals. The main objectives of performance management system are to enable employees plan their work, utilize their capabilities and maximize their contributions, to create a performance culture through continuous performance improvements of individual employees, teams and the organization and to gratify individual needs which encouraged towards individual commitment and engagement.

(h) Performance Linked Pay and other Reward Systems: Performance Linked Pay, Rewards and Incentives are necessary and are good ways of keeping up employee motivation, morale, reducing absenteeism, increasing retention, workforce engagement as well as contributing to their quality of life. RSP a unit of SAIL intends to introduce performance linked pay and recognition systems. SAIL believes in the philosophy that good performance should be recognized and rewarded. The quantum of rewards and the form of rewards depends upon many factors. The recognition and rewards may take many forms. Details of the performance linked pay and other rewards will be evolved after first year of the implementation of the employees' performance management system. In addition, RSP has introduced the following forms of non financial rewards such as: Job design, Praise, Long service awards, Work related trips, Chairman's Dinner, Directors' Dinner etc.

(i) Focus on Top-Performing Employees: High-performing organizations are focusing on engaging their top-performing employees. What high-performing firms are doing is what top-performing employees are asking for and this reduces the turnover of high-performing employees and as a result leads to top business performance. RSP recognizes that every individual's performance is dependent on the competencies of the officer concerned including his ability to manage and get the support he requires, his motivation as reflected in the effort he puts in to perform various KPAs and related activities he undertakes, and the support he receives to perform various tasks and activities. Performance planning will contribute significantly to role clarity, competency utilization, potential development and performance improvements.

Organizations should develop a performance management system which holds managers and employees accountable for the level of engagement they have shown. Conducting regular survey of employee engagement level at RSP helps to identify key factors that make employees engaged. After finalizing the survey, it is advisable to determine all the factors that driving engagement in the organization, then narrow down the list of factors to focus on two or three areas. It is important that organizations begin with a concentration on the factors that will make the most difference to the employees and put energy around improving these areas as it may be difficult to address all factors at once.. RSP executives should be behind such survey results and develop action-oriented plans that are specific, measurable, and accountable and time- bound to build the climate of workforce engagement.

CONCLUSION

Employee engagement is a hot topic circulating in corporate circles and being implemented in global corporations, government agencies, and nongovernmental organizations. Employee engagement is indeed a concept which if implemented properly makes a lot of sense. It is a simple idea rationalizing the fact that the engagement and commitment of employees towards their work and organization can make a huge difference. Engaged employees create winning organizations that are more profitable, a fun place to work in and offer superb customer services and other solutions for which the organization exists. Today, however, there is clear evidence that business leaders are not simply saying this - they are actually experiencing it too with the engagement tools. So that employee engagement has potential applications for HRM practices such as role definition, support and flexibility. People are a key component of any company's ability to execute its strategy and achieve its goals. Companies who are able to better engage their people also deliver better business performance and maximize the shareholders value. Now almost all of the organization has investing money towards people (HR-related practices). So that it create value for organizational performance. Increasing employee engagement is highly dependent on leadership and establishes two ways communication where people work and views are valued and respected. It is about building a truly great relationship with the workforce. Any organization that embraces fine management philosophy, recognition of employee's talent, potential and is committed to providing enriching professional experiences is bound to succeed. The drivers of employee engagement which are motivating employees to fully involve in their work and committed to their work, care about their organization and colleagues and are willing to go the extra mile for their organization to ensure its success.

An organization should thus recognize employees, more than any other variable, as powerful contributors to a company's competitive position. Therefore employee engagement should be a continuous process of learning, improvement, measurement and action. We would hence conclude that raising and maintaining employee engagement lies in the hands of an organization and requires a perfect blend of time, effort, commitment and investment to craft a successful endeavor.

References

1. Bates, S. (2004). Getting engaged, HR Magazine, 49 (2), 44-51.
2. Baumruk, R. (2004). The missing link: the role of employee engagement in business success, Workspan, 47, 48-52.
3. Britt, T. W., Adler, A. B., & Bartone, P. T. (2001). Deriving benefits from stressful events: The role of engagement in meaningful work and hardiness. Journal of Occupational Health Psychology, 6, 53-63.
4. Brown, S. P. (1996). A meta-analysis and review of organizational research on job involvement. Psychological Bulletin, 120, 235-255.
5. Colquitt, J. A. (2001). On the dimensionality of organizational justice: a construct validation of a measure. Journal of Applied Psychology, 86 (3), 386-400.
6. Cropanzano, R., & Folger, R. (1991). Procedural justice and worker motivation. In R. M. Steers & L. W. Porter (Eds.), Motivation and work behavior, (5th ed.), New York: McGraw-Hill, 131-143).
7. Csikszentmihalyi, M. (1990). Flow: The psychology of optimal experience. New York: Harper.
8. Csikszentmihalyi, Mihaly (1975). Beyond Boredom and Anxiety: Experiencing Flow in Work and Play, San Francisco: Jossey-Bass.
9. Csikszentmihalyi, Mihaly (1990). Flow: The Psychology of Optimal Experience. New York: Harper and Row.
10. Eisenberger, R., Huntington, R., Hutchison, S., & Sowa, D. (1986). Perceived organizational support. Journal of Applied Psychology, 71, 500-507.
11. Fleming, J. H., Coffman, C., & Harter, J. K. (2005). Manage your human sigma. Harvard Business Review, 83, 106-114.
12. Frank, F.D., Finnegan, R.P. and Taylor, C.R. (2004), "The race for talent: retaining and engaging workers in the 21st century", Human Resource Planning, 27(3), 12-25.
13. George, J. M., Reed, T. F., Ballard, K. A., Colin, J., & Fielding, J. (1993). Contact with AIDS patients as a source of work-related distress: Effects of organizational and social support. Academy of Management Journal, 36, 157-171.
14. Goffman, E. (1961), Encounters: Two Studies in the Sociology of Interaction, Bobbs-Merrill Co., Indianapolis, IN.
15. Gonzalez-Roma, V., Schaufeli, W.B., Bakker, A.B. and Lloret, S. (2006). Burnout and work engagement: independent factors or opposite poles?, Journal of Vocational Behavior, 68, 165-74.
16. Hackman, J.R. and Oldham, G.R. (1980). Work Redesign, Addison-Wesley, Reading, MA.

17. Hallberg, U. and Schaufeli, W.B. (2006). Same but different: can work engagement be discriminated from job involvement and organizational commitment? European Journal of Psychology, 11, 119-27.
18. Harter, J. K., & Schmidt, F. L. (2000). Validation of a performance-related and actionable management tool: A meta-analysis and utility analysis (Gallup Technical Report). Princeton, NJ: The Gallup Organization.
19. Harter, J. K., Schmidt, F. L., & Hayes, T. L. (2002). Business-unit-level relationship between employee satisfaction, employee engagement, and business outcomes: A meta-analysis. Journal of Applied Psychology, 87, 268-279.
20. Harter, J. K., Schmidt, F. L., & Keyes, C. L. M. (2003). Well-being in the workplace and its relationship to business outcomes: A review of the Gallup studies. In C. L. M. Keyes & J. Haidt (Eds.), Flourishing: Positive psychology and the life well-lived. Washington, DC: American Psychological Association, 205-224.
21. Kahn, W.A. (1990). Psychological conditions of personal engagement and disengagement at work, Academy of Management Journal, 33(4), 692-724.
22. Kahn, W.A. (1990). Psychological conditions of personal engagement and disengagement at work, Academy of Management Journal, 33, 692-724.
23. Kanungo, R. N. (1982). Measurement of job and work involvement. Journal of Applied Psychology, 67, 341-349.
24. Kanungo, R.N. (1982). Work alienation: An integrative approach. New York: Praeger Publishers, 82-97.
25. Lawler, E. E., III, & Hall, D. T. (1970). Relationship of job characteristics to job involvement, satisfaction, and intrinsic motivation. Journal of Applied Psychology, 54, 305-312.
26. Maslach, C., Schaufelli, W.B. and Leiter, M.P. (2001), Job burnout, Annual Review of Psychology, 52, 397-422.
27. May, D.R., Gilson, R.L. and Harter, L. (1994). The psychological conditions of meaningfulness, safety and availability and the engagement of the human spirit at work. Journal of Occupational and Organizational Psychology, 77, 11-37.
28. May, D.R., Gilson, R.L. and Harter, L.M. (2004), The psychological conditions of meaningfulness, safety and availability and the engagement of the human spirit at work. Journal of Occupational & Organizational Psychology, 77, 11-37.
29. Nelson, D.L. & Simmons, B.L. 2003. 'Health psychology and work stress: a more positive approach', In Quick, J.C. & Tetrick, L.E. (eds), Handbook of Occupational Health Psychology, Washington, DC: American Psychological Association, 97-119.
30. Rhoades, L. and Eisenberger, R. (2002). Perceived organizational support: a review of the literature. Journal of Applied Psychology, 87, 698-714.
31. Richman, A. (2006). Everyone wants an engaged workforce how can you create it? Workspan, 49, 36-9.
32. Robinson, D., Perryman, S. and Hayday, S. (2004). The Drivers of Employee Engagement, Institute for Employment Studies, Brighton.
33. Schaufeli, W.B. and Bakker, A.B. (2004). Job demands, job resources and their relationship with burnout and engagement: a multi-sample study. Journal of Organizational Behaviour, 25, 293-315.
34. Schaufeli, W.B., Bakker, A. and Van Rhenen, W. (2008). How changes in job demands and resources predict burnout, work engagement, and sickness absenteeism. Journal of Occupational Health Psychology, 22(7), 345-56.
35. Schaufeli, W.B., Salanova, M., Gonzalez-Roma, V. and Bakker, A.B. (2002). The measurement of engagement and burnout: a two-sample confirmatory factor-analytic approach. Journal of Happiness Studies, 3, 71-92.

36. Shaw, K. (2005). An engagement strategy process for communicators. Strategic Communication Management, 9(3), 26-9.

37. Shore, L.M. & Shore, T.H. (1995). Perceived organizational support and organizational justice. In Cropanzano, R.S. & K.M. Kacmar (Eds.). Organizational politics, justice, and support: Managing the social climate of the workplace, Westport, CT: Quorum, 149-164.

38. Sonnentag, S. (2003). Recovery, work engagement, and proactive behavior: a new look at the interface between non-work and work. Journal of Applied Psychology, 88, 518-28.

39. Sweeney, P. D., and McFarlin, D. B. (1993). Workers' evaluations of the "ends" and the "means": An examination of four models of distributive and procedural justice. Organizational Behavior and Human Decision Processes, 55, 23-40.

5

Employee Engagement Initiatives in India - A Comparative Study With Reference To IT & ITes Organizations

Binita Panda
Leena P. Singh
Dr. S. C. Sahoo

ABSTRACT

Employee engagement is generally the level of commitment and involvement an employee has towards their organization and its core values and beliefs. An engaged employee is presumed to be aware of business context, and work dynamics with colleagues and peer groups to improve performance within the job for the benefit and excellence of the organization. It is a positive attitude held by the employees towards the organization and its values. The paper focuses on how employee engagement is an antecedent of job involvement and what should company do to make the employees engaged. The scope of the study is limited to three organisations who are the major players in the service sector. The paper attempts to do a comparative analysis of employee engagement strategies adopted by these organisations on the basis of the widely accepted 10 Cs model of employee engagement.

Keywords: Employee engagement, Job involvement, Commitment, HR interventions

INTRODUCTION

Employee engagement initiative has a direct impact on the organization results. Also employee engagement is directly influenced by growth of the organization, value addition experienced by employees and employee perception of the organization. When managers become disengaged, employees are 37% more likely to be frustrated with company systems, processes, and procedures. (FLS Research 2008-09)

This paper is based on three case studies viz. Tata Teleservices, Infosys and Mind Tree. The paper has been divided into six sections. First section is all about introduction to employee engagement which elaborates the issues and its importance for organizations. Section two deals with the conceptual overview and the third includes the literature review. In section four strategies and initiatives linked to employee engagement has been described along with a comparative analysis of different initiatives taken by different Indian organizations and its implications based on ten Cs of employee engagement model used for analysis. It also elucidates the impact of employee engagement initiatives on organizations performance and employee retention. The fifth section includes the implications and initiatives and the last section i.e. sixth section concludes the paper.

EMPLOYEE ENGAGEMENT- AN OVERVIEW

The concept of engagement has naturally evolved from past research on high involvement, empowerment, job motivation, organizational commitment, and trust. All these research streams focus on employees' perceptions and attitudes about the work environment. In some ways they are variations on the same fundamental issue. Obviously, all organizations want their employees to be engaged in their work. But what can help them predict if their employees will "give their all"? Several standardized tools exist for assessing employee engagement and then providing feedback for making changes. These tools tend to have several common goals and characteristics:

- Create a simple and focused index of workplace engagement-Many organizations are using very short, simple, and easy-to-use measures that focus on the fundamentals of a great workplace. Instead of conducting broad culture or climate surveys with 100 or more questions, many organizations are opting for a focused approach that measures fundamental qualities of the workplace that likely will be important 10 years later (e.g., feedback, trust, cooperation).
- Allow for benchmarking-most organizations want to know how they compare with other organizations. Using a standard measure of engagement allows an organization to see how it measures up to other companies along a simple set of fundamental work qualities.
- Direct action-Engagement measures tend to be very actionable. This means that an organization can alter practices or policies to affect employees' responses to every item in the measure.
- Show relationship to company performance-without a link to the company's performance or other critical outcomes, measures of engagement have little value. The whole idea behind engagement is that it leads to enhanced performance. The link to performance outcomes is a necessary underlying assumption of all engagement measures.

Empirical research on "employee engagement" is relatively new. "Employee retention" has received the lion's share of the spotlight. This focus on retention however has spawned several studies on "engagement" - since retaining employees is dependent upon the need to "engage" them. Hence, engagement studies are beginning to take center stage. One of the most significant threads in the current research is the discovery that employee engagement is linked to customer satisfaction which is linked to organizational financial success. Employee engagement/satisfaction distinctly affects the bottom line. These findings are detailed in the studies referenced in this article. Engagement really happens at the team level - a framework called VOICE helps that process. VOICE is an acronym made up of its component parts, i.e., V is for vision, which is an emotion as well as a financial connection as to why people should be part of this organization, O is for opportunity. Are there opportunities to grow and develop?, I is for incentive. If you do a good job do you get both financial and non-financial rewards?, C is for community. Do I like the people I work with?, C - Communication, which is about "telling people about what is going on, and gives them the confidence that people care and E is for entrepreneurship, defined as things such flexibility on how people can work". "It's about things like flexibility in time so people don't feel they are being a slave to the organization."

LITERATURE REVIEW

Let us have a look on how employee engagement is defined by some of the consulting firms:

- Employees' willingness and ability to contribute to company success. (Towers Perrin)
- Staff commitment and a sense of belonging to the organization. (Hewitt)
- Employee's commitment to the organization and motivation to contribute to the organization's success. (Mercer)
- Employees' exertion of "discretionary effort". . . going beyond meeting the minimum standards for the job. (Hay)
- Creating the sense that individuals are a part of a greater entity. (Best Practices, LLC)

A research and information company Melcrum, recently surveyed 1,000 corporate communications and HR professionals and conducted 40 case studies and found that many respondents credit offering employee engagement programs with the following benefits: More than 50% report improvements in employee retention and customer satisfaction, 33% report higher productivity, 28% report improvements in employee advocacy, 27% improved status as a "great place to work", 27% report increased profitability and 25% report improved absenteeism. A snapshot of the corporations in this study shows that 74% began focusing on employee engagement between 2000 and 2004 and report performance improvements each year, 36% have a dedicated employee engagement program, 64% apply the philosophy to employee engagement to their people practices. The Forum for People Performance Management and Measurement at North-western University released their report in November 2004, The Impact of Employee Attitudes on Market Response and Financial Performance, which also links employee satisfaction to customer satisfaction and a company's financial success. This finding is true even if employees have no direct contact with customers. 110,000 surveys were mailed to media companies, with a 34% response rate. Below are key findings from the report:

- The key characteristic for explaining employee satisfaction is organizational communication as employee satisfaction is a key precursor to employee engagement.
- Organizational culture is a significant driver of employee engagement, where employees must be expected to work together and provide a voice for the customer within the organization.
- When individuals and teams compete to implement optimal behaviours oriented to the market and its customers, such competition can benefit both the organization and its customers.
- 64% apply the philosophy of employee engagement to their people practices.
- Organizations with engaged employees have customers who use their products more.
- It is an organization's employees who influence the behaviour and attitudes of customers, and it is customers who drive an organization's profitability through the purchase and use of its products.

Incentive programs, as a way to engage employees, have been found to increase organizational performance. The International Society for Performance Improvement released a study last year, Incentives, Motivation, & Workplace Performance, which showed that incentive programs can increase performance by as much as 44% among employee teams, 24% among individuals.

The study consisted of an analysis 45 existing scientific studies which were also compared to current practices through surveys of 145 U.S. organizations that use incentive programs. As per the key findings of the study it was found that incentive programs improve performance, incentive programs engage participants and increase interest in work, incentive programs attract quality employees, longer-term programs outperform short-term programs, executives and employees value incentive programs and quota-based incentive measures work best. Best Practices LLC, a research and consultant firm, recently released a new benchmarking report "Employee Engagement and the Service-Profit Chain" which shares best practices for engaging employees in their jobs and companies. Based on primary and secondary research of leading worldwide corporations, the report's key findings are as, a reduction in turnover rates by just two percentage points can result in a savings of $3 million annually, an effective performance management system is the cornerstone of engagement — from goal-setting to reward, recognition and incentive programs, 75% of high performing companies hold managers accountable for engaging their employees. This is in comparison to 35% across the entire study group that holds managers accountable, high performing companies engage employees by cutting across functional silos to create a sense of connectedness through communities of practice, cross-functional teams, and by creating common work areas, high performing companies recognize employees for their suggestions employ group brainstorming and utilize group list serves to enhance the feeling of connectedness, employee and customer loyalty attributes reflect each other, supporting the premise behind the importance of engagement which is based on a correlation between customer satisfaction and engagement, key factors in engagement are alignment of employees toward strategy, enabling employees to have the capability to engage themselves, and creating the sense of engagement — creating the sense that individuals are a part of a greater entity and top performing companies rank cross-functional teams and councils as the most effective vehicle to help employees understand how their — as well as team and/or business unit — efforts contribute to corporate performance. The research above is powerful - not only for organizations seeking to ensure their financial success, but for those seeking to harness their people power. For employees, or those seeking employment, it offers a tremendous sense of comfort. Their employers (or future employers), if enlightened by the type of research portrayed above, will be interested in finding ways to create an "engaging" workplace.

10 Cs OF EMPLOYEE ENGAGEMENT

"The Ten Cs of Employee Engagement", Gerard H. Seijts and Dan Crim (2006) tries and understand the various dimensions that can add value to the engagement level of an employee which can make people stay in the organisation for long. The ten Cs is elaborated as follows:

Connect: Employees should feel that their work is being valued and should feel a sense of connectivity with their superiors. Having a gap can lead to employee isolation and a sense of non-belongingness to the organisation.

Career: People in the organisation should be provided challenging and meaning full work with opportunities for career advancement. Most people want to do new things in their job. Good leaders have to challenge employee; but at the same time they must instil the confidence that the challenges can be met. People should be given tools and knowledge to be successful to keep them engaged.

Clarity: Success in life and organisations is, to a great extent, determined by how clear individuals are about their goals and what they really want to achieve. Leaders must communicate a clear vision employees need to understand what the organisations goals are, why they are important, and how the goals can be attained.

Convey: Leaders clarify their expectations about employees and provide feedback on their functioning in the organisation. Good leaders establish processes and procedures that help people master important tasks and facilitate goal achievement.

Congratulate: Exceptional leaders should give recognition to the employees for good performance. Recognising their efforts by praising them and giving them an applaud can boost their morale and ultimately make them enthusiastic towards their work.

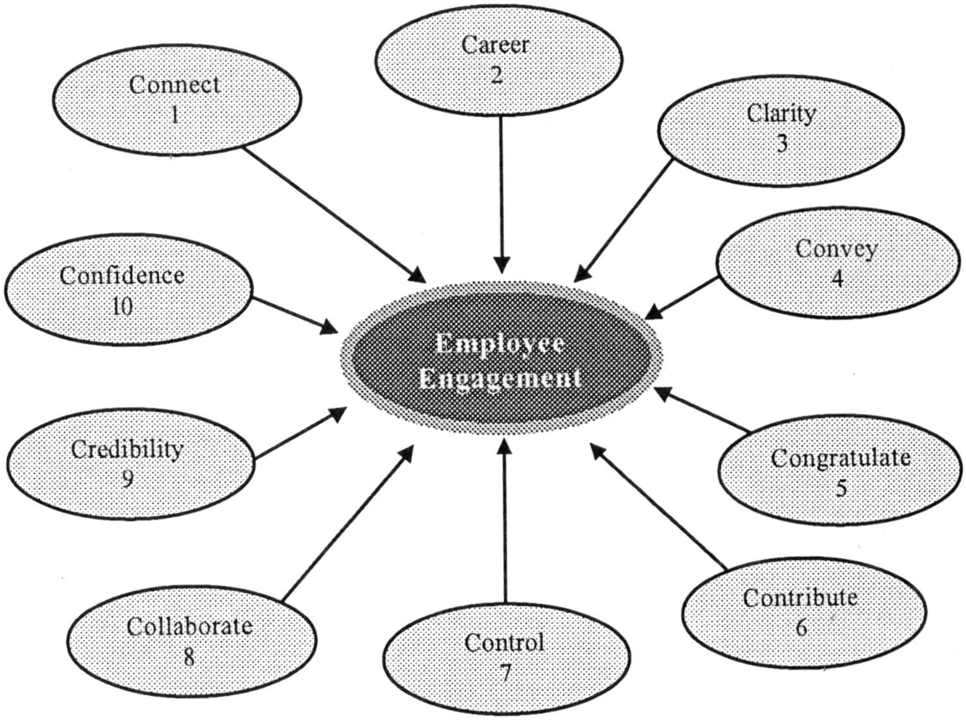

Fig. 5.1: Ten Cs of Employee engagement

Contribute: People want to know that their input matters and that they are contributing to the organisations success in a meaningful way. Efficient leaders should make sure that the employees feel their efforts are being used in the fulfilment of the overall goal and objectives of the organisation.

Control: Employees value control over the flow and pace of their jobs leaders can create opportunities for employees to exercise their control. Involving your people in decision making creates a culture wherein they can take the ownership of their own problems and can find solutions to them.

Collaborate: When employees work in teams and have the trust and cooperation of their team members, they outperform individuals and teams which lack good relationships. Great leaders are team builders: they create an environment that fosters trust and collaboration. Thus a continuous challenge for leaders is to rally individuals to collaborate on organizational, departmental and group goals, while excluding individuals pursuing their self-interest.

Credibility: Leaders should strive hard to demonstrate high ethical standards to their subordinates. People want to be proud of their jobs, their performance and their organisation.

Confidence: Efficient leaders help create confidence in a company by setting example of high ethical and performance standards. Instilling a sense of confidence is what is required from the leaders.

EMPLOYEE ENGAGEMENT INITIATIVES IN INDIAN ORGANIZATIONS

Case Study I: Tata Teleservices: HR Interventions and Employee Engagement

Tata Teleservices' (TTSL) many HR interventions have earned it the distinction of being an employer of choice. CN Nagakumar, CHRO, TTSL, believes that his company's commitment to employee engagement is what has earned it this accolade. The company's HR practices include a strong HR model that talks about alignment, assignment, engagement, empowerment and pride of the workforce. The annual employee engagement survey - Darpan - has been designed around the HR model. In order to foster a customer-centric and performance-driven culture in the organisation, the pillars of organisational culture were defined under the acronym CRISP - customer focus, responsibility for results, initiative with speed, self-confidence with consciousness and passion for achievement. A robust performance management scheme, a reward and recognition policy, and a career progression policy exist in the organisation, besides a number of engagement activities. The performance management system ensures the top down cascade of business goals. The key performance indicators of every employee are aligned to any one or multiples of the five key business levers, namely revenue, profit maximisation / cost optimisation, cash flow, customer satisfaction and employee engagement, aligning the entire organisation towards the vision, mission and business plans of the organisation.

The reward and recognition (R&R) policy aims to create a framework for recognising and rewarding the contributions of individuals and teams, and institutionalises a culture of openness, transparency and meritocracy. The recognitions include Spotlight (for on-the-spot recognition), Star of the Month, Super Stars for achievers, Customer First Reward and Valuable Reward. These awards are decided at both the circle and corporate level by various business units and circle R&R committees. TTSL strives to provide career growth in consonance with performance, merit and potential of an employee, while considering organisational needs. The opportunities include Career Progression Policy and CAS (Career Advancement Scheme), Job Rotation Policy and Internal Job Postings. The Career Progression Policy ensures career progression for all employees based on their performance rating, tenure in the role, SPARK Assessment Center scores and potential for growth. It also highlights the commitment to building a leadership pipeline by "grooming talent" from within. To ensure a supportive and encouraging environment, TTSL has focused its efforts towards institutionalising several initiatives like the employee health and well being policy, Long Service Award on completion of five and 10 years of service, Medical Insurance, Liberal Personal Accident Insurance coverage etc. For employees posted in remote geographies like the North-East, Assam, Jammu & Kashmir, a special geography benefit is provided. The Weavers initiative includes sports and recreation activities for employees, cultural and sports activities for employees' children, career counselling and corporate sustainability initiatives. These policies also seek to create and ensure "a meaningful relationship between the employee and the organisation." The company knows that a relationship of mutual respect and trust is the key to ensuring a motivated workforce. That is why TTSL engages in a number of activities to offer employees an opportunity to display the creative side of their personalities. At the circle level, the company organises various fun activities and games, including hoopla, tambola, carrom and table tennis, besides outdoor game championships for cricket, football and hockey. Many of these teams have participated in inter-corporate events and won for the company's pride.

Leadership development is one of the strategic pillars at TTSL. Assessment centres form the basic tool to identify high-potential employees who undergo a comprehensive leadership developmental programme. The Business Leadership Programme is carried out in association with the Tata Management Training Centre and involves all COOs and high-performing senior leaders. An in-house e-enabled multi-rater feedback system called Reflections has been put in place to enable senior leaders to get 360-degree feedback and create an individual development plan. Team-building initiatives at TTSL are not limited to the top management alone but touch all levels of management, aligning teams across the company towards achieving the organisational objectives.

Regular Townhalls are conducted by the MD and COOs at corporate and circle levels respectively to get to know the views of the people. Initiatives such as Lunch with MD, MD Online and Phone your MD also seek to increase interaction between employees and the MD. A chief ethics officer and local ethics officers have been appointed to deal with ethical issues. A women's welfare committee, comprising senior women employees, has been created to address women-related issues.

Training is an important component of employee engagement. Training employees through innovative workshops, cross-functional teams and collaborative working is also a key focus area in TTSL. TTSL encourages employees to enhance their skills and come up with innovative ideas and best practices through initiatives like Mind Beans, Propel (Six Sigma) and Promising Practices." Employees are also actively encouraged to develop their personalities. The portal Gyaan Jyoti enables people to enhance their skills through e-learning. Employees list their fields of interest and expertise on Gyan Tarang. TTSL then uses its in-house expertise to conduct various training workshops for others, thereby giving employees a chance to learn and teach. The motivated workforce is encouraged to give back to the community as well as TTSL has tie-ups with NGOs like SOS Children's Villages and the National Association for the Blind, and partners with various schools under the Samvedna initiative. It also has an active eco-club, Prakriti, which conducts activities such as tree plantation drives, energy conservation and wealth out of waste initiatives." The company's CSR activities include education and the environment as well, fully leveraging the company's core competencies, in addition to initiatives on affirmative action plans focused on employment generating schemes.

It is these and other similar activities that have helped TTSL gain the trust of its employees and ensured an atmosphere of enthusiasm and commitment in the workplace.

Case Study II: Infosys iEngage: Employee Engagement Platform

As companies grow, enabling collaboration and engagement among employees becomes increasingly difficult. Solid information and inefficient methods of communication lead to a slow pace of innovation and disengaged employees who make the wrong decisions. Consequently, it affects the company where it hurts the most - the bottom line. We live in a collaborative world. By leveraging and integrating different sources of knowledge, companies can drive innovation and ensure differentiation, resulting in a competitive advantage. Social media unleashes possibilities to collaborate and enhance your company's pool of knowledge, facilitate ideation and problem-solving among employees, and engage with external stakeholders.

Infosys iEngage employee engagement platform helps accelerate knowledge discovery, improve workforce productivity, deepen employee engagement and foster innovation. Our platform can be leveraged for employee engagement initiatives such as employee on-boarding, knowledge networks, new product development, sales collaboration, and alumni networks. The platform is delivered in the enterprise Software-as-a-Service (SaaS) model and offers convenient single point accountability, complete ownership of applications, infrastructure, professional services, Business Process Outsourcing and consulting. Benefits are as follows:

- **Accelerates Knowledge Discovery:** The employee engagement platform accelerates the discovery of intellectual capital hidden across organization silos. Employees can take better decisions by locating and discovering knowledge faster.
- **Improves Workforce Productivity:** The platform captures and shares information in new ways enhances team work and productivity. Employees across geographic boundaries can quickly form groups to solve problems and meet goals.
- **Deepens Employee Engagement:** It helps employees engage in a more integrated way. Relationships are enhanced through better access to corporate information, employee self-help, peer-to-peer collaboration and multi-channel interaction.
- **Enables Faster Innovation:** It helps introduce products faster to the market through social media, co-creation and testing of innovations with employees, customers and partners globally.
- **Networked Company:** Our platform helps you build a networked organization. It can be made available to all employees and can be extended to external business partners, alumni and customers.

Striving for a better tomorrow and making a difference through employee volunteerism Infosys has many voluntary employee CSR groups to participate in initiatives that enable sustainable community development. In 2008-09, they raised US $275,990 internally for various initiatives. These groups reach out to communities directly as well as through NGOs and participate in several activities across locations:

The CSR group at Infosys Australia partners with organizations that fulfil our CSR criteria and helps them with donations, volunteering and pro bono work. The group also supports citizens in times of natural disasters. In 2008-09, the group joined hands with the Centre for Multicultural Youth (CMY) to support the needs of young people in Australia from migrant and refugee backgrounds. Employees voluntarily donate through the Salary Sacrifice program to a few designated payroll giving charities / not-for-profit organizations. The Bangalore employee CSR group, Infinite Smiles, organized the Power of 100,000 to raise funds and provide the necessary classroom infrastructure to accommodate 240 school children. They also organized a planner sale to raise funds for the National Institute for the Blind. In Bhubaneswar, the Akanksha team, in collaboration with the Red Cross, organized a blood donation camp for thalassemia patients and contributed a total of 1,500 blood packets over a span of five years. More than 100 institutions have benefited through this unique initiative, which earned the Akanksha team recognition and felicitation from the Governor of Orissa in 2008. This year, the team introduced a new initiative called Soul Fund, to provide monetary support for accident victims needing critical care and are from economically weaker sections. They also have employee warning and surveillance system to control their employees.

At Infosys, growth is vertical. Growth is lateral. Growth is incremental. Growth is exponential. When people work in an ecosystem that spans so many countries and industries, it's bound to be. Infosys is serious about its employee's growth and have a plan for everyone with Infosys' Career Path Architecture. This unique model details organizational roles and career streams, as well as mechanisms for career growth. It provides guidelines for vertical and horizontal movements - within and across career streams.

At their Virtual Career Center, they help to decide upon a course of action. There's a wide range of information here - from internal job alerts to updates on career programs, from internal internship to career planning tools, from interaction with managers to leaders on careers. Empowerment and enlightenment are just a click away.

Infosys Technologies awarded the 2010 Force of Ideas Award for Strategic Engagement by Corporate Executive Board. This award recognizes management practices that redefine the way companies do business, creating sustainable value for organizations. Infosys has been awarded this honor under the category of 'Strategic Engagement' for its unique strategic planning methods engaging all stakeholders.

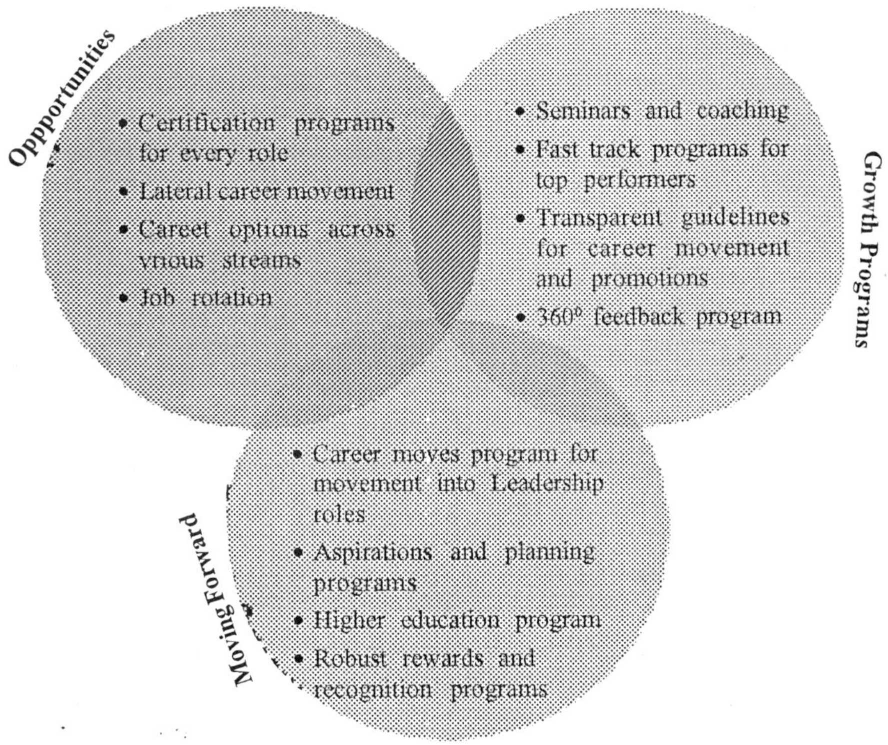

Fig. 5.2: Inspiration, Education, Recognition - Career Development Programs of Infosys

Source: *http://www.infosys.com/careers/why-infosys/career-growth.asp*

Case Study III: Mind Tree Enhances Employee Engagement with Cisco Soln

Life at Mind Tree is an adventure, a voyage of self-discovery. In this friendly, caring environment, employees have the opportunity to experiment and the freedom to explore - both as an employee as well as an individual. Their rock-solid value system is not imposed upon anyone - it is simply a part of life, an easy-to-assimilate set of guidelines that everyone at MindTree internalizes effortlessly. Each of the employees understands that growth can only be meaningful if it is inclusive; that is why they encourage one another to be the best that we can be, despite their limitations and shortcomings. Senior management here at MindTree is extremely approachable. Open interaction is encouraged, healthy competition rewarded, and outstanding performance recognized.

'Integrity means the world to us'; it is the very core of their existence. A breach of integrity is unacceptable at MindTree. They demand the highest standards of ethical behavior from our employees, from the senior most executive to the most recently hired trainee. And we hold ourselves to those standards - no matter what the cost. We insist - and take pride in - doing the right thing.

At MindTree, they place a premium on the ability to gain and share knowledge. Continuous learning is not only a part of their value system; it is a part of their psyche. Their learning initiatives are designed to achieve specific outcomes, for employees as well as for the organization.

The focus is on "learning," (which involves the acquisition, internalization and enhancement of knowledge by the learner), as opposed to "training," (which represents dissemination of knowledge by a trainer). Their approach to learning is, therefore learner-centric. Additionally, the company believes that all learning should be practitioner led; some of the finest minds in the industry partner with them to tutor and mentor Mind Tree Minds. All learning initiatives at Mind Tree are overseen by a dedicated group called C2; aligned to business goals and customer needs; and are in line with the diversity of the company's delivery mechanisms. These initiatives are also focused on building sustainable processes - sharing and knowledge dissemination that enhance personal learning, while building self sustaining learning systems. Above all, learning at Mind Tree is measured by a clearly definable metric: effectiveness. Following are some of the initiatives:

Mentor and Buddy System

Prior to any learning initiative, a specially assigned mentor assesses the preparedness level of each Campus Mind and customizes or shapes the program accordingly. Thereafter, a team of buddies interact with the Campus Minds to help them assimilate into the organization.

Outbound Learning

Outbound learning sessions are a lot of fun. However, they also help us understand and enhance Campus Minds' interpersonal, decision making, conflict management, team work and leadership skills.

Learning Bee

Learning bee is an intranet portal that allows you to view and register for ongoing learning opportunities. It works proactively: simply input your learning needs and receive updates whenever appropriate programs are scheduled to begin.

Mind Tree is an IT and IT services provider, which has gained recognition in recent times. Due to its focus on human capital development, it has consecutively been ranked as the No 1 enterprise in the Most Admired Knowledge Enterprise (MAKE) award ranking. The company, while moving forward with its HR initiatives, realised that open communication within the organisation set-up and interaction with each of the employees, or 'Mind Tree Minds' as they are referred to, was proving to be a challenge. Thus the company tries to create an environment through some engagement initiatives to connect to their employees. This internal annual event called the 'All Minds Meet Session' is an effort to communicate with each of the employees at Mind Tree about the organisation's health, important milestones achieved and growth areas for the times to come. "In the past, these interactions happened at one of the Mind Tree campuses itself, where everyone was physically present for a meeting each quarter. However, as Mind Tree grew in terms of locations and manpower, it was difficult to physically accommodate all the employees inside one campus," says Ramesh Kumar T, Associate Director for Infrastructure Management at Mind Tree. The company was looking for a technological solution that would allow real-time rich media communication as a substitute for physical presence which was decided to be provided by Cisco. As far as the physical IT infrastructure at Mind Tree is concerned, it was already live with networking infrastructure and LAN from Cisco as the company has offices in Bangaluru, Chennai, Pune and Hyderabad and are already using Cisco's LAN infrastructure, also looking for a similar IP multicast solution, which would be simple, lean, highly available, open and secure and meet our requirements." The IP multicast solution, when coupled with bandwidth conservation technology, reduced traffic and the number of servers needed by simultaneously delivering a single stream of information to thousands of employees India-wide. "Some of the examples of applications involving one-to-many and many-to-many communications include video and audio broadcasts, videoconferencing or collaboration, dissemination of stock quotes and news feeds, database replication, software downloads and website caching," says Kumar. Now Mind Tree employees participate in the company's quarterly meets sitting at their desktops. The live AV streams fed over a multicast solution have not only enabled them to connect with peers but have also helped them to reach a wider audience in the extended supply chain. There is a lot more, which the IT team has planned, with the multicast-based solution "In the future, we would be looking at integrating applications onto this solution, which would help us optimise the investment. Also, more and more internal events would be streamed using this solution," concludes Kumar.

It also has developed 'Career aspiration programmes', 'Mindtree certification' for becoming Mind Tree Certified Engineers and get promoted. Company has also made provisions for awarding and recognizing the employee achievements through 'Spot Awards' (for individuals and teams), Best Performer Award and Technical Appreciation Award.

It also practises a survey named as 'Mind Tree People Perception Survey' (MPPS) for collection of feedback from all departments regarding their functioning and project related advancements and requirements for facilitating contribution from employees.

A Comparative Analysis

Table 5.1: A Comparison of three IT & ITES companies using Ten Cs Model of Employee engagement

Ten Cs	TATA TELESERVICES *HR model integrating alignment, assignment, engagement, empowerment and pride of the workforce*	INFOSYS *iEngage*	MINDTREE *Link 'Mind Tree Minds'*
Connect	Reward and recognition (R&R) policy aims to create a framework for recognising and rewarding the contributions of individuals and teams, and institutionalises a culture of openness, transparency and meritocracy.	Social media unleashes possibilities to collaborate and enhance your company's pool of knowledge, facilitate ideation and problem-solving among employees	This internal annual event called the 'All Minds Meet Session' is an effort to communicate with each of the employees
Career	Career Progression Policy and CAS (Career Advancement Scheme), Job Rotation Policy and Internal Job Postings	Infosys' Career Path Architecture, Virtual Career Center helps to decide upon a course of action using wide range of information here - from internal job alerts to updates on career programs, from internal internship to career planning tools, from interaction with managers to leaders on careers.	Career aspiration programmes Mindtree certification for becoming Mind Tree Certified Engineers and promoted.
Clarity	—	—	Internal annual event called the 'All Minds Meet Session' is an effort to communicate with each of the employees and Team meetings at all levels of projects.
Convey	Key performance indicators of every employee are aligned to any one or multiples of the five key business levers, namely revenue, profit maximisation / cost optimisation, cash flow, customer satisfaction and employee engagement	Software-as-a-Service (SaaS) model and offers convenient single point accountability, complete ownership of applications, infrastructure, professional services and multi channel interaction	This internal annual event called the 'All Minds Meet Session' is an effort to communicate with each of the employees

Congratulate	Spotlight (for on-the-spot recognition), Star of the Month, Super Stars for achievers, Customer First Reward and Valuable Reward	Awards and Recognitions	Spot Awards(for individuals and teams), Best Performer Award, Technical Appreciation Award
Contribute	Encourages employees to enhance their skills and come up with innovative ideas and best practices through initiatives like Mind Beans, Propel (Six Sigma) and Promising Practices."	Employee on-boarding, knowledge networks, new product development, sales collaboration, and alumni networks	Participate in the company's quarterly meets sitting at their desktops through LAN and Mind Tree People Perception Survey (MPPS) i.e. collection of feedback from all departments.
Control	Organisational culture were defined under the acronym CRISP - customer focus, responsibility for results, initiative with speed, self-confidence with consciousness and passion for achievement	Employee Warning System and Employee Surveillance System, Performance management System	'All Minds Meet Session' as they talk about growth areas for the times to come
Collaborate	Lunch with MD, MD Online and Phone your MD also seek to increase interaction between employees and the MD.	Social media, Knowledge networks	CISCOs' networking & LAN Infrastructure
Credibility	Chief ethics officer and local ethics officers have been appointed to deal with ethical issues	Employee volunteerism through voluntary employee CSR groups to participate in initiatives that enable sustainable community development	–
Confidence	Business Leadership Programme is carried out in association with the Tata Management Training Centre	iEngage itself and voluntary participation of employees in many of its activities	Participate in the company's quarterly meets sitting at their desktops through LAN

IMPLICATIONS AND NEW INITIATIVES

The analysis gives us very clear picture that the three organisations are meeting most of the criteria of Ten Cs to a greater extent. Tata Teleservices has an excellent reward and recognition policy and a career progression policy which shows the concern parameter. It has different programs to congratulate its employees. Further it also provides a platform to the employees to collaborate and increase the interaction between superior and subordinates. The company is high on meeting ethical standards for which it has an ethical officer to deal with the local issues. The only criterion on which the company can work more on bringing role clarity for the individuals. It is suggested here that the company can clarify the roles of the employees from the very first step by giving them a realistic job preview and conducting a strong induction and orientation programme as a part of the performance management system. Employee counselling and mentoring techniques can be used to get the feedback from the employee about his role and job performance. On the other hand the iEngage platform of Infosys is a unique initiative adopted by it with an objective to be connected with all the employees located at different geographical regions. Their employee engagement practice enables employees to contribute, control and collaborate effectively. Infosys is also strong in communicating ethical standards. It develops appropriate leadership skills among individuals by empowering them through effective delegation. Mindtree employee engagement strategies are very strong in meeting the convey, career, collaborate and confidence. Strategies can be suggested to form some more communication forums including team meetings, conferences, monthly updates on corporate goals etc. to add more to the credibility component. Team building exercises like small team recreational activities e.g. bowling, skating; trips to cinemas etc. once in a month can also be introduced. Employee engagement is a direct reflection of how employees feel about their relationship with boss. Thus, quality of working relationships with peers, superiors and subordinates can be improved by providing more opportunities to collaborate. Though organisations are having their own models of practising employee engagement but to make the strategies more effective they can take into consideration the 10 Cs model of employee engagement and try to meet every 'C' as a parameter to the greatest possible extent.

CONCLUSION

Acquiring skilled workforce is just not enough in today's changing economy like ours; instead a lot needs to be done to retain, involve and make them committed to the organization and its goals. Thus, engagement is a state where an individual is not only intellectually committed but has great emotional attachment with his/her job that goes above and beyond the call of duty so as to further the interest of the company. Organizations like the above discussed ones are not only providing their employees a great infrastructure and other facilities but also freedom to make their work exciting and also give them an environment wherein they can say good-bye to a monotonous work. Thus working in a safe and cooperative environment adds to the engagement level of an employee.

References

(i) http://www.tata.com/media/articles/inside.aspx?artid=GAI3QG4hIfs=

(ii) Seijts, Gerard H. and Dan Crim (2006). "The Ten C's of Employee Engagement". Ivey Business Journal. http://web.ebscohost.com/ehost/pdf?vid=18&hid=109&sid=21a25099-6e82-4e66-849c-92a8d3ee0c6e%40sessionmgr102. Retrieved 2006-11-09.

(iii) BlessingWhite (December 2010). Employee Engagement Report 2011. http://www.blessingwhite.com/eee__report.asp. Retrieved 2010-12-12.

(iv) http://www.towersperrin.com/tp/getwebcachedoc?webc=HRS/USA/2008/200802/GWS_handout_web.pdf

(v) Konrad, Alison M. (March 2006). "Engaging Employees through High-Involvement Work Practices". Ivey Business Journal. http://web.ebscohost.com/ehost/pdf?vid=54&hid=120&sid=5d29fefe-0913-49de-82b6-9b95ee1a4f09%40sessionmgr105. Retrieved 2006-11-14.

(vi) "Engage Employees and Boost Performance". Hay Group. 2002. Archived from the original on 2006-11-23. http://web.archive.org/web/20061123123100/http://haygroup.ca/pdf/knowledge_engaged_performance_working_paper.pdf. Retrieved 2006-11-09.

(vii) Robinson, Dilys and Sue Hayday (2003). "Employee Engagement". In Brief (129). http://www.employment-studies.co.uk/news/129theme.php. Retrieved 2006-11-06.

(viii) Wilkinson, Adrien, *et al.* (2004). "Changing patterns of employee voice". Journal of Industrial Relations 46,3 (3): 298-322. doi:10.1111/j.0022-1856.2004.00143.x.

(ix) Lockwood, Nancy R. "Leveraging Employee Engagement for Competitive Advantage: HR's Strategic Role." HR Magazine Mar. 2007: 1-11. Search Spot. ABI/INFORM Global (PQ). McIntyre Library, Eau Claire. 22 Apr. 2007 <http://proquest.umi.com/pqdweb?did=1231781861&Fmt=4&VInst=PROD&VType=PQD&RQT=309&VName=PQD&>

(x) "Employee Commitment". Susan de la Vergne. 2005. http://www.auxiliumtraining.com/EmployeeCommitment.htm. Retrieved 2007-02-03.

(xi) "Employee Commitment Remains Unchanged....". Watson Wyatt Worldwide. 2002. http://www.watsonwyatt.com/research/resrender.asp?id=W-557&page=6. Retrieved 2006-11-07.

(xii) What Is Engagement?, Ken Scarlett, (2008). Retrieved on 2008-07-16.

(xiii) Harter, James K., Frank L. Schmidt, and Corey L. M. Keyes (2003). "Well-Being in the Workplace and its Relationships to Business Outcomes". Flourishing: the Positive Person and the Good Life: 205-244. http://media.gallup.com/DOCUMENTS/whitePaper--Well-BeingInTheWorkplace.pdf. Retrieved 2006-11-08.

(xiv) Ryan, Richard M. and Edward L. Deci (January 2000). "Self-Determination Theory and Facilitation of Intrinsic Motivation, Social Development, and Well-Being". American Psychologist Association 55: 68-78. Archived from the original on 2006-12-12. http://web.archive.org/web/20061212093251/http://www.psych.rochester.edu/SDT/documents/2000_RyanDeci_SDT.pdf. Retrieved 2006-11-06.

(xv) Hulme, Virginia A. (March 2006). "What Distinguishes the Best from the Rest". China Business Review.

(xvi) Derrick Hardman, Capital Incentives (part of Accor Services), Reward to Engage > rewards, benefits and employee engagement in today's organisations

(xvii) Robinson, D., S. Perryman, and S. Hayday (2004). "The Drivers of Employee Engagement". Institute for Employment Studies. http://www.employment-studies.co.uk/summary/summary.php?id=408. Retrieved 2006-11-07.

(xviii) Rawal Priyanka, Employee Retention "HRM REVIEW", April 2011

(xix) 2007 Employee Engaagement survey Comments Analysis for employees march 2008

(xx) www.frontlinelearning .com/article_employee_engagemnt_creating a culture of employee engagement.

(xxi) Ethical break downs ,Harvard Business Review South Asia, April(2011)

❖❖❖

6 Employee Engagement and Organisational Effectiveness: A Theoretical Construct

Mr. Bijaya Kumar Sundaray
Dr. Santosh Kumar Tripathy

ABSTRACT

Employee engagement has emerged as a popular organizational concept in recent years. It is the level of commitment and involvement of an employee towards the organization and its values. An engaged employee is aware of business context, and works with colleagues to improve performance within the job for the benefit of the organization. Employee engagement develops positive attitude among the employees towards the organization. This paper focuses on various factors which lead to employee engagement and what should company do to make the employees engaged. Proper attention on engagement strategies will increase the organizational effectiveness in terms of higher productivity, profits, quality, customer satisfaction, employee retention and increased adaptability.

Keywords: Employee engagement, organisational effectiveness, productivity, Employee retention.

INTRODUCTION

Today, society and business are witnessing unprecedented change in terms of the global nature of work and the diversity of the workforce. Organizations in the world are moving forward into a boundary-less environment. The ability to attract, engage, develop and retain talent will become increasingly important for gaining competitive advantage. Thus companies are competing for talent people who are have high performance and high competence in workplace (Berger and Berger, 2004). In the new economy, competition is global, capital is abundant, ideas are developed quickly and cheaply, and people are willing to change jobs often. The organisations, which are not able to provide a good treatment for their employees, will loose their talented people. In this situation engaged employees may be a key to competitive advantage. Organisations that understand the conditions that enhance employee engagement will have accomplished something that competitors will find very difficult to imitate. To the extent that employees are likely to face frequently with unanticipated and ambiguous decision-making situations, organizations must increasingly count on employees to act in ways that are consistent with organizational objectives. In addition, many employees are looking for environments where they can be engaged and feel that they are contributing in a positive way to something larger than themselves.

Employee engagement has emerged as a popular organizational concept in recent years, particularly among practitioner audiences (Saks, 2006; Bakker and Schaufeli, 2008). This is seemingly as attractive for organizations as it is for the professional societies and consulting groups who promote it. The outcomes of employee engagement are advocated to be exactly what most organizations are seeking: employees who are more productive in which they can work over the target within working time, profitable in which they spend the financial usage of company efficiently, safer, healthier, less likely to turnover, less likely to be absent, and more willing to engage in discretionary efforts (Buchanan, 2004; Fleming and Asplund, 2007; Wagner and Harter, 2006). Many organizations are now actively formulating engagement strategies with the belief that this will make them an "employer of choice" and concurrently improve organizational performance.

EMPLOYEE ENGAGEMENT: LITERATURE REVIEW

Employee engagement is a complex, broad construct that subsumes many well researched ideas such as commitment, satisfaction, loyalty and extra role behavior. An engaged employee extends themselves to meet the organization's needs, takes initiative, is proactive, reinforces and supports the organization's culture and values, is in the flow, shares the values of the organization, stays focused and vigilant and believes he/she can make a difference (Macey, 2006). In practice organizations typically define engagement as being a part of the organization, having pride and loyalty in the company, being committed, and going "above and beyond the call of duty". Kahn (1990) defined employee engagement as 'the harnessing of organization members' selves to their work roles. In engagement, people employ and express themselves physically, cognitively, and emotionally during role performances. The cognitive aspect of employee engagement concerns employees' beliefs about the organisation, its leaders and working conditions. The emotional aspect concerns how employees feel about each of those three factors and whether they have positive or negative attitudes toward the organisation and its leaders. The physical aspect of employee engagement concerns the physical energies exerted by individuals to accomplish their roles. Thus, according to Kahn (1990), engagement means to be psychologically as well as physically present when occupying and performing an organisational role.

Most often employee engagement has been defined as emotional and intellectual commitment to the organisation (Baumruk, 2004; Richman, 2006; and Shaw, 2005) or the amount of discretionary effort exhibited by employees in their job (Frank *et al.* 2004). Robinson et al. (2004) defined engagement similar to the established constructs such as 'organisational commitment' and 'organisational citizenship behaviour' (OCB). It is a desirable condition, has an organizational purpose, and connotes involvement, commitment, passion, enthusiasm, focused effort, and energy, so it has both attitudinal and behavioral components (Erickson, 2005). Brown (2006) viewed engagement as a progressive combination of satisfaction, motivation, commitment and advocacy resulting from employees' movement up the engagement pyramid. Engagement is the measure of an employee's emotional and intellectual commitment to their organization and its success. It is an outcome of employees' organizational experiences that are characterized by behaviors that are grouped in to three categories: say, stay and strive (Hewitt, 2005).

Employee engagement can be considered as cognitive, emotional and behavioral. Cognitive engagement refers to employees' beliefs about the company, its leaders and the workplace culture. The emotional aspect is how employees feel about the company, the leaders and their colleagues. The behavioral factor is the value added component reflected in the amount of effort employees put into their work (Lockwood, 2007). Mone and London (2010) defined employee engagement is "a condition of employee who feels involved, committed, passionate, and empowered and demonstrates those feelings in work behavior". Employee engagement is thus the level of commitment and involvement an employee has towards their organization and its values. An engaged employee is aware of business context, and works with colleagues to improve performance within the job for the benefit of the organization. The organization must work to develop and nurture engagement, which requires a two-way relationship between employer and employee. Thus Employee engagement is a barometer that determines the association of a person with the organization.

FACTORS OF EMPLOYEE ENGAGEMENT

There are some critical factors which lead to employee engagement. These factors are common to all organisations, regardless of sector. These factors create a feeling of valued and involved among the employees. But the components of feeling valued and involved, and the relative strength of each factor are likely to vary depending on the organisation. The factors which lead to employee engagement are;

- **Career Development Opportunities:** Organizations with high levels of engagement provide employees with opportunities to develop their abilities, learn new skills, acquire new knowledge and realize their potential. When companies plan for the career paths of their employees and invest in them in this way their people invest in them. Career development influences engagement for employees and retaining the most talented employees and providing opportunities for personal development.
- **Leadership:** Employees need to feel that the core values for which their companies stand are unambiguous and clear. Successful organizations show respect for each employee's qualities and contribution regardless of their job level. A company's ethical standards also lead to engagement of an individual
- **Empowerment:** Employees want to be involved in decisions that affect their work. The leaders of high engagement workplaces create a trustful and challenging environment, in which employees are encouraged to give input and innovative ideas to move the organization forward.
- **Equal Opportunities and Fair Treatment:** The employee engagement levels would be high if their superiors provide equal opportunities for growth and advancement to all the employees. Employees feel that they are not discriminated in any aspects within the organisation.
- **Training and Development Opportunities:** Redundancy of skills has been cited as one of the reasons for employee turnover, thereby indicating the necessity for training, re-training and multi-skill training. Much value is attached by employees to the availability of training opportunities which would prepare them for future roles.

- **Performance Appraisal:** Fair evaluation of an employee's performance is an important criterion for determining the level of employee engagement. The organisation which follows an appropriate performance appraisal technique will have high levels of employee engagement.
- **Pay and Benefits:** The organisation should have a proper pay system so that the employees are motivated to work in the organization. In order to boost his engagement levels the employees should also be provided with certain benefits and compensations.
- **Health and Safety:** Research indicates that the engagement levels are low if the employee does not feel secure while working. Therefore every organization should adopt appropriate methods and systems for the health and safety of their employees.
- **Job Satisfaction:** Only a satisfied employee can become an engaged employee. Therefore it is very essential for an organization to see to it that the job given to the employee matches his career goals which will make him enjoy his work and he would ultimately be satisfied with his job.
- **Communication:** The organisation should follow the open door policy. There should be both upward and downward communication with the use of appropriate communication channels in the organization. If the employee is given a say in the decision making and has the right to be heard by his boss than the engagement levels are likely to be high.
- **Family Friendliness:** A person's family life influences his work life. When an employee realizes that the organization is considering his family's benefits also, he will have an emotional attachment with the organization which leads to engagement
- **Co-operation:** Effective cooperation should be established between different departments and functions, and also between management and trade union. If the entire organization works together by helping each other, the employees will be more engaged.

OUTCOMES OF EMPLOYEE ENGAGEMENT

Employee engagement is a critical ingredient of individual and organizational success. The impact of engagement (or disengagement) can manifest itself through productivity and organisational performance, outcomes for customers of the organisation, employee retention rates, organisational culture, and advocacy of the organisation and its external image. Employee engagement is a key business driver for organizational success. High levels of employee engagement with in a company promote retention of talent, foster customer loyalty and improve organizational performance. It is also a key link to customer satisfaction, company reputation and overall stakeholder value (Lockwood, 2007). Kahn (1992) proposed that high levels of engagement lead to both positive outcomes for individuals, (e.g. quality of people's work and their own experiences of doing that work), as well as positive organisational-level outcomes (e.g. the growth and productivity of organisations). The Gallup Organisation (2004) found critical links between employee engagement, customer loyalty, business growth and profitability. Employee Engagement also acts as a catalyst towards the retention of staff. Greenberg (2004) says that employee engagement is critical to any organization that seeks not only to retain valued employees, but also increase its levels of performance. Hewitt Associates

LLC, (2005) established a conclusive relationship between engagement and profitability through higher productivity, sales, customer satisfaction, and employee retention. Engaged employees not only contribute more but also are more loyal and therefore less likely to voluntarily leave the organization. The various factors and outcomes of employee engagement have clearly depicted in the model (Fig 1) given below.

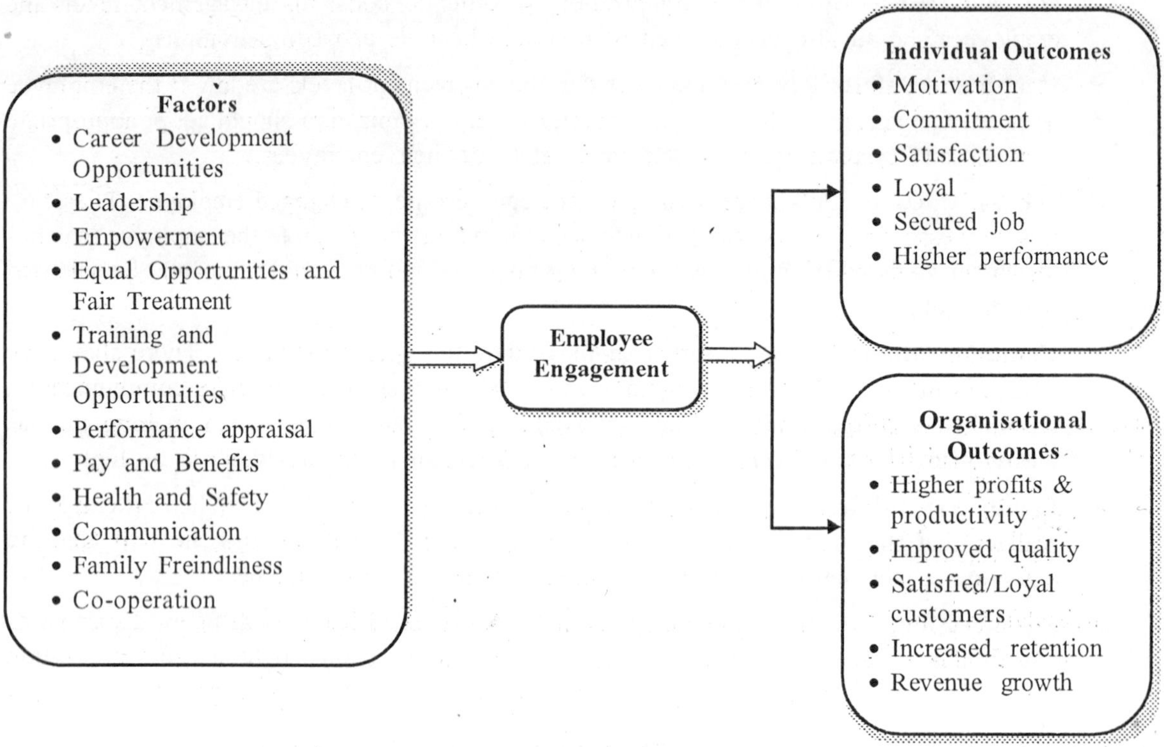

Fig. 6.1: Factors and Outcomes of Employee Engagement

CONCLUSION

Employee Engagement is a positive attitude held by the employees towards the organization and its values. It is rapidly gaining popularity and importance in the workplace and impacts organizations in many ways. An organization should thus recognize employees, more than any other variable, as powerful contributors to its competitive position. Engaged employees can help your organization achieve its mission, execute its strategy and generate important business results. Therefore employee engagement should be a continuous process of learning, improvement, measurement and action. This paper provides some noteworthy implications for practitioners. It focuses on the various factors which influence employee engagement. It has been observed that organisations with higher levels of employee engagement outperform their competitors in terms of profitability. Engaged employees give their companies crucial competitive advantages — including higher productivity, customer satisfaction and lower employee turnover. The relationship between employee engagement and organizational outcomes would be stronger if better measures were used. Thus, organisations need to better understand how different employees are affected by different factors of engagement and focus on those in order to achieve the strategic outcomes.

References

1. Bakker, A. and Schaufeli, W. (2008) Positive organizational behavior: engaged employees in flourishing organizations, *Journal of Organizational Behavior*, Vol. 29, Issue 2, pp. 147 – 154.
2. Baumruk, R. (2004). 'The missing link: the role of employee engagement in business success', *Workspan,* Vol 47, pp. 48-52.
3. Berger, L. and Berger, D. (2004). The talent management handbook. Mc Graw-Hill Companies. USA.
4. Brown, R. (2006). *Doing your dissertation in business and management: the reality of researching and writing*. London, SAGE.
5. Buchanan, L. (2004). The things they do for love. Harvard Business Review, *82*(12), 19-20.
6. Erickson, T. J. (2005). Testimony submitted before the U.S. Senate Committee on Health, Education, Labor and Pensions, May 26.
7. Fleming, J. H., and Asplund, J. (2007). Human sigma. New York: Gallup.
8. Frank, F.D., Finnegan, R.P. and Taylor, C.R. (2004) 'The race for talent: retaining and engaging workers in the 21st century', *Human Resource Planning,* Vol 27, No 3, pp.12-25.
9. Greenberg, J (2004) Increasing employee retention through employee engagement, *Alphameasure Incorporated Publication,* October, pp. 3.
10. Hewitt Associates LLC. (2005). Employee engagement. Retrieved April 29, 2011, from http:// was4.hewitt.com/ hewitt/services/talent/subtalent/ee_engagement.htm
11. Kahn, W. A. (1990). Psychological conditions of personal engagement and disengagement at work. *Academy of Management Journal,* Vol. 33, pp. 692-724.
12. Kahn, W.A. (1992) To be fully there: psychological presence at work. *Human Relations,* Vol. 45, pp. 321-50.
13. Lockwood, N. R. (2007). Leveraging Employee Engagements for Competitive Advantage: HRs Strategic Role. *HR Magazine,* 52(3), pp. 1-11.
14. Macey, W. H., (2006). *Toward a definition of engagement.* Paper presented at the Society for Industrial and Organizational Psychology 21st Annual Conference, May, Dallas, TX.
15. Mone, Edward M., and London, Manuel. (2010). Employee engagement; Through effective performance management. A practical guide for managers. Routledge Press. NY.
16. Richman, A. (2006) 'Everyone wants an engaged workforce how can you create it?' *Workspan,* Vol. 49, pp.36-39.
17. Robinson, D., Perryman, S. and Hayday, S. (2004) *The Drivers of Employee Engagement.* Brighton, Institute for Employment Studies.

18. Saks, A. M. (2006). Antecedents and consequences of employee engagement. *Journal of Managerial Psychology*, 21(7), pp. 600-619.

19. Shaw, K. (2005) 'An engagement strategy process for communicators', *Strategic Communication Management,* Vol 9, No 3, pp26-29.

20. The Gallup Organisation (2004) [online] Available at: www.gallup.com Accessed on 28th April 2011.

21. Wagner, R., and Harter, J. K. (2006). 12: The great elements of managing. Washington, DC: The Gallup Organization.

❖❖❖

7 Employee Engagement – Key to Organisational Success

Dr. Padmalita Routray
Dr. Kalyani Mohanty

ABSTRACT

Employee engagement can be a deciding factor in organizational success. Not only does engagement have the potential to significantly affect employee retention, productivity and loyalty, it is also a key link to customer satisfaction, company reputation and overall stakeholder value. In twenty first century all most all organizations in business world could realize the importance of human capital, it's talent, capability and creativity for organisation's growth and performance which can optimally used when people are committed and hope full. So, the present paper tries to explain the concept of employee engagement and its importance for business organisations. Again the growth of knowledge industry and demand for knowledge worker has created lot of competition in engagement practice and strategies among them. Hence in the paper the effect of and strategies for developing employee engagement are discussed. Though the industries have been working on HRD and OD for appreciating human value in organization since long, engagement needs a comparative and constant watch over things to make them committed which is known as corporate citizenship. So it is also described the ways for measuring and managing employee engagement as suggested in different research studies.

INTRODUCTION

The 21st century is all about engagement of people who will put their best selves into solving tough problems that require knowledge and insight. Employee engagement has emerged as a critical driver of business success in today's competitive market economy. Research by the CIPD has repeatedly demonstrated the links between the way people are managed, employee attitudes and business performance (Purcell 2006 and Truss *et al* 2006). Moreover, engaged employees have been found to outperform their disengaged counterparts. However, recent research in the UK and other countries shows that there are more disengaged employees than there are engaged employees in today's organisations. Employees with the highest levels of commitment perform 20 per cent better and are 87 per cent less likely to leave the organization, which indicates that engagement is linked to organizational performance (CLC, 2004). Further, employee engagement can be a deciding factor in organizational success. Not only does engagement have the potential to significantly affect employee retention, productivity and loyalty, it is also a key link to customer satisfaction, company reputation and overall stakeholder value. Thus, to gain a competitive edge, organizations are turning to HR to set the agenda for employee engagement and commitment.

CONCEPT AND DEFINITION OF EMPLOYEE ENGAGEMENT

Kahn (1990:694) defines employee engagement as "the harnessing of organization members' selves to their work roles; in engagement, people employ and express themselves physically, cognitively, and emotionally during role performances". The cognitive aspect of employee engagement concerns employees' beliefs about the organisation, its leaders and working conditions. The emotional aspect concerns how employees feel about each of those three factors and whether they have positive or negative attitudes toward the organisation and its leaders. The physical aspect of employee engagement concerns the physical energies exerted by individuals to accomplish their roles. Thus, according to Kahn (1990), engagement means to be psychologically as well as physically present when occupying and performing an organisational role. Employee engagement as described by Schmidt *et. al* (1993) as employee involvement with, commitment to and satisfaction with work. An engaged employee is one who is fully involved in and enthusiastic about his or her work and thus will act in a way that furthers their organisation's interests. Employee engagement is defined as "the extent to which employees commit to something or someone in their organization, how hard they work and how long they stay as a result of that commitment." (2) Research shows that the connection between an employee's job and organizational strategy, including understanding how important the job is to the firm's success, is the most important driver of employee engagement. In fact, employees with the highest levels of commitment perform 20% better and are 87% less likely to leave the organization, which indicates that engagement is linked to organizational performance. (3) In contrast, job satisfaction—a term sometimes used interchangeably with employee engagement—is defined as how an employee feels about his or her job, work environment, pay, benefits, etc. (4) The Gallup Organization, potentially the most widely recognized name associated with employee engagement due to their best selling book, "First, Break All the Rules," defines engaged employees as those who, "work with a passion and feel a profound connection to their company" and "drive innovation and move the organization forward" (GMJ, 2006). Melcrum Publishing recently produced a research report, "Employee Engagement: How to build a high performance workforce" that provides a very comprehensive review on the current state of employee engagement (Shaw, 2005). The author of Melcrum's report, Kieron Shaw (2005), highlights multiple definitions of employee engagement. For the purposes of his research, Shaw (2005) also created a definition of employee engagement, which is, "translating employee potential into employee performance and business success" and thus "changing the way employees perform by utilizing the tools in the armory of internal communication professionals." The International Survey Research (ISR) defines employee engagement as, "a process by which an organization increases commitment and continuation of its employees to the achievement of superior results." The ISR separates commitment into three parts; cognitive commitment, affective commitment, and behavioral commitment or think, feel and act. Dell Inc. defines employee engagement by stating, "To compete today, companies need to win over the minds (rational commitment) and the hearts (emotional commitment) of employees in ways that lead to extraordinary effort" (Vance, 2006). Employee Engagement is the means or strategy by which an organisation seeks to build a partnership between the organisation and its employees, such that:

- Employees fully understands and is committed to achieve the organisation's objectives, and
- The organisation respects the personal aspirations and ambitions of its employees.

It is seen largely the organisation's responsibility to create an environment and culture conducive to this partnership. According to Scarlett Survey (2010) "Employee Engagement" is a measurable degree of an employee positive or negative emotional attachment to their job, colleagues and organisation which profoundly influences their willingness to learn and perform at work.

Global studies suggest that there are three basic aspects of employee engagement:

- The employees and their own unique psychological make up and experience.
- The employers and their ability to create the conditions that promote employee engagement.
- Interaction between employees at all levels.

Employee engagement creates greater motivation within employees for the work they do and increases their commitment to the organisation. It is about creating an enthusiasm for their roles, their work and the organisation, and ensuring they are aligned with the values of the organisation, well informed and well integrated with their colleagues and the fabric or culture of the organisation. Engaged employees work harder, are more loyal and are more likely to go the 'extra mile' for the corporation.

Table 7.1: Levels of Employee Engagement

Engaged employees work with passion and feel a profound connection to their company. They drive innovation and move the organization forward.
Not engaged employees are essentially "checked out." They're sleepwalking through their work day, putting time — not energy or passion — into their work.
Actively disengaged employees aren't just unhappy at work: they're busy acting out their unhappiness. Every day, these workers undermine what their engaged co-workers accomplish.

Source: Adapted from "Engaged employees inspire company innovation." (2006, October 12). Gallup Management Journal, http://gmj.gallup.com

There are different levels of engagement (Table 1), and understanding the types of engagement provides perspective into employee behaviors that can either positively or negatively affect organizational success. Employee engagement can be considered as cognitive, emotional and behavioral. Cognitive engagement refers to employees' beliefs about the company, its leaders and the workplace culture. The emotional aspect is how employees feel about the company, the leaders and their colleagues. The behavioral factor is the value-added component reflected in the amount of effort employees put into their work.

Effects of Employee Engagement

Practitioners and academics tend to agree that the consequences of employee engagement are positive (Saks 2006). There is a general belief that there is a connection between employee engagement and business results; a meta-analysis conducted by Harter et al (2002:272) confirms this connection. They concluded that, "employee satisfaction and engagement are related to meaningful business outcomes at a magnitude that is important to many organisations". Kahn (1992) proposed that high levels of engagement lead to both positive outcomes for individuals, (e.g. quality of people's work and their own experiences of doing that work), as well as positive organisational-level outcomes (e.g. the growth and productivity of organisations). The Gallup Organisation (2004) found critical links between employee engagement, customer loyalty, business growth and profitability. They compared the scores of these variables among a sample of stores scoring in the top 25 per cent on employee engagement and customer loyalty with those in the bottom 25 per cent. Stores in the bottom 25 per cent significantly under-performed across three productivity measures: sales, customer complaints and turnover. The International Survey Research (ISR) team has similarly found encouraging evidence that organisations can only reach their full potential through emotionally engaging employees and customers (ISR 2005). In an extension of the Gallup findings, Ott (2007) cites Gallup research, which found that higher workplace engagement predicts higher earnings per share (EPS) among publicly-traded businesses. When compared with industry competitors at the company level, organisations with more than four engaged employees for every one actively disengaged, experienced 2.6 times more growth in EPS than did organisations with a ratio of slightly less than one engaged worker for every one actively disengaged employee. In 2005, a survey conducted by Gallup in Thailand revealed only 12 per cent of Thailand's employee population are 'engaged', 82 per cent are 'actively disengaged' and 6 per cent disengaged. Similar Gallup studies have found the levels of engagement in Australia, China, Japan, New Zealand and Singapore to be 18 per cent, 12 per cent, 9 per cent, 17 per cent and 9 per cent respectively (Gallup 2004). The study of employee engagement at a global level is worthwhile given the increasing number of multi-national organisations and use of outsourcing. It is important to consider whether or not the same engagement techniques work for employees in countries with different economies and cultures. Evidence from the USA (Johnson 2004) indicates roughly half of all Americans in the workforce are not fully engaged or they are disengaged. Furthermore, a Global Workforce Survey conducted in 2005 by consultancy firm Towers Perrin found disconcerting findings, again in the USA (Seijts and Crim 2006). The survey involved about 85,000 people who worked full-time for large and mid-sized firms; it found only 14 per cent of all employees worldwide were highly engaged in their job. Across industries, engagement is substantially higher in the non-profit sector than in every other sector looked at by Towers Perrin (2003). This would appear logical, given that people tend to be drawn to this sector through a sense of mission, rather than from any prospect of high pay or wealth accumulation. This finding is also consistent with the numerous definitions and views surrounding engagement, which identifies a 'passion for work' as being a key component factor (Truss *et al* 2006, Brim 2002 and Holbeche and Springett 2003). Indeed, the fact that the sector is traditionally not a high-paying one, relative to the others studied, emphasises the fact that it is not possible to 'buy' engagement in the conventional sense by offering better than average monetary awards. Conversely, in another study comparing the public and private sectors, Truss *et al* (2006) found that group in the public sector had a more negative experience of work, they reported more bullying and harassment than those in the private sector, and were less satisfied with the opportunities they had to use their abilities.

Employee Engagement Strategies

Purcell *et al* (2003) suggest that employee engagement is only meaningful if there is a more genuine sharing of responsibility between management and employees over issues of substance. The CIPD survey conducted by Truss *et al* (2006) suggests that strengthening employee voice can make a difference to organisational performance. Employee voice can be defined as the ability for employees to have an input into decisions that are made in organisations (Lucas *et al* 2006). It has been argued that one of the main drivers of employee engagement is for employees to have the opportunity to feed their view upwards (Truss *et al* 2006). Their survey concluded that currently many organisations are not very successful in doing this and as a result many employees felt they lacked opportunities to express their views and be involved in decisions. On the other hand, researchers at Towers Perrin (2003) found employers are doing well in giving employees the freedom to make decisions relating to their jobs; 62 per cent of respondents argued they have an appropriate amount of decision-making authority to do their job well. Research by Robinson (2006) suggests there is considerable evidence that many employees are greatly under-utilised in the workplace through the lack of involvement in work-based decisions. Employee involvement is seen as a central principle of 'soft' HRM, where the focus is upon capturing the ideas of employees and securing their commitment (Beardwell and Claydon 2007). The concept of employee involvement is strongly grounded in unitarist views of organisations, as it assumes that managers and employees have the same interests.

Recent research suggests that high-involvement work practices can develop the positive beliefs and attitudes associated with employee engagement, and that these practices can generate the kinds of discretionary behaviours that lead to enhanced performance (Konrad 2006). High involvement workplaces use "a system of management practices giving their employees skills, information, motivation, and latitude and resulting in a workforce that is a source of competitive advantage" (Guthrie 2001:181). According to Lawler and Worley (2006) for a high-involvement work practice to be effective and for it to have a positive impact on employee engagement, employees must be given power. They argue this will lead to employees having the ability to make decisions that are important to their performance and to the quality of their working lives, thus engaging them in their work. Furthermore, Lawler and Worley (2006) contend that power can mean a relatively low level of influence, as in providing input into decisions made by others or it can mean having final authority and accountability for decisions and their outcomes. Involvement is maximised when the highest possible level of power is pushed down to the employees that have to carry out the decision, resulting in gaining the maximum level of engagement possible from employees. Purcell *et al's* (2003) study found a number of factors to be strongly associated with high levels of employee engagement. The one thing all of these factors had in common was that they were connected with an employee's involvement in a practice related to their work. For example, effective communications was found to be a factor as engagement levels were affected by the amount of information employees received about how well the company was performing and how they contributed to the company achieving its business objectives. Furthermore, employees having involvement in decisions' affecting their job or work was also associated with high levels of engagement. "High-involvement" work systems as having combinations of five characteristics: On-line work teams, problem-solving groups, job rotation, suggestion programs, and decentralization of quality efforts. Research has shown that implementing any or all of these work practices can result in considerable improvement in overall performance, especially in labor-intensive settings such as manufacturing. Improved quality, higher productivity, lower scrap rates, and lower turnover are just some of the results seen when these work practices are used successfully. Pil and MacDuffie (1999) found that three factors drive the success of efforts to adopt high-involvement practices:

- The level of complementary organizational practices and technologies that enhance the benefits from the new practices (e.g. flexible automation, such as robotics, enables companies to harness the workforce flexibility of high-involvement systems in ways that hard/fixed automation does not).
- The performance levels the organization is achieving from its current practices. Poor performers were more likely to undertake change than mediocre performers. The latter were more likely to focus on squeezing additional performance out of existing practices.
- Organizational actions that alter the cost of introducing new practices. As an example, the authors found that unfreezing of existing practices happens naturally at many companies (e.g. during new product introductions), and that many organizations use these occasions to undertake change. They urge caution, however, in using these opportunities, because factors that result in unfreezing of existing practice also make it difficult to identify performance changes from introducing new practices. Introducing new work systems in periods of stability makes it easier to focus attention on optimizing the practices, and assessing their effect on performance.

MANAGING AND MEASURING EMPLOYEE ENGAGEMENT

ISR's (2004) study identified four issues as global factors in managing engagement; career development, leadership, empowerment, and image (which refers to the company's image to customers and the public). Career development was found to influence engagement for employees in each of the ten countries studied, with the key message being organisations with high levels of engagement provide employees with opportunities to develop their abilities, learn new skills, acquire new knowledge and realise their potential. The logic behind this is that when companies invest in their people in this way, their people invest in them.

Table 7.2: Ten Common Themes: How Companies Measure Engagement

1. Pride in employer.
2. Satisfaction with employer.
3. Job satisfaction
4. Opportunity to perform well at challenging work.
5. Recognition and positive feedback for one's contributions.
6. Personal support from one's supervisor.
7. Effort above and beyond the minimum.
8. Understanding the link between one's job and the organization's mission.
9. Prospects for future growth with one's employer
10. Intention to stay with one's employer

Source: Vance, R. J. (2006). Effective practice guidelines: Employee engagement and commitment. Alexandria, VA: SHRM Foundation.

Measuring employee engagement is a smart business strategy to improve productivity and attain business objectives. It allows the organization to track progress, or slippage, and determine what gaps exist in terms of organizational engagement, attendance and retention, motivation and aspirations.

The financial and competitive advantage of employee engagement efforts can be demonstrated by measuring engagement and commitment initiatives (Table: 2). The level of engagement determines whether people are productive and stay with the organization—or move to the competition. Research highlights that the employee connection to the organizational strategy and goals, acknowledgment for work well done, and a culture of learning and development foster high levels of engagement. Without a workplace environment for employee engagement, turnover will increase and efficiency will decline, leading to low customer loyalty and decreased stakeholder value. Ultimately, because the cost of poor employee engagement will be detrimental to organizational success, it is vital for HR to foster positive, effective people managers along with workplace policies and practices that focus on employee well-being, health and work/life balance.

References

1. (2006). Gallup Study: Engaged employees inspire company innovation. Gallup Management Journal (GMJ), http://gmj.gallup.com/content/default.aspx?ci=24880&pg=1.
2. Shaw, K. (2005). Employee engagement, how to build a high-performance workforce. Melcrum Publishing Limited, ISBN: 0-9547741-3-2.
3. Vance, R. J. (2006). Employee engagement and commitment, A guide to understanding, measuring and increasing engagement in your organization. Society for Human Resource Management,1-45.
4. Corporate Leadership Council(CLC). (2004). Driving performance and retention through employee engagement. Washington, DC: Corporate Executive Board.
5. Lockwood, Nancy R. (2007).Leveraging Employee Engagement for Competitive Advantage: HR's Strategic Role, SHRM®Research Quarterly
6. Purcell, J., Kinnie, N., Hutchinson, S., Rayton, B. and Swart, J. (2003) Understanding the People and Performance Link: Unlocking the Black Box. London, CIPD.
7. Purcell, J. (2006). Change Agenda, Reflections on Employee Engagement. London, CIPD.
8. Truss, C., Soane, E., Edwards, C., Wisdom, K., Croll, A. and Burnett, J. (2006) Working Life: Employee Attitudes and Engagement 2006. London, CIPD
9. Kahn, W.A. (1990). 'Psychological conditions of personal engagement and disengagement at work', Academy of Management Journal, Vol 33, pp692-724.
10. Beardwell, J. and Claydon, T. (2007) Human Resource Management, A Contemporary Approach. 5th ed. Harlow, Prentice Hall.
11. Brim, B. (2002). 'The longer workers stay in their jobs, the more disheartened they become', GallupManagementJournal,March.Availableat:http://www.gallupjournal.com/GM/Jarchive/issue5/2002315c.asp [Accessed 1st August 2007]
12. Guthrie, J.P. (2001).'High involvement work practices, turnover and productivity: Evidence from New Zealand' Academy of Management Journal, Vol 44, pp180–190.
13. The Gallup Organisation (2004).[online] Available at: www.gallup.com.
14. Harter, J.K., Schmidt, F.L. and Hayes, T.L. (2002) 'Business-unit level relationship between employee satisfaction, employee engagement, and business outcomes: a meta- analysis', Journal of Applied Psychology, Vol 87, pp268-79.

15. Holbeche, L. and Springett, N. (2003). In Search of Meaning in the Workplace. Horsham, Roffey Park.

16. ISR (2004). International Survey Research. [Online] Available at: www.isrsurveys.com

17. Johnson, M. (2004). 'Gallup study reveals workplace disengagement in Thailand', The GallupManagementJournal,12thMay.[online]Availableat:http://gmj.gallup.com/content/16306/3/Gallup-Study-Reveals-Workplace-Disengagementin.aspx.

18. Konrad, A.M. (2006). 'Engaging employees through high-involvement work practices', Ivey Business Journal, March/April, pp1-6.

19. Lawler, E and Worley, C.G. (2006). 'Winning support for organisational change: Designing employee reward systems that keep on working', Ivey Business Journal, March/April.

20. Ott, B. (2007).'Investors take note: Engagement boosts earnings', The Gallup Management Journal, 14thJune.[online]Availableat:http://web.ebscohost.com/ehost/pdf?vid=4&hid=21&sid=8470b965-28f0-4f5a-95226c297e68b789%40sessionmgr8

21. Robinson, I. (2006). Human Resource Management in Organisations. London, CIPD.

22. Saks, A.M. (2006). 'Antecedents and consequences of employee engagement', Journal of Managerial Psychology, Vol 21, No 6, pp600-619.

23. Seijts, G.H and Crim, D. (2006).'What engages employees the most or, the ten C's of employee engagement', Ivey Business Journal, March/April, pp1-5.

24. Frits K. Pil and John Paul MacDuffie(1999).Why Efforts To Implement High-Involvement Work Practices Fail Published: October 13, in Knowledge@Wharton

Websites

www.opcuk.com

www.gallup.com

www.towersperrin.com

www.corporateleadershipcouncil.com

www.scarlettsurveys.com

8

Work Culture: A Promising Tool for Employee Engagement

Kalpana Sahoo
Nihar Ranjan Agasti

ABSTRACT

Organizations in the modern days are undergoing transformation in the wake of industrialization and globalization. In the face of a globally expanding and highly competitive world, now the organizations are seeking fundamental insights to help, nurture, harvest, and manage the immense potential of employee's knowledge assets for capability to excel at the leading edge of innovation. It has become more significant for HR professionals to devise new and innovative management practices and ideas towards engaging their employees motivated, satisfied and always available for giving their best efforts towards achieving organizational goals and objectives. Retention of skills and competencies and maintaining a motivated and contended workforce are, perhaps the biggest challenges before the HR professionals. However, it largely depends on the organizational culture where employees' willingness and commitment can create a sharing environment. This paper highlights that what extent the organizational culture can affect attitudes of the employees towards the participation in employee's involvement and secondly, the extent to which appropriate, positive knowledge cultures can be crated by deliberate management efforts.

Keywords: Employee Engagement, Work Culture, Work Culture and employee engagement, Employee Engagement & Culture Change.

INTRODUCTION

In pursuit of objectives, all organizations rely on the availability and effectiveness of several kinds of resources, which can be divided into finance, technology and people. Some organizations emphasize their financial resources others rely on the quality of its employees, its human resources. Regardless of the particular resource emphasis in an industry, the human resource is almost always the key ingredient for organizational success (Nankarvis, Compton & Baird, 2002). HR practice could not form the basis for sustainable competitive advantage but human capital pool has greater potential to constitute a source of sustainable competitive advantage Wright, Dunford & Snell, (2001). Wright *et al.* (2001) have explained human capital pool means skillful employees in the organization.

Employee engagement is a big and a constant challenge for every organization today whether to talk of any corporate sector or any educational institution. It is a herculean task for most organizations in the modern era of globalization and competitive business. Successful organizations realize the importance of employee retention and talent management .These are integral to sustaining their leadership and growth in the market place. Becoming an employer of choice by engaging high caliber employees in today's labour market should be the highest priority. HR professionals all over the world are breaking their heads to formulate Employee Engagement Strategies. (ESS). Engaging quality workforce is a tough task for many HR professionals in today's aggressive job scenario. And now with the job market slowly opening up, the challenge now is to retain the best by offering incentives which ensures employee engagement and empowerment.

There is an old saying that you can take a horse to the water but you cannot force it to drink: it will drink only if it is thirsty-so with people. They will do what they want to do or otherwise motivated to do whether it is to excel on the workshop floor, they must be motivated or driven to do it either by themselves or through external stimulus, thus it is imperative on the part of an employee to be engaged, motivated so that a productive workplace can be maintained and developed and employees derive satisfaction from their job.

EMPLOYEE ENGAGEMENT

An organization's productivity is measured not in terms of employee satisfaction but by employee engagement. Employees are said to be engaged when they show a positive attitude toward the organization and express a commitment to remain with the organization. Where engagement leads, performance follows. A highly engaged workforce is 50% more productive than an unengaged workforce. A major Right Management study of engagement involving nearly 30,000 employees in 15 countries worldwide suggests that an organization's culture can play a special role in driving engagement and that leaders can take many concrete steps to create a culture of engagement. The extent to which employees commit to something or someone in the organization, and how long they stay as a result of that commitment, Corporate Executive Board. *Driving performance and retention through employee engagement. (2004).* Washington, DC. Loyal employees (versus satisfied employees) stay because they want to. They go above and beyond the call of duty to further their company's interests. *Walker loyalty report.* (2003, September). Indianapolis, IN: Walker Information. Engagement is the state in which individuals are emotionally and intellectually committed to the organization as measured by three primary behaviors: Say, Stay and Strive, *Employee engagement at double-digit growth companies.* (2004). Hewitt Research Brief. The extent to which employees put discretionary effort into their work in the form of brainpower, extra time, and energy, *Understanding what drives employee engagement.* (2003) . The latest idea is employee engagement, a concept that holds that it is the degree to which an employee is emotionally bonded to his organization and passionate about his work that really matters. The BW-HR Anexi Blessing White Employee Engagement Survey 2008 shows significant differences between what motivates workers in India and what motivates workers in other countries. The term 'employee engagement' represents an alignment of maximum job satisfaction with maximum job contribution. The global survey shows that 34 per cent of the employees in India are fully engaged and 13 per cent disengaged. As many as 29 per cent are 'almost engaged'. Focus on Employee Engagement by industry: With the exception of the government sector (which has relatively low engagement levels in all countries), some high-tech industries (pharma, biotech) score low whereas some service-focused industries (retail, consumer products) score high. Engagement by level: Our survey shows that people higher up in the organization experience higher engagement. The survey reveals a large disparity between men and women: Men count 8 per cent more fully engaged and 6 per cent less disengaged than women. What Employees Want Factors influencing satisfaction: In the survey, respondents were asked to pick one of eight factors that they believed would most influence their satisfaction at work. Career development opportunities and training (30 per cent), more challenging work (20 per cent), and more opportunities to do what I do best (19 per cent) were the three factors at the top of Indian workers' wish lists, consistent with the top three global demands. The Employee People higher up in the organization expectedly show higher levels of engagement as they are closer to the centre of decision making, have more say in the direction of the organization and presumably were promoted at least partly on the basis of their ability to deliver in tune with the organization's goals.

Key employee retention and making them engaged is a critical to the success of a business which is a long term plan. Now since the job market has become a battleground over talent. Now Indian corporations are busy weaving out new strategies to attract and retain and engaged the talent. For bigger players, cash incentives and full variable payouts are the primary areas to concentrate upon. Whereas, smaller players need to differentiate themselves by concentrating on performance-based variables and through empowerment. There are many tools used by the human resource (HR) departments across industries to retain and stimulate the best talents, which propel talented peoples to stay motivated and remain in the organizations.

WORK CULTURE

Culture plays larger part in determining the quality of organizational life. Culture perpetuates and reproduces itself through the socialization of new member entering the group. The culture and ethos of an organization includes both the way in which it sees itself and manages itself internally and the way in which it sees and interacts with its clients and others outside the organization. Organizational cultures are central aspects of organization and serve important communication functions further people who create and participate in them. These functions include providing employees with sense of individual and collective identity contributing to the establishment of structure and control within the organization, aiding the socialization of employees through learning about the customs and traditions of the organization and fostering cohesiveness among employees. Work culture is a combination of qualities in an organization and its employees that arise from what is generally regarded as appropriate ways to think and act. Culture is the vehicle through which individuals coordinate their activities to achieve common goals .Culture helps individuals understand how their roles fit within the larger picture The culture of a group can now be defined as: a pattern of shared basic assumptions that the group learned as it solved its problems of external adaptation and internal integration, that has worked well enough to be considered valid and therefore, to be taught to new members as the correct way to perceive, think, and feel in relation to those problems. (Schein, 1993). Gareth Morgan describes culture as "an active living phenomenon through which people jointly creates and recreates the worlds in which they live." For Morgan, the three basic questions for cultural analysts are:

- What are the shared frames of reference that make organization possible?
- Where do they come from?
- How are they created, communicated, and sustained? (Morgan, 1997)

Morgan proposes four essential strengths of the organizational culture approach:

- It focuses attention on the human side of organizational life, and finds significance and learning in even its most mundane aspects (for example, the setup in an empty meeting room).
- It makes clear the importance of creating appropriate systems of shared meaning to help people work together toward desired outcomes.
- It requires members—especially leaders—to acknowledge the impact of their behavior on the organization's culture. Morgan proposes that people should ask themselves: "What impact am I having on the social construction of reality in my organization?" "What can I do to have a different and more positive impact?"
- It encourages the view that the perceived relationship between an organization and its environment is also affected by the organization's basic assumptions. Morgan says:

The "work culture" of an organization is a product of its history, traditions, values, and vision. "a pattern of basic group assumptions that has worked well enough to be considered valid, and, therefore, is taught to new members as the correct way to perceive, think and feel." Desirable work culture includes shared institutional values, priorities, rewards and other practices which foster inclusion, high performance, and commitment, while still allowing diversity in thought and action. Work cultures, that mix of practices and ideologies arising from the interactions of people with their work environments, have been shaped in all by diversity—diversity of employment opportunities, population, and housing. The ways in which people find jobs, the rhythms of employment, the size of the workplace, the process of getting to and from work, how the workday is organized, power relationships and hierarchies, how workers learn and manage their tasks, how they socialize and organize family life, how informal worker behavior interacts with sanctioned authority and rules—all these things constitute work culture. Culture can encourage openness, knowledge sharing and mutual support among employees, while generating attitudes like altruism, trust, error tolerance, and understanding. Organizational culture can create positive or negative outcomes for individuals within the organization (Deal & Kennedy, 1992).

There are many different work cultures, reflecting the differences between skilled and unskilled labor, professional, white-collar, and service work, and workers' identities by race, gender, age, and ethnicity. The work culture can be improved in a number of ways by, for example: Improving communications between management and staff in both directions.

Ensuring that all employees have sufficient variety of tasks to enable them to use different muscles and postures and to make their job more satisfying.

Providing adequate rest breaks to prevent the build up of fatigue and by ensuring that the breaks are taken. Identifying and removing stress factors from the workplace.

Giving workers control over their pace of work and how they plan their day.

Removing bonus, performance or monitoring schemes which make workers push themselves beyond their capacities.

Employees shape the Culture. Personalities and experiences of employees create the culture of an organization. For example, if most of the people in an organization are very outgoing, the culture is likely to be open and sociable. If many artifacts depicting the company's history and values are in evidence throughout the company, people value their history and culture. If doors are open, and few closed door meetings are held, the culture is unguarded. If negativity about supervision and the company is widespread and complained about by employees, a culture of negativity, that is difficult to overcome. For that purpose, work culture matters a lot. Here, a model that lays out the roadmap to increase employee engagement. A major point is that the best way to increase employee engagement is to focus on creating a culture of engagement. Once the culture is created, engagement becomes 'the way we do things around here' and it does not have to be recreated year after year.

WORK CULTURE & EMPLOYEE ENGAGEMENT

Employees are engaged when many different levels of employees are feeling fully involved and enthusiastic about their jobs and their organizations. Engagement is the willingness and ability to contribute to company success, the extent to which employees put discretionary effort into their work, in the form of extra time, brainpower and energy" according to a Towers Perrin study On the left side of the model are the five most important drivers of a culture of engagement. Each driver must be translated into practical systems, practices and structures that are embedded in the organization.

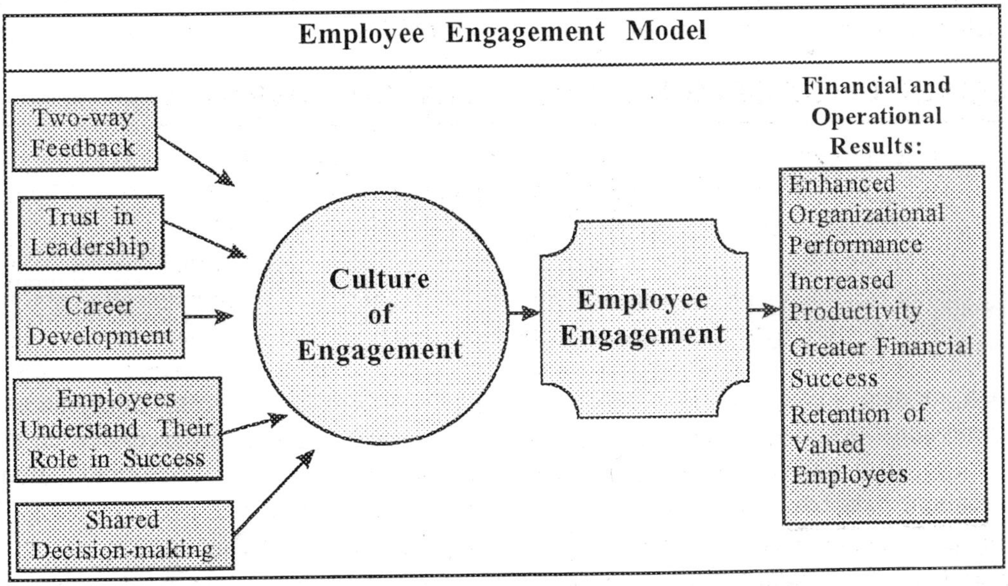

- **Two Way Feedback:** Most organizations do well in terms of communication down from management to employees. These are mechanisms for employees to communicate up on a regular basis. Relying on a suggestion box and an annual employee survey just doesn't do the job. Two helpful ways to ensure the upward flow of feedback are employee's regular meetings and quarterly, brief, online surveys that capture the changing concerns of employees.

- **Trust in Leadership:** Trust can be shattered instantly when executives appear to suddenly change directions or seem to break promises. Building trust is a slower process. Executives build trust by developing a clear vision of the organizations' future and communicating this to all employees.
- **Career Development:** Finding—and keeping—quality workers can be difficult for even the most competitive firms. The rules have changed: today, borderless offices include local employees, expatriates abroad, offsite consultants and others, all of whom have different attitudes toward their careers. Engagement levels rise when there is a formal career development system that includes components such as formal career tracks, mobility systems to help employees move about in the organization, and annual career conversations.
- **Employees Understand their Role in Success:** Employees need to understand how their job fits into the big picture and what they must do more of and do differently to help the business succeed. HR can help by clarifying what are the competencies, the capacities that this particular organizations needs to grow and helping employees upgrade their skills to match the needs of the future.

Shared Decision-making

When employees participate in making decisions, they take feel more engaged in the organization. Decision-making needs to be pushed down to the lowest possible level. It gives them empowerment and enrichment. Employee empowerment emerges as another key value for business success.

EMPLOYEE ENGAGEMENT AND CULTURE CHANGE

Today's business environment is changing. 21st century capitalism is shifting focus from making money to making meaning (ends vs. means, trailing indicators v leading indicators). This is good and necessary. The average work day is longer and people are more mobile than ever before as businesses try to compete in a global marketplace.. The key remaining question, therefore, is "how can we go about creating employee engagement for the organization?" Communication and training can help support a solid, honest employee engagement initiative. But they cannot create one based on a camouflaged top-down leadership approach that is not committed to changing its own ways of managing before asking employees to show more engagement at work. The most effective, and perhaps the really only way, to inspire employee engagement is through going directly to the core of human needs that spur action. In "Employee Engagement for Change" programme, these human needs in the statement, "The Dignity to be and the Freedom to Do." Employees need to feel appreciated and recognized as unique human beings before they begin to consider giving you any of their hearts and minds. The second, human need that must be met is for employees to apply their talent, in their own way, to achieve organizational goals. This is the way people create themselves through their work. Work becomes a way for self-actualization. Dedication to work becomes self-generated. Engagement becomes something employees seek for their own inner rewards. Only then will engagement occur and deliver results for the organization.

THE SIX PRINCIPLES OF EMPLOYEE ENGAGEMENT FOR CHANGE

1. People are not "assets" or "resources" the organization owns or manages. People are the organization. The Organization is nothing but people. People manage the organization. The organization does not manage people. This qualitative shift in the way we view the organization and the people who manage it is necessary for the success of any employee engagement initiative. Change is about people, not process, technology, or numbers. Financial results do not engage people. Engaged people achieve financial results, and every other worthwhile value for the organization.
2. We must become the change we want to see in the world. This is what Gandhi, the great leader of India's independence, said. Our Employee Engagement for Change Program puts this powerful concept to work by asking people to become the change they are talking about. People are asked to take a pledge to refrain from three negative behaviors (complaining, criticizing, and gossiping) in the first three weeks of the program. After experiencing the power of change first-hand in them, people then move to make the changes needed in their workplace.
3. Change Is Positive and Carries Its Own Rewards. Employees do not resist change. They resist the way some in management try to change them. Employees embrace the change that they participate in making. The Employee Engagement for Change Program is designed to make organizational change a positive and exciting process. It integrates fun and camaraderie in every aspect and every step of the process. People don't have to be dragged to participate. They ask for it and invite others to join in. There is nothing as powerful and meaningful for people as the feeling that they are the ones in control of their own change and of the changes they create for the organization.
4. Change is Social a social process. Employee Engagement for Change methodology leverages the powerful human need for belonging, socializing, and community. The program enables participants to think, behave, and create change. This approach accelerates the change process as it makes it more in harmony with people's need for social interaction. The process of effecting change together creates the strongest bonding between team members and dramatically heightens morale and employee engagement
5. Work outside the Box with a Bias for Action-The Employee Engagement for Change Program puts creativity in the change process: The activities and exercises are the part of the Change Programmes are designed to push participants beyond their comfort zone of traditional thinking and business-as-usual limitations. Inviting participants to think and work outside the box. In the Employee Engagement for Change Program, to encourage people for writing a detailed "strategic plan" that ends up collecting dust on executives' desks. Involving people to quickly experience the power of change first in themselves, in their own behavior. People then move, with their just acquired self-confidence and sense of success, to confront the aspects of the business that need to be changed. They learn on the job. They gain from experience. They grow and achieve dramatic results
6. There Are No Ordinary People .The "Employee Engagement for Change" Program is guided by the assumption that there are no ordinary people. Each person has the potential to achieve

extraordinary accomplishments and is only waiting for the opportunity and condition that makes this possible. Our change process provides people with such opportunity, and they jump right in to participate. Because "Employee Engagement for Change" is people-based and is designed to touch people's hearts and minds, the rewards people receive from it are intrinsic, personal, and powerful. There is nothing as powerful and meaningful for people as the feeling that they are the ones in control of their own change and of the changes they create for the organization.

CONCLUSION

In the '90s the role of HR was primarily accepted to be that of a support and an administrative one. The HR professionals focused on activities and deliverables. The decision makers of companies also thought it to be sufficient to have them at line manager levels, and not have them involved in strategic business activities. In today's connected world, no function is an island, and HR holds one of the keys to unravel business intelligence. Globalization has forced companies to grow at a faster pace, grow business across the globe, look at optimizing all the business processes, and has even forced companies to look at strategic employee engagement. These changes have had varying effects on all resources, most so on the "human" type. Some studies have shown that mergers and acquisitions which have failed have been primarily because of the failure in managing the human resources; either having key employees separating, or teams not able to integrate and work together as planned. Hence, the twenty-first century has brought about the thought of seeking the involvement of employees at the strategic planning level.

References

1. Corporate Executive Board. Driving performance and retention through employee engagement. (2004). Washington, DC.
2. Deal, T.E.,& Kennedy, A. A. (1982), Corporate Culture: The Rites and Rituals of Corporate Life. Reading, MA:IRWIN.
3. Morgan, G. (1997). Images of Organization. Thousand Oaks, CA: Sage Publications.
4. Nankarvis, A., Compton,. R., & Baird, M. (2002). Strategic Human Resource Management, (4th ed). Melbourne: Nelson Thompson Learning.
5. Schein, E. (1993). Organizational Culture and Leadership. In Classics of Organization Theory. Jay Shafritz and J. Steven Ott, eds. 2001. Fort Worth: Harcourt College Publishers. pp. 373-374.
6. Walker loyalty report. (2003, September), Indianapolis, IN: Walker Information.
7. Employee engagement at double-digit growth companies. (2004). Hewitt Research Brief.
8. Wright, P.M., Dunford, B.B., & Snell, S.A. (2001), Human resource and the resource based view of the firm. Journal of Management, 27, pp. 701-721.
9. Understanding what drives employee engagement. (2003). The 2003 Towers Perrin Talent Report.
10. http://expertscolumn.com/content/human-resource-management-nature-scope-objectives-and-function assessed on (27/04/2011, 7:45PM).

11. -http://www.socialfunds.com/news/article.cgi/493.htmlassessed on (29/04/2011, 9:00PM).

12. Boosting staff wellbeing can improve financial performance, research reveals-http://www.personneltoday.com/articles/2010/05/11/55493/boosting-staff-wellbeing-can-improve-financial-performance-research-reveals.html assessed on (24/04/2011, 6:00PM).

13. http://www.questia.com/googleScholar.qst?docId=5009356449 assessed on (28/04/2011, 7:45PM).

14. http://www.simplehrguide.com/your-hr-management-goals-and-clear-hr-focus.html assessed on (29/04/2011, 8:00PM).

❖ ❖ ❖

9 Employee Engagement - A Critical Review of Literature

Dr.Sujit Kumar Acharya
Vandana Mohanty

ABSTRACT

Employee engagement is the level of commitment and involvement an employee has towards his/her organization and its values. Moreover an engaged workplace encourages commitment, energy and productivity from all those involved to help improve business performance. Many companies have come to realize that maximum productivity doesn't come from just a "satisfied" or "happy" employee. They know that the most productive and loyal employee is known as an engaged employee. This employee goes beyond the basic job responsibility to delight the customers and drive the business forward. Moreover, in times of diminishing loyalty, employee engagement is a powerful retention strategy. The most valuable resource of a company walks out of the door every evening and sometimes it never comes back. Employee engagement is the means or the strategy to ensure that the most valuable resource again back to the same position. It is about creating an enthusiasm for the roles and the job, the people perform and ensuring they are aligned with the values of the organization, well informed, well integrated with their colleagues and the fabric or culture of the organization. The review aims to add value to the current state of knowledge by critically evaluating the existing literature on employee engagement and providing a reflective stance on existing debates and findings. The review of literature covers the following areas pertinent to today's organization, with the focus being on individual differences, employee involvement, productivity in relation to employee engagement.

Keywords: Employee Engagement, Satisfaction, Engaged Employee, Literature Review Employee Involvement.

INTRODUCTION

Due to the market conditions and new business processes, organizations today have become lean. We find the new organizational set up has led to leaving some of the executives over worked. The Pareto principle seems to still stick around – 'the vital few and trivial many is' plaguing organizations even now. Organisations are continuously searching for ways to increase their competitiveness as a means to survive in the global economy. More recently approaches have focused on the role that people perform in bringing about competitive advantage. Ray (2003, p.1) asserts that organizations, over the past decades, have explored many ways to improve competitiveness including improved selling, marketing, and refining strategy. It is further stated that this decade's competitive advantage lies in staff improvement and engagement. Employee engagement remains an area that throws up new challenges to managers.

'Employee engagement' is a relatively new term in HR literature came to prominence from 2000 onwards. Coffman and Gonzalez-Molina (2002, p.2) assert that when engaged employees utilise their natural talents, they provide an instant, and constant, competitive edge. Jamie Neil, chief executive of Archer Young Performance Improvement Agency, is quoted in the Financial Times (2003, p.1) as saying that "the sixties were about improving manufacturing; the seventies about better selling; the eighties smarter marketing; and the nineties refined strategy; then this decade's competitive edge will be delivered via staff improvement and engagement".

This literature survey examined peer-reviewed journal articles, working papers, textbooks, and other published resources relevant to employee engagement. Articles were found through the search facility of on-line journal databases. The review aims to add value to the current state of knowledge by critically evaluating the existing literature on employee engagement and providing a reflective stance on existing debates and findings. As a result, it addresses concerns about the lack of agreement on what engagement is and how issues surrounding it can be addressed.

Employee Engagement Defined

The concept of 'employee engagement' is rapidly gaining popularity and use in the workplace. The term employee engagement has been used at different times to refer to psychological states, traits, and behaviors, as well as their antecedents and outcomes.

The first published use of the term employee engagement was in the Academy of Management Journal article "Psychological Conditions of Personal Engagement and Disengagement at Work" (W. Kahn, 1990), but since then many varied and conflicting definitions of employee engagement have made it difficult to compare and contrast research findings. To determine a common definition, Shuck and Wollard reviewed 140 articles that mentioned employee engagement and observed four areas of consistency or inconsistency:

1. Engagement is a personal decision, not an organizational decision as implied by some definitions.
2. While early definitions treated engagement as an atomic concept, later definitions divided it into three basic concepts: emotional, behavioral and cognitive engagement.
3. Employee engagement has "no physical properties, but is manifested and often measured behaviorally". Different definitions look at behavior as the employee's basic job performance or extended effort or the success of the employer.
4. Employee engagement is about the behaviors that meet or exceed organizational goals.

Synthesizing the reviewed definitions, Shuck and Wollard define employee engagement as "an emergent and working condition as a positive cognitive, emotional, and behavioral state directed toward organizational outcomes".

According to Macey and Schneider (2008), the sources of confusion in definitions of engagement are due to the fact that some defined engagements with regard to attitude and behaviour. As a concept that has developed over time, engagement has been defined in numerous, often inconsistent, ways in the literature, so much so that the term has become ambiguous to many and it is rare to find two people defining it in same way (Macey and Schneider, 2008a). It has variously been conceived as a psychological or affective state (eg commitment, involvement, attachment etc.), a performance construct (eg role performance, effort, observable behavior, organizational citizenship behavior etc; Macey and Schneider, 2008a) or an attitude. Some even relate the concept to other specific constructs such as altruism or initiative (Macey and Schneider, 2008a) and little consensus has been reached in the literature as to which of these definitions is the definitive, or at least, 'best fit' model of engagement.

Kahn (1990) defined personal engagement as "expression of a person's preferred self in task behaviors that promote connections to work and to other's, personal presence (physical, cognitive, and emotional), and active, full role performance" (p.700). Dvir, Eden, Avolio, and Shamir (2002) defined active engagement behaviorally as a "high level of activity, initiative, and responsibility" (p.737).Wellins and Concelman (2005) also defined engagement behaviorally. They suggested that engagement is a "passion, commitment, extra effort... the illusive force that motivates employees to higher (or lower) levels of performance"(p.1). They broke the idea of engagement into a number of individual elements: Focused work (with strategy, empowerment), Individual value (support and recognition), and Interpersonal support (teamwork and collaboration).

Colbert, Mount, Harter, Witt, and Barrick (2004) defined engagement attitudinally as a "high internal motivation state" (p.603).As pointed out in Rafferty et al (2005), the concept of employee engagement has, two well-researched precursors – employee commitment and organizational citizenship behavior as its foundation.

In defining engagement, Macey and Schneider (2008a p.6) split engagement into these three areas and propose that 'trait engagement' is an inclination to see the world from a particular vantage point and this is reflected in the individual's 'state engagement' which leads to 'behavioral engagement', defined in terms of exerting discretionary effort. This proposition has, however received criticism by Newman and Harrison (2008) who argue that when engagement is broken up into the separate aspects of state, trait and behavior, state engagement becomes a redundant construct and tells us nothing more than an individual's attitude towards their job which, as they point out, has been suitably measured by other constructs in the past. Instead, they argue that the defining features of employee engagement are the simultaneous presence of three behaviors in employees,

namely their performance in the job, citizenship behavior and involvement. However, this proposition shies away from defining the psychological state of engagement and merely describes its outcomes.

The Table 9.1 shows some common definitions and phrases, found out by reviewing the definitions on engagement.

Table 9.1: Based on 18 Definitions of Employee Engagement

Concept	Percentage Used
Commitment-cognitive, effective, behavioral	5.5%
Commitment-rational & emotional	5.5%
Discretionary effort — going above and beyond	11%
Drive innovation	5.5%
Drive business success	22%
Energy, involvement, efficacy	11%
Passion and frofound connection	5.5%
Positive attitude toward company	5.5%
Psychological presence-attention and absorption	5.5%
Shared meaning understanding-active participation	5.5%
Stay, say, strive	5.5%
Think, feel, act, during performance	11%
Translate employeee potential into performance	5.5%

Source: Colin Dicke, American Express Graduate Research Assistant to CAHRS in his article "EMPLOYEE ENGAGEMENT: I WANT IT, WHAT IS IT"

The Gallup Organization, potentially the most widely recognized name associated with employee engagement due to their best selling book, "First, Break All the Rules," defines engaged employees as those who, "work with a passion and feel a profound connection to their company" and "drive innovation and move the organization forward" (GMJ, 2006).

The International Survey Research (ISR) defines employee engagement as, "a process by which an organization increases commitment and continuation of its employees to the achievement of superior results." The ISR separates commitment into three categories cognitive commitment, affective commitment, and behavioral commitment or think, feel and act.

Employee engagement focuses more on how psychological experiences of work and work contexts of employees influence them in presenting or absenting themselves during task performance. Kahn (1990, p. 693) distinguishes amongst three dimensions of employee engagement, namely emotional, cognitive or physical. Of these, emotional and cognitive dimensions are key constructs for psychological engagement and organizational behaviors.

Some Definitions on Employee Engagement

Barclays suggests a formal definition of employee engagement might be, 'the extent to which an employee feels a sense of attachment to the organization he or she works for, believes in its goals and supports its values.' Barclays also suggest that it is possible to 'gain a good sense of someone's engagement by asking a simple question, would you recommend Barclays as a good place to work?(Barclays, 2008). Dell refers to being engaged as 'giving time and talent to team building activities'.(Dell, 2008)

Nokia Siemens Networks describes being engaged as 'an emotional attachment to the organization, pride and a willingness to be an advocate of the organization, a rational understanding of the organization's strategic goals, values, and how employees fit and motivation and willingness to invest discretionary effort to go above and beyond'.(Nokia Siemens Networks, 2008).

It is clear that some of the major employers in the UK (Royal Bank of Scotland and the NHS for example) take employee engagement seriously and are actively implementing measures to increase engagement levels. Engagement in these organisations is not seen as merely an issue for HR. Rather, it is seen as a strategic issue at Board level, impacting standards of service delivery in the public and private sectors as well as profitability in the private sector.

The evidence shows that the impact of employee engagement (or disengagement) can manifest itself through:

- productivity and organizational performance
- outcomes for customers of the organization
- employee retention rates
- organizational culture, and
- advocacy of the organization and its external image.

There is no discernable difference between the dynamics of engagement within the public sector as opposed to the private sector. Rather, differences in engagement levels result from organisational characteristics; in whichever sector that organisation sits. However, studies suggest that the public sector performs weaker in areas relating to strategic vision and change management, both of which are important to employee engagement. The report concludes that the primary driving force behind engagement is the organisation, its view of engagement and how it acts to create an environment conducive to engaging employees.

Important areas in which an organisation can work to improve engagement include:

- training and career development
- effective management
- promoting a clear strategic vision
- communication
- fair treatment
- pay and benefits
- job satisfaction
- cooperation and trust

These factors vary between those that tend to be taken as given and written explicitly into the contract of employment (i.e. pay and benefits) and those that are organisational-dependent, cannot be taken for granted and require the organisation to take an initiative (i.e. ensuring two-way communication, promoting a strategic vision and building trust).

DRIVERS OF EMPLOYEE ENGAGEMENT

Research shows that committed employees perform better. If we accept that engagement, as many believe, is 'one step up' from commitment, it is clearly in the organisation's interests to understand the drivers of engagement. However, the strongest driver of all is a sense of feeling valued and involved. This has several key components:

- involvement in decision making
- the extent to which employees feel able to voice their ideas, and managers listen to these views, and value employees' contributions
- the opportunities employees have to develop their jobs
- the extent to which the organisation is concerned for employees' health and wellbeing.

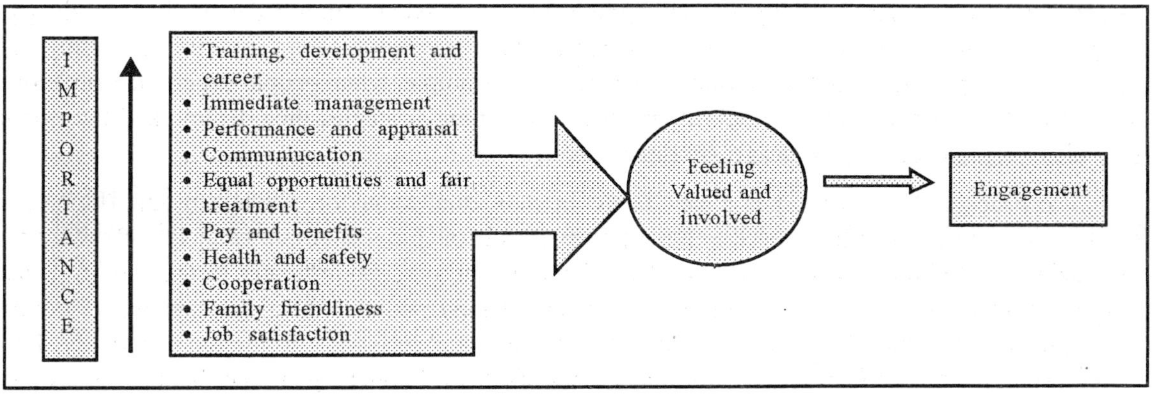

Fig. 9.1

Source: Robinson *et al* (2004)

Research conducted by Institute of Employment Studies (IES) in 2004 (Robinson et al., 2004) found considerable variation in the views of authors in what drives engagement and pointed out that 'there is no easy answer as far as engagement is concerned – no simple pulling of one or two levers to raise engagement levels' (p. 26). It is unlikely that a 'one size fits all' approach is effective, as levels of engagement and its drivers vary according to the organization, employee group, the individual and the job itself (Robinson, 2007). There is 'no definitive all purpose list of engagement drivers' (CIPD, 2007). Employee engagement is likely, therefore, to be influenced by many interrelated factors. Such variation is illustrated in the work of The Conference Board (2006) who found that 26 different drivers of engagement were proposed in 12 largely consultancy based studies of engagement. The most commonly reported drivers were trust and integrity; the nature of the job; the line of sight between individual performance and company performance; career growth opportunities; pride in the company; relationships with co workers/team members; employee development and the personal relationship with one's manager (The Conference Board, 2006, p. 6).

Kahn (1990) found that the presence of three psychological conditions influenced people to personally engage in their work and the absence of which encouraged disengagement. These are meaningfulness, safety and availability. Kahn suggests that people vary their degree of engagement in a given situation according to their perception of the benefits and the guarantees, and also by the resources they perceive themselves to have.

Engagement levels can vary according to demographic and job related factors. It is thus noted from the model above that some of these factors are what would be fundamental or contractual requirements for the organization (the 'hygiene' factors), such as pay and benefits and health and safety, whereas others are the areas where the organization must 'go the extra mile' to ensure effective communication, management and cooperation.

Engagement and Individual Differences

It is argued that individual differences play a vital role in determining an employee's potential level of engagement (Robinson 2006). Kahn (1990), for instance, argued that psychological differences may have an impact on individuals' ability to engage or disengage in their role performance, just as they shape a person's ability and willingness to be involved or committed at work. Accordingly, people would engage differently "given their experiences of psychological meaningfulness, safety and availability in specific situations" (Kahn 1990:718). For example, when people experience situations as unsafe, it is a matter of individual differences what coping strategies they deploy, and the extent to which they engage or disengage (Portello 1996).

The process of perception is a key factor in individual behavior. Buchanan and Huczynski (2004:215) define perception as "the dynamic psychological process responsible for attending to, organizing and interpreting sensory data". To a large extent, perception relates to the way in which individuals make sense of their environment and interpret and respond to the events and people around them. Equally, it is important to emphasize that each individual receives information differently. This is because individuals do not receive information about what is happening around them passively and dispassionately or in the same way as others. According to Robinson (2006) individuals categorise and make sense of events and situations according to their own unique and personal frame of reference, which reflects their personality, past experiences, knowledge, expectations and current needs, priorities and interests. Personality is a key influence on the process of perception. Bowditch and Buono (2001:46) suggest that, "our personality acts as a kind of perceptual filter or frame of reference which influences our view of the world". Therefore, it is argued that it is our personal perception of our social and physical environment that shapes and directs how engaged an employee is, rather than some objective understanding of an external reality.

The Towers Perrin (2003) study of engagement identified both emotions and rationality as core components. They found that emotional factors are linked to an individual's personal satisfaction and the sense of inspiration and affirmation they get from their work and from being a part of their organization. For example, a key element here is having a sense of personal accomplishment from one's job. By contrast, the rational factors generally relate to the relationship between the individual and the broader corporation, for instance the extent to which employees understand their role and their unit's role, relative to company objectives.

According to Towers Perrin (2003), building engagement is a process that never ends and it rests on the foundation of a meaningful and emotionally enriching work experience. Furthermore, it is not about making people happy, or even paying them more money. As important as pay and benefits are in attracting and retaining people, it was found they play a less important role in engaging people in their work. The elements found to be fundamental for engagement were strong leadership, accountability, autonomy, a sense of control over one's environment and opportunities for development; there are no substitutes for these fundamentals.

Gender differences have also been found, such that men experience enrichment from work to family, while women experience depletion from work to family. While women experience enrichment from family to work, men experience no links from family to work (Rothbard 1999).A CIPD study in 2006 says, women were found, in general, to be more engaged than men, but they also tend to be doing different kinds of jobs. Women are more satisfied with their work and hold more positive views of their senior management team than do men. They are more loyal to their organization as an employer and report higher levels of loyalty to their customers and clients than men. This is in contrast to the NHS survey result conducted by IES and analyzed by Robinson *et al* (2004), where it was found that there was no discernable difference between engagement levels between men and women. Workers aged 55+ are more engaged with their work than younger employees, and they are also happier with their work-life balance, working shorter hours than others. Employees aged under 35 are significantly less engaged with their work than older workers (CIPD, 2006).

Engagement and Employee Involvement

Whilst some argue that employees are 'engaged' if they have a positive attitude towards work, others such as Purcell et al (2003) suggest that employee engagement is only meaningful if there is a more genuine sharing of responsibility between management and employees over issues of substance. The CIPD survey conducted by Truss *et al* (2006) suggests that strengthening employee voice can make a difference to organizational performance. Employee voice can be defined as the ability for employees to have an input into decisions that are made in organizations (Lucas *et al* 2006). It has been argued that one of the main drivers of employee engagement is for employees to have the opportunity to feed their view upwards (Truss *et al* 2006). Employee involvement is seen as a central principle of 'soft' HRM, where the focus is upon capturing the ideas of employees and securing their commitment (Beardwell and Claydon 2007). The concept of employee involvement is strongly grounded in unitarist views of organizations, as it assumes that managers and employees have the same interests. Critics have argued that employee involvement has management firmly in control and very limited real influence is given to employees (ibid).

Hyman and Mason (1995) argue that employee involvement schemes "extend little or no input into corporate or higher level decision making" and generally do not entail and significant sharing of power and authority. Similarly, Blyton and Turnbull (2004:272) argue that employee involvement is 'soft on power'. However, Purcell et al's (2003) study found involvement in decisions affecting the job or work to be an important factor, which was strongly associated with high levels of employee engagement thus demonstrating it is an important driver. In any work role or situation, employees have a degree of choice and discretion over how they perform their tasks and responsibilities (Robinson 2006).

Purcell et al's (2003) study found a number of factors to be strongly associated with high levels of employee engagement. The one thing all of these factors had in common was that they were connected with an employee's involvement in a practice related to their work. For example, effective communications was found to be a factor as engagement levels were affected by the amount of information employees received about how well the company was performing and how they contributed to the company achieving its business objectives. Furthermore, employees having involvement in decisions' affecting their job or work was also associated with high levels of engagement.

According to Lawler and Worley (2006) for a high-involvement work practice to be effective and for it to have a positive impact on employee engagement, employees must be given power. They argue that this will lead to employees having the ability to make decisions that are important to their performance and to the quality of their working lives, thus engaging them in their work. Furthermore, Lawler and Worley (2006) contend that power can mean a relatively low level of influence, as in providing input into decisions made by others or it can mean having final authority and accountability for decisions and their outcomes. Involvement is maximized when the highest possible level of power is pushed down to the employees that have to carry out the decision, resulting in gaining the maximum level of engagement possible from employees.

Clearly employee engagement also depends on the manager or supervisor. (Cufaude 2004) argues that when managers employ a philosophy of 'servant-leadership', whereby a manager's primary role is in supporting and serving those around them, the environment becomes 'highly engaged'. Research has demonstrated that employee engagement tends to be based on factors such as the relationship they have with their managers (Blizzard 2003). Yet other theorists claim that employee engagement depends on offering empowerment and that jobs should fit employees' interests (Lloyd 2004 and MacDonald 2002).

Engagement and Performance

There is an increasing awareness that employee engagement is pivotal to successful commercial and business performance, where engaged employees are the 'backbone of good working environments where people are industrious, ethical and accountable' (Levinson, 2007a; Cleland et al, 2008). Organizations with higher engagement levels tend to have lower employee turnover, higher productivity, higher total shareholder returns and better financial performance (Baumruk, 2006). Towers Perrin (2007) found that organizations with the highest percentage of engaged employees increased their operating income by 19 per cent and their earnings per share by 28 per cent year to year. Highly engaging organizational cultures may also have an attractive employer brand, being an employer of choice which attracts and retains the best talent (e.g. Martin and Hetrick, 2006). By building a culture that enables employees to engage in their work, organizations may benefit from staffs who are willing to go the extra mile and achieve better financial performance (Baumruk, 2006).

Research studies (Kahn (1990, p.692), Buckingham and Coffman (1999 p.32), Towers Perrin Report (2003, p.5)) have indicated that employees who are engaged are more likely to be satisfied and productive. The Corporate Leadership Council (CLC) (2009) completed a study of engagement levels of over 50,000 employees across the globe and found that those employees who are most committed:

- Perform 20% better, which CLC (2009) claims infers that moving from low to high engagement levels will induce an increase in employee performance of 20 percentile points; and

- Are 87% less likely to leave the organization, which CLC (2009) states indicates the significance of engagement to organizational performance.

On the other hand, in reporting on the costs of employee disengagement, Meere (2005) discusses a survey carried out by ISR on 360,000 employees from 41 companies in the world's 10 largest economies and finds that in companies with low engagement both operating margin and net profit margins reduced over a three year period, whilst in companies with high levels of engagement both these measures increased over the same time period. In order to determine whether increases in profit are due to an engaged workforce, it is necessary to measure an organization's engagement and performance over a period of time and compare the changes during this period. If engagement is the cause of profit increase then an increase in engagement levels should precede an increase in profit. Such a study by Hewitt Associates (2004, cited in The Conference Board, 2006), found indications that engagement does indeed drive profit. It is important that the organization find ways to clearly communicate successes that demonstrate how the organization is performing, and especially to find ways to socialize stories of superior performance. Clear, well-planned, high-impact messages can help employees not only see the connection between their work and these successes, but also understand how they support overall organizational performance, which ties directly to engagement levels.

Employee Engagement and Satisfaction

The nature of work is thought to be one of the distinctive facets of job satisfaction (Spector, 2006). However, Macey and Schneider (2008) found that the nature of work is a component that directly and indirectly affects state engagement; job satisfaction is one of the components of state engagement. However engagement is beyond satisfaction. Macey and Schneider (2008) quoted Ericson's 2005 study that indicated "Engagement, in contrast, is about passion and commitment – the willingness to invest oneself and expend one's discretionary effort to help the employer succeed" (p.8).

Recent work by Saks (2006: 613) determined that engagement levels are predicted by perceived support granted to employees by the organization and that measures of engagement themselves predict levels of job satisfaction, commitment measures, intentions to quit, and positive behaviors within the organization. Additionally, in a meta-analysis of data collected by The GalupOrganization, Harter, et al. (2002) had similar findings, citing the strong effects employee satisfaction and engagement can have on turnover and levels of customer satisfaction and loyalty. A weaker, but practically significant, effect was also found between measures of engagement and satisfaction and business-level outcomes. In another meta-analytic study, Riketta (2002) found a correlation between measures of attitudinal organizational commitment—defined as "the relative strength of an individual's identification with and involvement in a particular organization" (Mowday, Steers, & Porter, 1979: 226)—and job performance. Interestingly, the strength of this correlation was found to be moderated by the type of data collected and was stronger when self ratings were used as compared to objective and supervisor-rated measures. Additionally, Luthans & Peterson (2001) examined the role of managers with regard to employees' levels of engagement and determined that levels of manager self efficacy partially mediated the relationship.

Engaged employees work with passion and feel a strong connection to their company. This is ultimately what our interviewees keep striving to accomplish. They indeed focus on the employee, because they believe that the employee is a key factor on the performance of an organization. Therefore, they try to keep employees engaged by empowering them, delegating responsibilities, making them actively participate in the decision-making processes that take place within the organization, and by giving them benefits or incentives.

Role of HR Manager In Employee Engagement

When the concept of employee engagement first emerged, there was apprehension among HR professionals, line managers, and researchers over the connection between the levels of engagement of an employee and the quality of their work. In essence, employee engagement requires a realistic employee value proposition from the Human Resource function in an organization, because HR's values-add is integrally linked to or influenced by its employee value proposition. Human Resources' value-add will certainly be judged by how it builds and maintains employee engagement and commitment, and how it positions itself as a key driver in this process (Tsukudu, 2008). It is therefore, the role of HR professionals to understand and determine what drives engagement

The reasons for teams and people in them not delivering their best can be many. These reasons may also vary from time to time. So it is necessary that the HR manager monitors teams and individuals by interacting with each team's manager. HR plays a very crucial role in keeping the employees engaged. A survey has revealed that only a meager four percent of HR senior managers concentrate on employee engagement. But on the other hand 90 per cent of these managers were highly concerned about employee retention. The fact of the matter is that both employee engagement and retention are closely related. And this relationship has an impact on the top revenues and the bottom-line.

The importance of good management and effective communication has been highlighted as key vehicles through which employee engagement can be implemented. As(Robinson et al 2004) highlight, organizations must work to engage employees and establish a two-way relationship between the employer and employee. (Michelman 2004) notes that the defining contribution of great managers is that they boost the engagement levels of the people who work for them. (Michelman 2004) suggests that they achieve this through concentrating on four core areas of managing people:

- Selection;
- Expectation setting;
- Motivation; and
- Development

Michelman (2004) points out that in leading engagement, great managers will seek the right fit for a person's talent, they work to see that employees are rewarded for their performance and they endeavour to ensure that talent is developed through progressively more challenging and meaningful assignments. HR professionals are responding to employee engagement by flattening their chains of command, providing training and improving internal communications. They agree that changes on employee engagement will not happen overnight; therefore, they keep working in order to achieve their goals. According to Phil Gerbyshak (2007) if managers want to build a great team that makes a huge impact on the bottom line of the company, there is a need to get employees engaged and loyal. At a local level, managers can influence employees' most basic needs by setting clear expectations and providing needed resources. Moreover, they can energize their employees by showing them that they care, personally and professionally. Personally, managers can create a meaningful relationship within workgroups and position employees so that they can do what they do best. Professionally, managers can provide challenging work and opportunities to learn, grow, and make significant contributions (Fleming and Asplund, 2007). When HR succeeds in making the employee see himself as part of the organization and that his contribution is valuable, is what sets the pace for total employee engagement. Shaw (2005) suggests that employee engagement falls into two basic approaches: The philosophical approach where engagement is more of a "management philosophy" to consider when making overall HR decisions, and the pragmatic approach where a company has a "dedicated program" for engagement where they try to articulate and measure engagement. But, neither process is stated to provide a clear winner in achieving an 'engaged' workforce.

Conclusion and Findings

Having engaged employees is harder than it was in the past, when most people worked at one job all their lives or continued their parents' working line. Nowadays, there is a competing workforce and there are competing organizations. Globalization and technology have changed the world and now it is easier for employees to look for another company that will give them the money they need, the benefits they want, or the respect they deserve. In the other hand, it is harder for companies to keep up with the changing workforce; turnover is expensive, so they need to retain employees. What is even more harmful to the company is that the good employees are the ones who have more opportunities to get another job, and the ones who the company needs to retain. This is the importance of employee engagement, that the best employees stay motivated at the company.

It is evident that by giving employees the opportunity to feed their views and opinions upwards is a key driver of employee engagement. In addition, employees want to be kept 'in the know' about what is happening in their organization. People want a sense of involvement with their employer. Employers can increase employee engagement by going beyond downward communication and making sure that people are not just treated as employees; instead they should be treated as valued individuals, as the research on individual differences suggests.

Research has shown that there may be a link between levels of engagement and organizational performance. Human resource practices that have a strong focus on people have demonstrated a significant impact on improvements in productivity, satisfaction and financial performance. In addition, engagement needs to be viewed as a broad organizational strategy that involves all levels of the organization (Frank *et al* 2004), a string of actions and steps (Shaw 2005), which require the contribution and involvement of organizational members (Robinson *et al* 2004), as well as consistent, continuous and clear communications (Truss *et al* 2006).

Employee engagement matters as it impacts on companies bottom line, both through HR related impacts (such as recruitment and retention) and through wider impacts on productivity ,profit and achieving the aims and objectives of the organization. It is clear that employee engagement has moved beyond HR discussion papers and concepts into the main stream of strategic and operational management. It is a reality for many organizations that view it as having benefits and are using it as tool to further the organization's objective.

Employee engagement is a concept with multiple definitions, arguably no form of direct measure, and bewildering crossover with other longer standing concepts. Engagement affects both micro and macro levels of the organization from many different directions. In order to reduce the overarching ambiguity around employee engagement further research must be done to clarify what employee engagement is and what makes it unique. Any company hoping to achieve controllable results using employee engagement, as it is currently understood, is advised to proceed with caution using deliberate steps and the expectation of creating a custom approach based on extensive research of company strengths and weaknesses, related concepts, and the 'unknowns' of employee engagement. An engaged staff can contribute significantly to reaching positive outcomes. This review suggests that employee engagement is a meaningful construct that is clearly worthy of future research.

References:

1. Anne-Marie Kontakos. (2007). "Employee engagement and fairness in the workplace" CAHRS.
2. Bates, S. (2004) 'Getting engaged', HR Magazine, Vol. 49, No. 2, pp. 44-51.
3. Blizzard, R. (2004), Engagement vs. satisfaction among hospital teams, Gallup Poll Tuesday Briefing, The Gallup Organisation, 9th March.
4. Baumruk, R. (2004). 'The missing link: the role of employee engagement in business success', Workspan, Vol. 47, pp. 48-52.
5. Beardwell, J. and Claydon, T. (2007). Human Resource Management, A Contemporary Approach. 5th ed. Harlow, Prentice Hall.
6. Blyton, P. and Turnbull, P. (2004). The Dynamics of Employee Relations. 3rd ed. Basingstoke: Palgrave.
7. Buchanan, D. and Huczynski, A. (2004). Organisational Behaviour. An introductory text, 5th ed. Harlow, FT/Prentice Hall.
8. Buckingham, M. (2001). 'What a waste', People Management, 11 October, pp. 36-39.
9. Burke, M. (2008). On the skilled aspect of employee engagement. Industrial and Organizational Psychology, 1(1), pp. 70-71.
10. Cleland A, Mitchinson W, Townend A (2008). Engagement, Assertiveness and Business Performance – A New Perspective, Ixia Consultancy Ltd.
11. Conference Board (2006). Employee Engagement: A review of current research and its implications, The Conference Board.
12. Corporate Leadership Council (2004). Driving Performance and Retention Through Employee Engagement, Corporate Executive Board.
13. Coffman, C., & Gonzalez-Molina, G. (2002). Follow this path, How the world's greatest organizations drive growth by unleashing human potential. Warner Books.
14. Corporate Leadership Council (2004). Driving performance and retention through employee engagement (summary, website extract).
15. Chartered Institute of Personnel and Development (CIPD) (2005). Reward Managementsurveys. Available online at http://www.cipd.co.uk/subjects/pay/_rewrdmansurv.htm?IsSrchRes=1
16. Chartered Institute of Personnel and Development (CIPD) (2006c). Working Life: Employee attitudes and engagement 2006, Research Report.
17. Chartered Institute of Personnel and Development (CIPD) (2007a). Employee engagement. Available online at http://www.cipd.co.uk/subjects/empreltns/general/empengmt.htm?IsSrchRes=1
18. Colbert, A. E., Mount, M. K., Hater, J.K., Witt, L., & Barrick, M. R. (2004). Interactive effects of personality and perceptions of the work situation on workplace deviance. Journal of Applied Psychology, 89, pp. 599-609.

19. Crabtree, S. (2005). 'Engagement keeps the doctor away; A happy employee is a healthy employee, according to a GMJ survey', Gallup Management Journal, 13th January.
20. Cufaude, J. (2004). in Lanphear, S. (2004). 'Are Your Employees Highly Engaged?' Credit Union Executive Newsletter, 19, 1-2. Credit Union National Association, US.
21. Dicke, Colin (2007). "Employee Engagement : I want it, What is it" CAHRS.
22. Dvir, T., Eden, D., Avolio, B. J., & Shamir, B. (2002). Impact of transformational leadership on follower development and performance: A Filed experiment. Academy of Management Journal, 45, pp. 735-744.
23. The Gallup Organisation (2004) [online] Available at: www.gallup.com.
24. Gallup Poll (2008). Employee Engagement Overview Brochure.Washington, DC: Consulting University Press.
25. Harter, J. K., Schmidt, F. L., & Hayes, T. L. (2002). Business-unit-level relationship between employee satisfaction, employee engagement, and business outcomes: A metaanalysis. Journal of Applied Psychology, 87(2), pp. 268-279.
26. Hyman, J. and Mason, B. (1995). Managing Employee Involvement and Participation. London, Sage. ISR (2004). International Survey Research. [Online] Available at: www.isrsurveys.com
27. Johnson, G. (2004). 'Otherwise engaged', Training, Vol 41, No 10, pp. 4.
28. Johnson, M. (2004). 'Gallup study reveals workplace disengagement in Thailand', The Gallup Management Journal, 12th May. [online] Available at: http://gmj.gallup.com/content/16306/3/Gallup-Study-Reveals-Workplace-Disengagementin. aspx.
29. Johnson, Rebecca (2006) Singular focus (employee engagement), IN People Management, Vol 12 No 18, 14 Sept. 2006, pp. 36,38.
30. Kahn, W.A. (1990). 'Psychological conditions of personal engagement and disengagement at work', Academy of Management Journal, Vol 33, pp. 692-724.
31. Kular, Sandeep. Gatenby, Mark. Rees, Chris. Soane, Emma. Truss, Katie. (2008). Employee Engagement: A literature Review : Working Paper Series – 19. Kingston University.
32. Konrad, A.M. (2006). 'Engaging employees through high-involvement work practices', Ivey Business Journal, March/April, pp. 1-6.
33. Lawler, E and Worley, C.G. (2006). 'Winning support for organisational change: Designing employee reward systems that keep on working', Ivey Business Journal, March/April,
34. Levinson E (2007a), Developing High Employee Engagement Makes Good Business Sense, www.interactionassociates.com/ideas/2007/05/ developing_high_employee_engagement_makes_good_business_sense.php
35. Lloyd, J. (2004). 'Offer empowerment to encourage engagement', Triangle Business Journal, Vol 15, No 1.
36 Locke, E.A. and Taylor, M.S. (1990). 'Stress, coping, and the meaning of work', in Brief, A. and W.R. Nord (Eds) Meanings of Occupational Work, pp. 135-170. Lexington, Lexington Books.
37 Lucas, R., Lupton, B. and Mathieson, H. (2006). Human Resource Management in an International Context. London, CIPD.
38. Luthans F, Peterson SJ (2002), 'Employee engagement and manager self efficacy
39. Implications for managerial effectiveness and development', Journal of Management Development, 21(5), pp. 376–387.
40. MacDonald, M. (2002). 'How companies can find renewed focus during uncertain times', Journal of Communication Management, Vol. 6, No. 3, pp. 220-227.

41. Macey, W., & Schneider, B. (2008). The Meaning of Employee Engagement. Industrial and Organizational Psychology, 1(1), pp. 3-30.
42. Macleod David and Clarke, Nita. A report to Government on Engaging for success: enhancing performance through employee engagement.
43. May, D.R. Gilson, R.L. and Harter, L.M. (2004). 'The psychological conditions of meaningfulness, safety and availability and the engagement of the human spirit at work', Journal of Occupational and Organisational Psychology, Vol. 77, pp. 11-37.
44. Melcrum Publishing (2005). Employee Engagement: How to build a high-performance workforce. An independent, Melcrum Research Report Executive Summary.
45. Mowday, R. T., Steers, R. M., & Porter, L. W. (1979). The measurement of organizational commitment. Journal of Vocational Behavior, 14, pp. 224-247.
46. Newman DA, Harrison DA (2008). Been there, bottled that: are state and behavioural work engagement new and useful construct 'wines'?, Industrial and Organisational Psychology, 1, pp. 31–35
47. Portello, J. (1996). 'Dimensions of managerial and professional women's stress: Interpersonal conflict and distress', Dissertation Abstracts International: Section B: the Sciences and Engineering, US: University Microfilms International, 57 (6-B)
48. Purcell, J., Kinnie, N., Hutchinson, S., Rayton, B. and Swart, J. (2003). Understanding the People and Performance Link: Unlocking the Black Box. London, CIPD.
49. Purcell, J. (2006). Change Agenda, Reflections on Employee Engagement. London, CIPD.
50. Rafferty, A.N *et al.* (2005). What makes a good employer? Geneva: International Council of Nurses. Available online at http://www.icn.ch/global/Issue3employer.pdf
51. Ray, A. (2003). Engage your staff. **Financial Times**. http://www.mca-group.com/ArtEngageStaff.htm
52. Richman, A. (2006) 'Everyone wants an engaged workforce how can you create it?' Workspan, Vol. 49, pp. 36-39.
53. Robinson, I. (2006) Human Resource Management in Organizations. London, CIPD.
54. Riketta, M. (2002). Attitudinal organizational commitment and job performance: a meta-analysis. Journal of Organizational Behavior, 23 pp. 257-266.
55. Robinson, D., Perryman, S. and Hayday, S. (2004). The Drivers of Employee Engagement. Brighton, Institute for Employment Studies.
56. Rothbard, N. (1999). 'Enriching or depleting? The dynamics of engagement in work and family'. Dissertation Abstracts International US: University Microfilms International, 59 (10- A).
57. Saks, A.M. (2006). 'Antecedents and consequences of employee engagement', Journal of Managerial Psychology, Vol. 21, No. 6, pp. 600-619.
58. Spector, P. E. (2006). Feelings about work: Job Attitudes and Emotions. Industrial And Organizational Psychology: Research and Practice. (216-244). New Jersey: John Wiley & Sons, Inc. USA.
59. Truss, C., Soane, E., Edwards, C., Wisdom, K., Croll, A. and Burnett, J. (2006). Working Life: Employee Attitudes and Engagement 2006. London, CIPD.
60. Towers Perrin (2003) Working today: understanding what drives employee engagement.
61. Wellins, R., & Concelman, J. (2005). Creating a culture for engagement. Workforce Performace Solutions (www.wpsmag.com). Retrieved, October 2, 2008, from www.ddiworld.com/pdf/wps_engagement_ar.pdf
62. Wikipedia, (2008). Employee Engagement. Retrieved October 2, 2008, from Wikipedia's website: http://en.wikipedia.org/wiki/Employee_engagement.

10 Understanding Employee Engagement — Concepts and Practices

Chinmay Kumar Podder

Engagement is the aggregate energized feeling; one has about one's worth that emerges as product of the feeling of urgency , focus , intensity and enthusiasm. An engaged employee is one who is fully involved in, and is enthusiastic about his or her work and thus will act in a way that furthers their organization's interest. Employee engagement is measurable degree of an employee's positive or negative emotional attachment to the job , colleagues and organization which profoundly influence their willingness to learn and perform at work. Thus engagement is distinctly different from satisfaction, motivation, culture, climate, and indeed difficult to measure . Engagement deals with the emotional content-challenging role, growth opportunities while satisfaction is the function of the hygiene factors.

CHARACTERISTICS/ATTRIBUTES OF EMPLOYEES WHO ARE HIGHLY ENGAGED

- They will always speak positive about the company to others including clients, customers, colleagues or friends.
- They are committed to stay with organization no matter what even at the cost of a financially better opportunity.
- They are intellectually and emotionally involved in their work , give 100% , feel passionate about its goals and align themselves with the values of the organization.
- They are highly productive and stay focused.
- They are not easily distracted. They are not the ones who will frequently look at the clock to find whether it is time to leave the office.
- They enjoy their work and are proud to tell people that they work for the company. They go the Extra mile to help their customers and colleagues and they would like to stay and develop a career with the company.

Work Place Engagement - What it Impacts?

- Employee engagement has a direct impact on the organization results. Engaged employees positively impact organizational results and return to stakeholders as they perform better than others
- Employee engagement has direct impact on retention rate too. Employee engagement can serve as a great management tool to retain talent. Engaged employees will stay with the company, be an advocate of the company and its products and services and contribute to business success.
- Engagement has a significant impact on the motivation of employees. While the reverse may not necessarily be true, engaged employees have always been found to be inspired and motivated.

CULTURE AND ENGAGEMENT

Culture is intangible for some but it has a major impact on the feeling or climate in any organization Whilst there is no right culture, there are certain environments which build engagement, where as others do the opposite and leaders can play an important role in building a culture which draws employees in rather than pushes them away. The TCS culture has prominence of job content (efficient and less stressful); merit based performance and flexible working hours . A major culture difference that TCS has over other companies is its philosophy and commitment to employee development. Microsoft culture has been profoundly influenced by its growth. The constant promotion and rotation of existing personnel into new jobs gives the company an edge to make employees stay for long. Managers emphasize both values and business results to create a high performance culture, enabling the organization to consistently achieve solid performance through the actions of motivated employees who are aligned with the goals and mission of the company.

FACTORS THAT DRIVE EMPLOYEE ENGAGEMENT

Factors that drive employee engagement include leaders who inspire confidence in future managers who recognize employees and emphasize quality and improvement , opportunity to grow and farms showing genuine commitment to employees. Employee engagement is directly influenced by following facts-

- Growth of the organization
- Value addition experienced by employees
- Employee perception of the organization

Key Levers for Employee Engagement

They are 4 primary organization levers that needs to be managed-reward system that differentiates between level of performance , culture that fosters mutual reliance and friendship , role designed to make people feel that their strengths are leveraged and resource allocation process that are just and fair. If we manage the basic processes most of the disillusionment that employees face will be taken care.

Some Ways to Ensure Workplace Engagement

- The process of engagement is what tells employees down the line about the differences they make. No matter how small their part, they must be given the power to see that they are building an edifice, not just brick-wall.
- Many times all that required is genuine appreciation in the form of a complaint, not even formal recognition; a pay hike or an award. Understand your employees needs as what might motivate one may not be necessarily liked by everyone.
- Convey to employees that they are valued individuals, people who make a difference to the Organization and you count on them at every step. Take feedback from them and be honest on how you are going to act on their feedback.
- Work on attendance policies that help correct work and family balance. Try to implement regular review of performance in the organization.
- Make an effort to inspire and motivate employees on a regular basis. Thank them for their work provide an atmosphere that shows value and constant appreciation.
- Build an attitude that encourages and provide support to achieve their career goals.

PROMOTING ENGAGEMENT AT WORKPLACE-HR STRATEGIES

There are several HR strategies to promote workplace engagement. The number can however be shortlisted to fire and can be better expressed in the form of a acronym V.O.I.C.E where each letter denotes an important component and is instrumental in promoting and sustaining engagement.

V-Vision – which is an emotion as well as a financial connection as to why people should be part of the organization. HR's role is therefore to set a shared and inspiring vision.

O-Opportunity – It is necessary to assess and find whether organization provides adequate opportunity to grow and develop. If not create adequate opportunities for growth both at horizontal and vertical level.

I-incentive – If you do a good job, do you get both financial and non-financial reward? Whether the performance management system provides for adequate rewarding the performers? HR must probe and get an answer to these fundamental questions. If the answer is not affirmative HR should facilitate developing systems which intelligently discriminates between high performers and non-performers and reward accordingly.

C-Communication – Communication is about telling people about what is going on and gives the confidence that people are cared.

E-Entrepreneurship – It is defined as things such as flexibility on people can work. Such flexibility generates a feeling that they are not slave to the organization. HR's initiatives have to incorporate and introduce flexibilities which gives employees freedom of choice.

Workplace Engagement Surveys

A workplace engagement survey is the key to develop a high performance fully engaged workforce. Employee surveys are becoming a popular management tool. They not only help management investigate whether employees align with corporate values but also identify problem areas and elicit information to increase engagement.

SOME FINDINGS OF STUDIES ON ENGAGEMENT

- Disengaged employees are 53% less productive than their engaged counter-parts.
- One in three employees is disengaged and is not putting forth his/her maximum effort. Studies across multiple organizations indicates that the cost of disengaged employee is substantially high.
- Indian companies ranked the highest as compared to the global peers when it comes to the employee confidence and effective leadership in the firm. While comparing the country level employee engagement differences India is ranked highest (71%) and Japan ranked lowest (38%)

Why Engagement Initiatives Often Fail?

One of the reasons why large scale engagement initiatives are hit and miss is that what is motivating for one worker might be demotivating for another. For ex-research conducted by Genos international found that 53% employees are motivated by a role that involves contribution to society but 47% are not. Similarly 43% of employees are motivated where engagement is highly competitive while 57% are not. And 58% find well established policies and procedures motivating while 42% do not.

Managers need to understand the motivational drivers of the workers who report them and treat Individuals accordingly.

Engagement-It is Primarily Line Manager's Responsibility

HR professionals.are only the custodians of the engagement process-it is the line manager who has to become a great manager and has to engage his/her team. If a line manager doesn't take the responsibility of developing his own people, assessing them, giving them adequate feedback, supporting them when required, helping them to grow professionally and in the organization HR cannot drive engagement under any circumstances. The responsibility of engaging team lies with the line manager-HR is only a felicitator

CONCLUSION

Workplace engagement is all about generously caring for your employees. They should be aware of their employer's attitude towards them which means that there should be ways and means to convey employee's concern to his employer. Employer must make clear that they care for them. This should be part of the company policy, so that employees can actually benefit from it. This policy will reap long term results for the followers. It should however be remembered that engagement is something that cannot be forced upon. So it is important to work towards developing an inspired workforce with an attitude that values constructive employees feedback, and be accountable and work hard to incorporate changes as deemed necessary. In the best organization engagement is more than a human resource initiative. It is a strategic function for the way they do the business

11 Employee Engagement and Retention Strategy

By Dr. Mahendra Kumar Mohanty

ABSTRACT

Most organizations today realize that a 'satisfied' employee is not necessarily the 'best' employee in terms of loyalty and productivity. It is only an 'engaged employee' who is intellectually and emotionally bound with the organization. Employee engagement is the level of commitment and involvement an employee has towards his organization and its values. An engaged employee is aware of the business context, and works with colleagues to improve performance within the job for the benefit of the organization. It is the positive attitude held by the employees towards the organization and its values. Engaged employees who are inspired and guided by the leadership, equipped with the right tools and managed by the right systems and processes deliver superior performance. The paper discusses the importance of the employee engagement, and the role of the organization to make the process successful to keep the employees engaged. A case study HCL Technologies on employee engagement is also discussed.

Keywords: Employee engagement, Commitment, Satisfaction, Employee, Organisation.

INTRODUCTION

In a world that is changing both in terms of the global nature of work and the diversity of the workforce, engaged employees may be a key to competitive advantage. Companies that understand the conditions that enhance employee engagement will have accomplished something that competitors will find very difficult to imitate. Employees who are engaged in their work and committed to their organizations give companies crucial competitive advantages—including higher productivity and lower employee turnover. Thus, it is not surprising that organizations of all sizes and types have invested substantially in policies and practices that foster engagement and commitment in their workforces. Indeed, in identifying the three best measures of a company's health, business consultant and former General Electric CEO Jack Welch recently cited employee engagement first, with customer satisfaction and free cash flow coming in second and third, respectively. In addition, many employees are also looking for environments where they can be engaged and feel that they are contributing in a positive way to something larger than themselves.

EMPLOYEE ENGAGEMENT DEFINED

Engagement is the extent of employees' commitment, work effort, and desire to stay in an organization. To compete today, companies need to win over the MINDS (rational commitment) and the HEARTS (emotional commitment) of employees in ways that lead to extraordinary effort. Engagement describes how an employee thinks and feels about, and acts toward his or her job, the work experience and the company. Engagement is the extent to which employees commit to something or someone in their organization, how hard they work and how long they stay as a result of that commitment. Engagement is the extent to which people enjoy and believe in what they do, and feel valued for doing it. According to The Gallup Organization, Employee engagement is the involvement with and enthusiasm for work. Engagement is the state of emotional and intellectual commitment to an organization or group producing behavior that will help fulfill an organization's promises to customers - and, in so doing, improve business results. Engaged employees have an intense desire to be a part of the organization and they stay with that organization; they advocate for the organization by referring potential employees and customers, are positive with co-workers and are constructive in their criticism; and exert extra effort and engage in behaviors that contribute to business success. Engagement is a positive attitude held by the employee toward the organization and its values. An engaged employee is aware of business context, and works with colleagues to improve performance within the job for the benefit of the organization. The organization must work to develop and nurture engagement, which requires a two-way relationship between employer and employee. Engagement is above and beyond simple satisfaction with the employment arrangement or basic loyalty to the employer. Engagement is about passion, commitment, and the willingness to invest oneself and expend one's discretionary effort to help the employer succeed. Organizational effectiveness depends on more than simply maintaining a stable workforce; employees must perform assigned duties dependably and be willing to engage in activities that go beyond role requirements. Harter and Schmidt propose that employee engagement reflects a deeper level of involvement and enthusiasm from the employee than the terms "job satisfaction" or "organizational commitment" might imply.

COMMITTING TO THE WORK AND THE COMPANY

Some experts define commitment as both a willingness to persist in a course of action and reluctance to change plans, often owing to a sense of obligation to stay the course. People are simultaneously committed to multiple entities, such as economic, educational, familial, political and religious institutions. They also commit themselves to specific individuals, including their spouses, children, parents and siblings, as well as to their employers, co-workers, supervisors and customers. Commitment manifests itself in distinct behavior. For example, people devote time and energy to fulfill their on-the-job responsibilities as well as their family, personal, community and spiritual obligations. Commitment also has an emotional component. People usually experience and express positive feelings toward an entity or individual to whom they have made a commitment. Finally, commitment has a rational element also. Most people consciously decide to make commitments, then they thoughtfully plan and carry out the actions required to fulfill them. Because commitments require an investment of time as well as mental and emotional energy, most people make them with the expectation of reciprocation.

10 Common Themes: How Companies Measure Engagement

Employers typically assess their employees' engagement levels with company-wide attitude or opinion surveys. A sampling of the criteria featured in such instruments reveals 10 common themes related to engagement:

- Pride in employer
- Satisfaction with employer
- Job satisfaction
- Opportunity to perform well at challenging work
- Recognition and positive feedback for one's contributions
- Personal support from one's supervisor
- Effort above and beyond the minimum
- Understanding the link between one's job and the organization's mission
- Prospects for future growth with one's employer
- Intention to stay with one's employer

Employer practice that ultimately affect the business results

Fig. 11.1

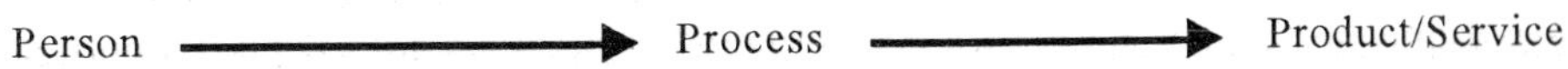

Fig. 11.2

Employers naturally want to encourage workers to perform prescribed and voluntary activities while avoiding proscribed ones. To achieve these goals, organizations use a number of HR practices that directly affect the person, process and context components of job performance. Employees' reactions to these practices determine their levels of engagement and commitment.

Drivers of Engagement

An organization's HR System is the primary driver of employee engagement. The HR system's staffing, training and development practices contribute to the development of employee competencies that enhance competitive advantage and help to ensure organization and employee fit. Rewards, benefits, and performance management practices help motivate employees to behave in ways that benefit the organization. Organizational and job designs help create a work environment that is conducive to employees' development and effective work systems. Lastly, effective management and leadership development helps to ensure a productive, fair, and supportive working environment in which employees feel motivated to achieve organizational objectives. A rich body of literature has identified key drivers of employee engagement that are the result of the proper alignment of HR practices, including: job characteristics, role clarity and fit, coworker and management relations, leadership, and perceptions of fairness.

Job and Task Design

Workers' negative responses to job design in early 20th century America spurred organizational scientists to examine the human component of work more closely. By the 1950s, several theories of job satisfaction and work motivation had emerged that related to job design, particularly the beneficial effects of job enlargement (broadening the scope of job tasks) and job enrichment (providing more complex and challenging tasks). With publication of the job characteristics model in the early 1970s, interest in the impact of job design on worker motivation and productivity intensified. This model proposed five "core" or motivational job characteristics: skill variety, task identity, task significance (which collectively contribute to a sense of work meaningfulness), autonomy and performance feedback. Jobs that have these characteristics promote internal motivation, personal responsibility for performance and job satisfaction — in short, engagement. Analysis of work-design research revealed that social characteristics strongly influence both employee engagement and commitment. Research shows that managers who provide enriched work (jobs that are high in meaningfulness, variety, autonomy and co-worker trust) stimulate engagement and enthusiasm in their employees. In turn, engagement and enthusiasm encourage employees to define their work roles broadly. Broad definition of job roles then enhances workers' willingness to take ownership of challenges that lie beyond their immediate assigned tasks. These challenges inspire people to innovate and to solve problems proactively. Thus, job enrichment promotes engagement in both prescribed and voluntary work activities.

Recruiting

The messages an organization conveys while seeking to attract job applicants also can influence future employees' engagement and commitment. If the firm has designed jobs specifically to engage employees, then you'll want to ensure that recruiting ads extol these positions' attractive features— such as challenging work assignments, a highly skilled team environment or minimal supervision. Applicants who notice and respond to these ads will more likely be motivated by these features.

Employee Selection

Once the recruiting efforts produce a pool of promising job candidates, selection is made among them to fill available positions. When the selection of the right individuals for the right jobs is made, the new hires carry out their work more smoothly and experience fewer performance problems. The result is greater enjoyment of — and engagement in — the job. To enhance engagement through selection of employees, first identify those candidates who are best-suited to the job and organization's culture. Also need for use is the candidate assessment methods that have obvious relevance to the job in question.

Training and Development

Training and development can serve as additional levers for enhancing engagement and commitment. For new hires, training usually begins with orientation. Orientation presents several important opportunities — including explaining pay, work schedules and company policies. Most important, it gives a chance to encourage employee engagement by explaining how the new hire's job contributes to the organization's mission. Through orientation, it can be described how the company is organized, introduce the new employee to his or her co-workers, give the person a tour of the area where he or she will be working and explain safety regulations and other procedural matters. In short, foster person-organization fit which is vital for developing productive and dedicated employees. Through training, new and current employees can acquire the knowledge and skills they need to perform their jobs. And employees who enhance their skills through training are more likely to engage fully in their work, because they derive satisfaction from mastering new tasks. Training also enhances employees' value to your company as well as their own employability in the job market. In addition, most companies offer higher wages for skilled workers, to compensate them for their greater value and to discourage turnover.

Compensation

Like the HR practices discussed above, compensation can powerfully influence employee engagement and commitment. Some compensation components encourage commitment to employers, while others motivate engagement in the job. It is possible to stimulate one and not the other, though it's generally better to foster both. Incentive pay, also known as pay-for-performance, can directly influence employees' productivity (and thus their engagement) as well as their commitment to the organization (as workers learn to trust that they will be rewarded for good performance).

Management

Effective managers are those who get the work done with the people they have and do not try to change them; they attempt to capitalize on the competencies their people have, not what they, the manager, wished they had. The relation with one's immediate manager can have a dramatic impact on an individual's perceptions of the work environment. A supportive, and non-controlling, relationship should foster perceptions of safety and enhance employee creativity. Supervisors who foster a supportive work environment:

- Display concern for employees' needs and feelings
- Provide positive feedback
- Encourage employees to:
  - *Voice their concerns*
  - *Develop new skills*
  - *Solve work-related problems*

Such supportive actions enhance employee self-determination and interest in their work. Employees who are self-determined experience "a sense of choice in initiating and regulating one's own actions." These individuals are likely to feel safer to engage themselves more fully, try out novel ways of doing things, discuss mistakes and learn from these behaviors when they are in such supportive environments. Supervisory supportiveness of employees' self determination and congruent perceptions between supervisors and employees have also both been linked with enhancing trust.

Performance Management

The right performance management practices also can enhance employee engagement and commitment. Encouragement by managers to include employees in the goal-setting process is quite useful. This technique helps to ensure that workers understand the goals. It also promotes acceptance of challenging objectives, because people generally feel more committed to goals they have helped define. Performance management processes operate on a continuous basis. Therefore, they provide perhaps the best ongoing opportunities for employers to foster employee engagement and commitment. An employee's aspirations and career goals can receive careful attention during performance appraisal meetings. Without inquiring into an employee's personal life, a supervisor can nevertheless explore ways to enhance the compatibility between the worker's commitment to the organization and the employee's other life commitments. Through such means, the organization personalizes its relationship to each employee and provides support, while also expressing appreciation for their contributions, which are key drivers of engagement and commitment. Of course, effective performance management systems also identify employees who are not meeting expectations. Failing to address problem, performance can erode other employees' engagement and commitment, as their workloads increase and they conclude that the company is willing to tolerate poor performance. If feedback, coaching and remedial training are of little avail, the manager may need to move the person to a different position within the company where he or she can make a more valuable contribution, or let the individual go if there is no good match elsewhere in the organization.

Creation of an Engagement Culture

The need is to establish a receptive foundation for engagement initiatives by creating an "engagement culture." Communication of the value of employee engagement through company mission statement and other executive communications are necessary for this. Follow up and ensuring that all units execute their engagement action plans. Monitor progress on engagement-improvement efforts, and adjust your strategies and plans as needed. Equally important, be sure to recognize and celebrate progress and results.

Leadership

There has been a great deal of research indicating that leaders who engage in "transformational/charismatic" behaviors produce transformational/charismatic effects. Transformational leaders enhance employee engagement by fostering a sense of passion for work as well as the employees' capacity to think independently, develop new ideas, and challenge convention when no longer relevant. Leaders also play an important role by defining and communicating the organization's vision, purpose, and goals. Top management openness, defined as the degree to which top management is believed to encourage and support suggestions and change initiatives from below, has also been shown to enhance employee engagement.

Perception of Fairness

Fairness consists of three types of subjective perceptions, typically referred to as distributive justice, procedural justice, and interactional justice. Much of the equity theory research was derived from initial work conducted by Adams, who used a social exchange theory framework to evaluate fairness, which was used to help define distributive justice. According to Adams, people were not concerned about the absolute level of outcomes per se, but whether those outcomes were fair. Adams suggested that one way to determine whether an outcome was fair was to calculate the ratio of one's outcomes (e.g., compensation, promotions, and development) to their contributions or inputs (e.g., effort, time, education, intelligence, and experience) and then compare that ratio with that of a comparison other. When employees feel that they are being treated fairly, they reciprocate through the performance of organizational citizenship behaviors (OCB).

Gallup Q12 Model

There is the famous Gallup's Q12 model for determining the employee's engagement level. An employee engagement measure used by many organizations, measures important actionable aspects of the work environment that lead to employee engagement. The Gallup Q12 is a survey designed to measure employee engagement. The instrument was the result of hundreds of focus groups and interviews. Researchers found that there were 12 key expectations, that when satisfied, form the foundation of strong feelings of engagement. So far 87,000 work units and 1.5 million employees have participated in the Q12 instrument. Comparisons of engagement scores reveal that those with high Q12 scores exhibit lower turnover, higher sales growth, better productivity, better customer loyalty and other manifestations of superior performance. The Gallup organization also uses the Q12 as a semi-annual employee engagement Index – a random sampling of employee across the country. The engagement index slots people into one of three categories.

- **Engaged** employees work with passion and feel a profound connection to their company. They drive innovation and move the organization forward.
- **Not-Engaged** employees are essentially "checked out." They are sleepwalking through their workday. They are putting in time, but not enough energy or passion into their work.
- **Actively Disengaged** employees aren't just unhappy at work; they're busy acting out their unhappiness. Every day, these workers undermine what their engaged co-workers accomplish.

The results of the latest engagement index:

Engaged employees – 28 %

Not-engaged employees – 54%

Actively Disengaged – 17%

In other words, 71% of the workforce is either underperforming or actively undermining their work.

CASE STUDY OF HCL TECHNOLOGIES: EMPLOYEE FIRST, CUSTOMER SECOND

Company Overview

Hindustan Computers Ltd (HCL) is a $5.9 billion IT major based in India. The three decade old enterprise, founded in 1976, is one of India's original IT garage start ups. Its range of offerings span R&D and Technology Services, Enterprise and Applications Consulting, Remote Infrastructure Management, BPO services, IT Hardware, Systems Integration and Distribution of Technology and Telecom products in India. The HCL team comprises 80,000 professionals of diverse nationalities, operating across 31 countries including 500 points of presence in India. HCL has global partnerships with several leading Fortune 1000 firms, including several IT and Technology majors.

In April 2005, Vineet Nayar, the newly appointed president of HCL Technologies (HCL), took on the challenge of bringing the company to a leadership position in the IT services industry. It was a formidable task given that HCL was, at the time, plagued with many problems, not least an attrition rate of almost 17% — much higher than that of its main competitors — and a demoralized work force. In February 2006, Vineet announced a radical new strategy, "Employee First, Customer Second," (EFCS) at HCL's first global customer meeting. The strategic goals for the EFCS transformation were to create a unique employee organization, drive an inverted organizational structure, create transparency and accountability within the organization, and encourage a value driven culture.

Indian IT Sector

The IT services sector in India had been a demand-driven industry. While alternate outcome-based pricing models had received a lot of attention, estimates suggested that in most of the major companies in this sector, revenues that were not linear in billable hours accounted for only 5% to 30% of the total revenues from IT services in 2008. Hence, scale up was almost a direct multiple of employee head count, making hiring and attrition rates critical to the growth of an IT services company. This was in contrast to most technology-product companies, where scale up was not a direct linear function of head count. Thus, human-resources strategies were critical ingredients of the growth plans for companies in the IT services sector. Customer accounts had grown as customers started leveraging the lower-cost offshore model. Indian IT services companies used quality as a key differentiator, and by 2008, all of them could boast of Capability Maturity Model Integration (CMMI) Level 5 processes. Customers had started to take continuous improvements in cost, productivity, quality, and delivery excellence for granted.

Challenges in IT Sector

Demand growth and the increasing complexity of engagements raised many challenges on the supply side. An obvious one was the need to hire in large numbers to sustain growth. Yet it was not just a numbers game. Productivity of new hires tended to be low and training costs relative to other costs tended to be higher for Indian IT services vendors than for similar companies in the United States. The shortage of suitably trained employees was apparent at both the low and high ends of the education spectrum. Commenting on the 2006 report by the Association for Computing

Machinery's (ACM's) Job Migration Task Force, David Patterson, a Berkeley computer science professor and former president of ACM, noted with surprise that India produced fewer than 50 PhDs a year in computer science, a number smaller than the output of the San Francisco bay area alone.

Transformation at HCL Technologies

In July 2005, during a three-day Blueprint meeting of the company's top 100 managers, Vineet and his senior management team announced a paradigm shift in HCL's strategic focus. There were to be two main points of departure from the company's own past as well as that of other Indian IT service companies' approaches at that time. HCL's primary focus would shift from volume to value and from processes to people. The transformation was to occur in three phases. The goal for the first phase was to create more engaged employees through EFCS. Vineet wanted to create a strong service brand by focusing on customer interactions with energized employees. In the second phase, Vineet wanted to form strategic partnerships with other companies to offer more value and end-to-end services to the customer. The plan for the third phase was to implement a radical shift in HCL's core business model, with 50% of revenues in 2010 coming from services that did not exist in 2005.

Smart Service Desk

To create a unique employee organization, HCL wanted to create a uniform experience for employees of all ranks. Enabling functions such as administration, human resources, finance, accounts, and IT support were to be accountable to employees. To help create uniformity of experience, HCL implemented Smart Service Desk (SSD), a ticket-based online system that decreased resolution times and provided more transparency across all enabling functions. Any employee could submit a ticket electronically to any enabling function, and only the employee who submitted a ticket could close the ticket.

360-degree Feedback

To create an inverted organizational structure, Vineet Nayar instituted reverse accountability—essentially holding managers accountable to their direct reports. All managers were required to go through the 360- degree-feedback mechanism, regardless of their level in the organization. The feedback was to be purely developmental and was not to be used for appraisal purposes.

Opinion Polls

For policy matters that would affect a large part of the organization, HCL management gathered employee opinions using opinion polls. In the 45 opinion polls conducted in 2006–07, the number of participants ranged from 450 to 10,000 (averaging 2,000 per poll).

"Directions"

"Directions" was an annual company-wide event that took strategic discussions out of closed-door meetings to all employees. The CEO and the leadership team were present at these meetings to share the vision and strategy of the company as well as respond to questions in interactive sessions. Directions allowed everyone in HCL to speak the same language and understand how their individual contributions fit in a larger organizational framework.

U&I Initiative

The U&I initiative, launched at the end of 2006, provided an online forum for employees to interact directly with the CEO — allowing them to raise seemingly unresolvable issues. Initially, transactional issues such as compensation packages and delayed appraisals dominated the questions.

CEO's blog

The CEO's blog performed the reverse function: Vineet posed questions or posted information about events, and the employees responded.

"Natasha"

"Natasha" was an animated online assistant and guide for users on the HCL intranet. It served as a virtual face for HCL's processes and policies.

iGen

Value-creation activities were promoted by creating capability through learning- and knowledge-management systems. In keeping with the philosophy that thinking was not the monopoly of a central group, there were many venues for employees to contribute ideas.

Innovation at HCL

In a monthlong innovation contest held in 2008 to recognize innovations created by various project teams, a company-wide contest was held for project managers and higher ranked staff associated with customer-delivery projects to submit entries to innovation at HCL. The line of business (LOB) heads evaluated ideas on a set of metrics that included cost savings, innovativeness, effective usage of tools, and unique differentiation from the competition.

CONCLUSION

Engaged employees can help the organization achieve its mission, execute its strategy and generate important business results. This paper has highlighted ways in which different HR practices, including job design, recruitment, selection, training, compensation and performance management can enhance employee engagement. But these examples also show that employee engagement is more complex than it may appear on the surface. Organizations define and measure engagement in a variety of different ways, suggesting there is no one "right" or "best" way to define or stimulate engagement in your workforce. The decision to invest in strengthening engagement or commitment (or both) depends on an organization's strategy and the makeup of its workforce. For these reasons, it is vital to consider any particular organization's view of engagement, as well as its strategy and workforce composition when deciding which HR practices will receive scarce investment.

References

1. Abrahamson, M., & Anderson, W. P. (1984). People's commitments to institutions. *Social Psychology Quarterly*, 47, pp. 371-381.
2. Borman, W. C., & Motowidlo, S. J. (1997). Task performance and contextual performance:The meaning for personnel selection research. *Human Performance, 10*, pp. 99-110.
3. Cohen, A. (2003). *Multiple commitments in the workplace: An integrative approach.* Mahwah, NJ: Lawrence Erlbaum Associates.
4. Kahn, W. A. (1990). Psychological conditions of personal engagement and disengagement at work. *Academy of Management Journal, 33*, pp. 692-724.
5. Katz, D., & Kahn, R. L. (1978). *The social psychology of organizations* (2nd ed). New York: John Wiley & Sons.
6. Meyer, J. P., & Allen, N. J. (1991). A three-component conceptualization of organizational commitment. *Human Resource Management Review, 1*, pp. 61-89.
7. Meyer, J. P., Becker, T. E., & Vandenberghe, C. (2004). Employee commitment and motivation: A conceptual analysis and integrative model. *Journal of Applied Psychology*, 89, pp. 991-1007.
8. Organ, D. W., & Ryan, K. (1995). A meta-analytic review of attitudinal and dispositional predictors or organizational citizenship behavior. *Personnel Psychology*, pp. 775-802.
9. Ramsay, C. S. (2006, May). Engagement at Intuit: It's the people. In J. D. Kaufman (Chair), *Defining and measuring employee engagement: Old wine in new bottles?* Symposium conducted at the Society for Industrial and Organizational Psychology 21st Annual Conference, Dallas, Texas.
10. Ramsay, C. S., & Finney, M. I. (2006). *Employee engagement at Intuit.* Mountain View, CA: Intuit Inc.
11. Robinson, D., Perryman, S., & Hayday, S. (2004). *The drivers of employee engagement.* IES Report No. 408. Brighton, UK: Institute for Employment Studies.
12. Vance, R. J. (2006). Organizing for customer service. In L. Fogli (Ed.), *Customer service delivery: Research and best practices* (pp. 22 – 51). San Francisco, Calif.: Jossey-Bass.
13. Van Maanen, J. (1976). Breaking in: Socialization to work. In R. Dubin (Ed.), *Handbook of work, organization, and society* (pp. 67 – 130). Chicago: Rand McNally & Co.
14. Welch, J., & Welch, S. (2006, May 8). Ideas the Welch way: How healthy is your company? *Business Week*, 126.

APPENDIX

The Q12 Index

1. Do you know what is expected of you at work?
2. Do you have the materials and equipment to do your work right?
3. At work, do you have the opportunity to do what you do best every day?
4. In the last seven days, have you received recognition or praise for doing good work?
5. Does your supervisor, or someone at work, seem to care about you as a person?
6. Is there someone at work who encourages your development?
7. At work, do your opinions seem to count?
8. Does the mission/purpose of your company make you feel your job is important?
9. Are your associates (fellow employees) committed to doing quality work?
10. Do you have a best friend at work?
11. In the last six months, has someone at work talked to you about your progress?
12. In the last year, have you had opportunities to learn and grow?

12 Organisational Culture for Employee Engagement: A Study at VIOM Networks

Ms. Lopamudra

ABSTRACT

The concept of organizational culture has gained attention in last decades. Organizations have understood it is the culture of the organization which aligns the employee objective with that of the organization. Therefore organization takes effort build a true engagement culture where employees will be committed, motivated and willing to go the extra miles. In engagement culture employees are encouraged to offer loyalty and commitment to the organization. This article is a descriptive study to understand factors contributing towards engagement culture. The article discusses the effort of Viom Network towards building an engagement culture. The findings will be arrived at analyzing the data collected from the secondary sources. The findings will provide quantum of insights into the HRM innovative practices to the HR professionals, academicians, researchers and practitioners.

Keywords: Employee engagement, Organization culture, Engagement culture, Viom Network.

INTRODUCTION

Barry Marcus said that the greatest asset of any business lies in its human capital, the employees. Today organisations also understood that employees are central to the smooth functioning of the business. It is also realised that to look after the employee is crucial for the management. Therefore organisation these days enriched its human resource functions by adopting many employee oriented practices. As a way to understand human resources organisation culture also gained acceptance. Because it is the culture of the organisation which provides platform for HR practices. In a favourable culture organisation can cultivate commitment and loyalty within the employees. Therefore favourable organisational culture promotes employee engagement. The engaging culture employs focuses on seeing that employees engage in what they do, rather than just do it. Organizations with highly engaged employees experience a decrease in customer complaints. By engagement we mean passion, commitment, extra effort — the illusive force that motivates people to high performance. High engagement manifest itself as high energy, commitment, job ownership and pride, productivity, loyalty, discretionary effort, wise use of time, passion, excitement, execution, and bottom line results.

OBJECTIVE OF THE STUDY

The study is an effort

- to understand the factors contributing towards an culture of engagement.
- to understand how Viom Network successfully built a culture of engagement.

Method

This article is a descriptive study to understand factors contributing towards engagement culture. The article discusses the effort of Viom Network towards building an engagement culture. Data collected from both primary and secondary resources. Personal interview method is used as primary method. The study interviewed various HR executives and employees of Viom Network. Non probability sampling method is used to select the respondents. As secondary method books, journals, periodicals and internet is used.

Employee Engagement

An effective leader dedicates to develop their employees with focus on engagement. To promote this he builds engagement culture. According to Kahn (1990), engagement means to be psychologically as well as physically present when occupying and performing an organisational role.[1] Kahn (1990) also defines employee engagement as "the harnessing of organization members' selves to their work roles; in engagement, people employ and express themselves physically, cognitively, and emotionally during role performances".[2] The cognitive aspect of employee engagement concerns employees' beliefs about the organisation, its leaders and working conditions. The emotional aspect concerns how employees feel about each of those three factors and whether they have positive or negative attitudes toward the organisation and its leaders. The physical aspect of employee engagement concerns the physical energies exerted by individuals to accomplish their roles. Employee engagement determines the association of a person with the organisation. Most often employee engagement has been defined as emotional and intellectual commitment to the organisation (Baumruk 2004).[3] Truss *et al* (2006) define employee engagement simply as 'passion for work', a psychological state which is seen to encompass the three dimensions of engagement discussed by Kahn (1990).[4]

It is acknowledged that employee engagement has been defined in many different ways, it is also argued the definitions often sound similar to other better known and established constructs such as 'organisational commitment' and 'organisational citizenship behaviour' (OCB) (Robinson *et al* 2004).[5] Thus Robinson *et al* (2004) defined engagement as 'one step up from commitment'.[6]

Gallup being one of oldest the consulting organisation {in conducting engagement survey} creates a feedback system for employers that would identify and measure elements of worker engagement most tide to the bottom line. Things such as sales, growth, productivity and customer loyalty are all accessed. Gallup researchers found (Gallup 2010) that companies in the top 10 percent on employee engagement bested their competition by 72 percent in earnings per share during 2007-08. For companies that scored beneath the top quartile, earnings fell 9.4 percent below their competition.

A satisfied employee is not necessarily the best employee in terms of loyalty and productivity. It is only an engaged employee who is intellectually and emotionally bound with the organization who feels passionate about its goals and is committed towards its values thus he goes the extra mile beyond the basic job. When employees are effectively and positively engaged with their organization, they form an emotional connection with the company. Employee engagement is a barometer that determines the association of a person with the organisation. It is about creating the passion among associates to do things beyond what is expected from him. Hence engagement can be defined as a measure of the emotional and intellectual commitment that employees have to their organisation. [7]

Employee engagement requires a supportive organisational climate. Hence their exist a definite interface amongst employee commitment, organisational climate and accountability and ownership, which can stand for engaged employee.[8]

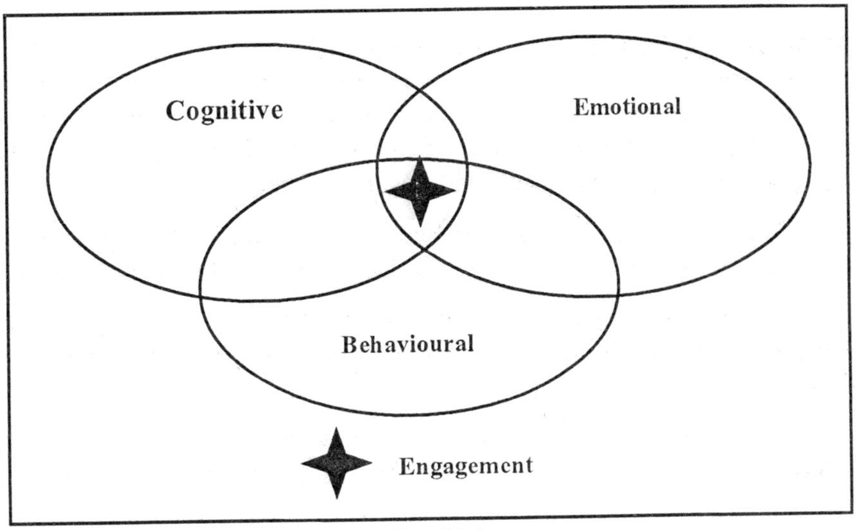

Fig. 12.1

The views of ISR Surveys reflect that engagement is the interface of the three components such as the Cognitive component or the think component, which relates to the employees logical evaluation, of company's goals and values; the second is the emotional component or the feel component or the affective component, which taps into whether employees have a sense of belonging and pride in the company, and the third one is the behavioural component or the act component, which captures the out comes that employees desire such as retention and willingness to "go the extra distance" for the company when necessary. Engagement it self is actually a measure of these three components.

According to the Gallup the Consulting organization there are there are different types of people:-

Engaged—"*Engaged*" employees are builders. They want to know the desired expectations for their role so they can meet and exceed them. They're naturally curious about their company and their place in it. They perform at consistently high levels. They want to use their talents and strengths at work every day. They work with passion and they drive innovation and move their organization forward.

Not Engaged – *Not-engaged* employees tend to concentrate on tasks rather than the goals and outcomes they are expected to accomplish. They want to be told what to do just so they can do it and say they have finished. They focus on accomplishing tasks vs. achieving an outcome. Employees who are *not-engaged* tend to feel their contributions are being overlooked, and their potential is not being tapped. They often feel this way because they don't have productive relationships with their managers or with their co-workers.

Actively Disengaged--The "*actively disengaged*" employees are the "cave dwellers." They're "Consistently against Virtually Everything." They're not just unhappy at work; they're busy acting out their unhappiness .They sow seeds of negativity at every opportunity. Every day, actively disengaged workers undermine what their engaged coworkers accomplish. As workers increasingly rely on each other to generate products and services, the problems and tensions that are fostered by *actively disengaged* workers can cause great damage to an organization's functioning .

EMPLOYEE ENGAGEMENT—THE DRIVERS

To implement engagement organisation need to understand the drivers of engagement. Organisation culture is the most important driver of engagement. The strongest driver of all is a sense of feeling valued and involved. This has several key components:

As engagement is all about people, people are one of the most important drivers of employee engagement. The superior, the peer, customers , all have their role to make engagement effective.

As engagement makes the employee get involved in their job/work, so work is another driver of employee engagement. It includes the work activities, the resources to perform the work and the process of the work etc.

Reward is one of the motivators for employee. If employees get motivated it will ultimately increase their commitment towards the job. Reward can be in the form of pay, benefits and recognition.

Opportunities in the form of career opportunity and learning and development opportunity play an important role towards employee engagement. Today employees are pretty career and development oriented. If these purposes get solved in the organisation then employee's commitment will get increased.

Company practices should have a objective towards employee engagement. Every practices have direct or indirect impact on employee engagement.

If a company provides better quality of life it ultimately motivated the employee and their involvement in their job gets increased.

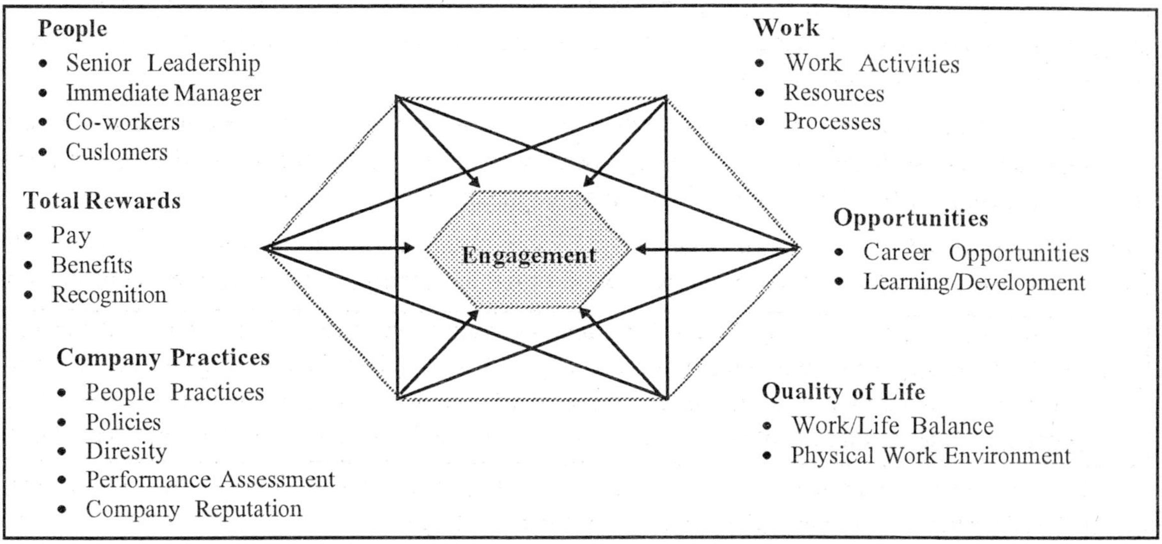

Fig. 12.2

Source: Hewitt research.

Organisation Culture of Viom Network Supporting Engagement

Viom Networks Limited, a joint venture between Tata Teleservices and Quippo, a SREI Group enterprise, is the pioneer in the Shared Passive Telecom Infrastructure industry in India. In 2009, the parent company - Quippo Telecom Infrastructure Limited (QTIL) announced its partnership with Tata Teleservices Ltd. (TTSL) with the merger of their passive infrastructure businesses, resulting in the formation of a unified entity – Viom Networks. Viom is an independent entity with over 39,000 towers and with over 83,000 tenants.

The Work Culture at Viom Networks is defined by the compassion of its employees and the core values of the organization. The supportive organisational culture of Viom facilitates employee engagement activities.

Viom focuses on productivity norms and attrition. Where the aim is to increase the productivity and decrease the employee attrition. They identified insufficiency in job profile the reason for which people remain disengaged. Either of the under occupied and over occupied people remain disengaged in the organisation.

Based on the engagement parameter Viom also has categorised people in to engaged, passively engaged and disengaged people. And their intention is always to reduce the disengaged zone as disengaged employee can pull the passively engaged people to their zone. To manage the under occupied employees action plan is prepared, so that they will remain engaged. Similarly people who are over occupied their supervisor; the management always remain concerned for them. Management show their care for this person which motivates them. Even works of such people sometimes get squeezed to short term projects.

Viom has a wide range of engagement activities. Their work culture gets vibrant with the fun at work place. Viom remains a fun place to work 24 × 7 × 365, as stringent deadlines and tough commitments go hand-in-hand with strategies designed to help employees unwind and beat unwanted stress. Hobby club, sports club, partying, festivals, birthdays, anniversaries, and achievements reflect that every day is a fun day in Viom.

Skip level meeting of Viom is an excellent step to unveil various problems and challenges. It is formal team feedback session facilitated by HR as well as the supervisor where they get to know their team members, build trust with them, and understand their problems.

The concept of *"your opinions counts"* of Viom founded on the original approach of the suggestion box. This effort of Viom allow a wide range of employees to make their contributions

At the centre of the building which they name as inspiration zone, the bell and the thank you board reflects the appreciation and inspiration culture of Viom. When the bell rings all get gathered at the inspiration zone then gratitude is expressed in the thank you board. This is a brilliant idea to express gratitude so that people get motivated and ultimately their commitment gets enhanced.

Engagement calendar lists various activities/events of engagement that can be carried every month for the employees. The calendar is prepared by a team.

Communication is the base of any business activity. In the engaged culture passion is communicated amongst the employees to such an extent that they do things beyond what is expected of them. Similarly it is highly essential to know the status of employee and to prepare the action plan accordingly. The Employee Communication Forum at the end of every quarter is helpful to know the position of the team, the circle, the employees.

To rate its engagement activity Viom network is also get tied with Great Place to Work Institute.

The engagement activity of Viom can be represented as:

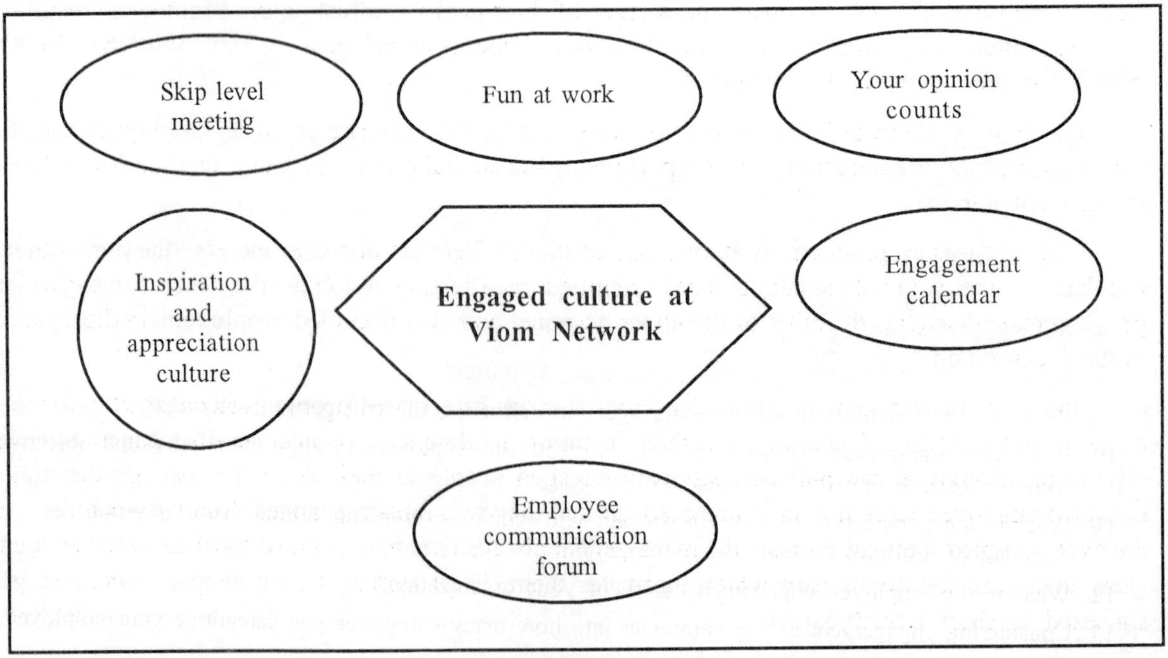

Fig. 12.3

CONCLUSION

Employees are the greatest asset for the organisation. The more they will remain engaged the more will be the productivity and the growth of the organisation. Viom invest a great deal in human capital, convinced of its perfectly engaged and empowered workforce that will help to achieve the vision of being the Most Valuable And Independent Telecom Infrastructure Company Offering Integrated Value Added Services.

References:

1. Kahn, W.A. (1990), 'Psychological conditions of personal engagement and disengagement at work', *Academy of Management Journal,* Vol. 33, pp. 692-724.
2. *Ibid.*
3. Baumruk, R. (2004), 'The missing link: the role of employee engagement in business success', Workspan, Vol. 47, pp. 48-52.
4. Truss, C., Soane, E., Edwards, C., Wisdom, K., Croll, A. and Burnett, J. (2006). Working Life: Employee Attitudes and Engagement 2006. London, CIPD.
5. Robinson, I. (2006), Human Resource Management in Organisations. London, CIPD.
6. *Ibid.*
7. http://was7.hewitt.com/bestemployers/europe/slovakia/
8. Mishra B.N., Dash R.K.S.Mangesh, Employee engagement in service sectors: some views in line with organisational practices, Souvenir New Age HR: Opportunities and challenges, Srusti Academy of Management, pp. 7.
9. http://www.citehr.com/255482-please-help-me-understand-employee-engagement.html
10. http://search.ebscohost.com.
11. http://viomnetworks.com/our-culture.html

Questions:

1. How do you define the term employee engagement?
2. What are the regular practices you are doing to facilitate employee engagement?
3. What are the need-based practices you are doing to facilitate employee engagement?
4. Out of all your practices which one is popular by the employees?
5. What complains in general people have which indicates that employees are not engaged?
6. What are the disengaged behavior of the employees?
7. What are the engaged behavior of the employees?
8. What budget you allocate for the engagement activities?
9. What are the reactions of the line managers in delivering the engagement activities?
10. How your engagement activities are able to create the employees to align their individual objectives with the organizational objectives?
11. What is the perspective of your organization in employer branding efforts vis-à-vis employee engagement efforts?
12. What is the employee engagement score of your organization?
13. Considering engagement as the parameter into how many categories you categorize your employees?
14. What are the major difficulties of your engaged employees?
15. How do you integrate the employee engagement practices with your organizational culture?

13 Transition from Employee Involvement to Employee Engagement as a Retentional Strategy

Ms. Susri Sangita Mohanty
Ms. Swati Mishra
Ms. Lopamudra Hati

ABSRACT

The role of employee engagement in organization has been evolving dramatically in recent times especially after global recession. Employee engagement is increasingly receiving consideration as a strategic partner because it assists to utilize human power effectively which ultimately helps the companies to beat the competition and to gain the competitive advantage. Employee engagement can be critically important to competitiveness in the contemporary business environment as well as it is a positive concept to human resource management.

This article aims at providing a transparent and indisputable transition of retention strategies in four successive stages; these are employee involvement, employee satisfaction, employee motivation and employee engagement. The primary focus of the paper is to showcase how employee engagement plays a dominant role over all other three stages to retain employees and also discussed how it helps to flourish and survive the organization in a highly competitive world.

Keywords: Employee involvement, Employee satisfaction, Motivation and Employee engagement.

INTRODUCTION

"The roadways have been graded and the retention pond for the lake has been dug, although there are embankments to prevent it from filling with runoff water"

— *Don Hoth*

This article clearly shows how transition of employee retention practices has been moved from employee involvement to employee satisfaction to employee motivation and finally towards employee engagement. Employee involvement is the first strategy in which companies feels that in order to make employee more productive and to retain them employees should be involved in various management practices like workers participation in management, forming Quality circle and emphasizing total quality management. In Mid 90ies it is realized that only employee involvement practices are not sufficient so companies started focusing on employee satisfaction with the belief that happy workers are productive workers through increased rate of pay, work responsibilities, variety of tasks, promotional opportunities and democratic management style. It was found that more or less employee satisfaction focuses on tangible factors where as in order to compete with cross cultural environment and globalised economy intangible factors plays a significant role. Therefore companies' focus shifted from satisfaction to employee motivation. Motivation as a psychological phenomenon uplifted the potential of the employees but faulty identification of motivational requirement for different employees forced the companies to initiate some innovative strategies. One of such strategy is employee engagement which takes its momentum after global melt down. Unless and until employees are engaged and identified themselves to the company they cannot be retained for a long period of time.

TRANSITION FROM EMPLOYEE INVOLVEMENT

The transition of retention strategies takes in four successive stages these are as follows:

1st phase of retention strategy: employee involvement

2nd phase of retention strategy: employee satisfaction

3rd phase of retention strategy: employee motivation

4th phase of retention strategy: employee engagement

1st Phase of Retention Strategy: Employee Involvement

Employee involvement is an old idea constantly being revitalized by organizations. It is identified as a 1st key contributor to retain employees. Generally employee involvement means employees participate directly to help an organization fulfill its mission and meet its objectives by applying their ideas, expertise, and efforts towards problem solving and decision making. Although employee involvement is not a new management concept, it has only recently seen a revival in popular support along with the concomitant rise in HRM.

Historically, it has been an integral part of labor movements, unions. In the United States the oldest documented system of formal employee involvement is Eastman Kodak Company's employee suggestion system, established in 1898. During World War II employee suggestion system named National Association of Suggestion Systems (NASS). At fiftieth anniversary celebration in Chicago in 1992, the name change to "Employee Involvement Association" was adopted to reflect increasing impact of employee involvement to retain employee. In recent 2010 annual conference the membership voted to adopt our current name of Ideas America (IA). It clearly depicts that employee involvement is an old concept for corporate practitioners.

Lawler (1986) points out that if people at all levels of an organization manage their own work then they will find their jobs more rewarding. In fact Lawler is not alone with this point of view; Peters and Kanter also promote a similar message and support it with business success stories (Peters and Waterman, 1982, Kanter 1983, Holden 1994)

Another important contribution for employee involvement as retention strategy was done by Tannenbaum and Schmidt (1958) and Sadler (1970), who gives a most approved employee involvement process model which is as follows:

(a) **Tell:** the supervisor makes the decision and announces it to staff. The supervisor provides complete direction.

(b) **Sell:** the supervisor makes the decision and then attempts to gain commitment from staff by "selling" the positive aspects of the decision.

(c) **Consult:** the supervisor invites input into a decision while retaining authority to make the final decision herself.

(d) **Join:** the supervisor invites employees to make the decision with him.

While in Japan in the mid 1950s, employee involvement draws attention through quality circles which consist of small groups of employees who meet voluntarily to identify and solve productivity problems. The Japanese emphasize decentralized decision making and use the small group as the organization unit to promote collective decision making and responsibility. While quality circles were introduced in the United States in the mid-1970s.

Employee involvement programs include employee involvement relating to production, quality, safety and health, training or voluntary dispute resolution.

It has benefited organization in several ways like increased employee productivity, increased organizational effectiveness by improving employee performance, improved organizational decision-making capability, improved attitude regarding work, and reduced costs through elimination of waste and reduced product cycle times.

In 1980s it is realized that only employee involvement practices are not sufficient as Employees started presenting vague interest so companies started focusing on employee satisfaction as another tool to retain employee.

2nd Phase of Retention Strategy: Employee Satisfaction

Then the focus quickly shifted to employee satisfaction as a tool to retain employees. Here an employee is satisfied with the company and the work that he does but is simply not motivated to put forward his best performance. He is satisfied and yet may not be a willing team player. An offer of better pay, perks, working conditions, location etc. may invariably lure the employee away from the current assignment.

Job satisfaction describes how content an *individual* is with his or her job. The happier people are within their job, the more satisfied they are said to be. Job satisfaction methods include *job rotation, job enlargement*, *job enrichment* and *job re-engineering*.

Factors that has impact on employee satisfaction are rate of pay, work responsibilities, variety of tasks, promotional opportunities, the work itself and co-workers, management style and culture, employee involvement, empowerment and autonomous work position

Management gurus like Elton Mayo, F.W Taylor, Maslow, Edwin A. Locke contributes a lot with respect to employee satisfaction as a strategy to retain employee.

Elton Mayo of the *Harvard Business School* in his Hawthorne experiment (1924–1933) found the effects of various conditions (most notably illumination) on workers' productivity. These studies showed that to some extent employee satisfaction has impact on productivity. *Frederick Winslow*

Taylor's 1911 in his book, Principles of Scientific Management contributed to a change in industrial production philosophies, causing a shift from skilled labor and *piecework* towards the more modern of *assembly lines* and *hourly wages*. The initial use of scientific management by industries greatly increased productivity because workers were forced to work at a faster pace. However, workers became exhausted and dissatisfied, thus leaving researchers with new questions to answer regarding employee satisfaction.

Some argue that *Maslow's hierarchy of needs* theory, a motivation theory, laid the foundation for employee satisfaction theory. This theory explains that people seek to satisfy five specific needs in life – physiological needs, safety needs, social needs, self-esteem needs, and self-actualization.

Edwin A. Locke's Range of Affect Theory (1976) is arguably the most famous job satisfaction model. This theory postulates that satisfaction is determined by a discrepancy between what one wants in a job and what one has in a job. Also it states that how much one values a given facet of work. This leads to a special degree of satisfaction when expectations are met or dissatisfaction when they aren't met. The application of that theory in the daily life turns out to be much more complicated since there are normally a couple of factors which influence the employee satisfaction.

After all these theories, companies pay their attention to employee satisfaction but gradually they started to feel that only employee satisfaction is not sufficient to retain the employees but also other factor required and that is employee motivation.

3rd Phase of Retention Strategy: Employee Motivation

In the mid 90ies organization came to know that employee involvement and satisfaction are not sufficient to retain the employees. Eminent psychologist like H. Maslow, Herzberg and others postulate motivational theories which is an important tool for motivation as motivation arouses the energy or drive in the individual to proceed in an activity.

Content theorist of motivation said that employees will be primarily motivated by monetary factors. Many organizations at that time focuses on hygiene factors like company policy, working conditions, payment bonus EPF etc to motivate employees. But as globalization came into existence companies started realizing that only monetary factors does not leads to motivation. Rather work itself achievement recognition responsibility leads to motivation.

Common motivational tools used by the organization

(a) Build foundation

(b) Create a positive environment

(c) Put people on right path

(d) Educate the masses

(e) Do not forget fun

(f) Acknowledge contributions

(g) Provide incentives

(h) Honor your promises

(i) Provide career coaching
(j) Match task to talent
(k) Focus n non contingent interaction
(l) Share information and power

Benefits Out of Employee Motivation

Increased employee performance, Job satisfaction, Employee retention, Employee participation, Commitment towards the organization, Innovative thinking, and improved moral are the major benefits of employee motivation.

Flaws with Employee Motivation

- Different people has different motivational requirement. So applying a common motivational tool for everyone may leads to failure.
- Excessive motivation may pressurize the employee and deviates them from their normal functioning
- Human needs are unlimited, so categorization of motivation is difficult task

The drawbacks of this mechanism forced the corporate to change their attention towards a booming concept i.e. employee engagement.

4th Phase of Retention Strategy: Employee Engagement

As we all know the universal truth i.e. "survival of the fittest", which is the rule of the game in today's corporate. So in order to survive companies have to go for uniqueness. The organization may have same resource, technology, investment structure etc but what makes them unique and different is the manpower they have. In such situation where global market has already faced economic crisis, and this pressured the companies to give birth employee engagement strategies in order to retain employee and to gain uniqueness. The field of employee engagement has certainly come to an evolutionary crossroads. It has evolved quite rapidly during the past few years. Employee engagement, also called work engagement or worker engagement, is a *business management* concept. An "engaged employee" is one who is fully involved in, and enthusiastic about, his or her *work*, and thus will act in a way that furthers their *organization*'s interests. According to Scarlett Surveys, "Employee Engagement is a measureable degree of an employee's positive or negative emotional attachment to their job, colleagues and organization which profoundly influences their willingness to learn & perform at work". Thus engagement is distinctively different from satisfaction, motivation, culture, climate and opinion and very difficult to measure.

The quest to find out the best practices to retain and engage employees has forced HR gurus to carry out surveys on it. One of the important survey done regarding employee engagement by Blessing White (global consulting firm) and HR Anexi (HR consulting firm in Mumbai) on January-march 2008. The survey defines 'employee engagement' as an alignment of maximum job satisfaction with maximum job contribution.

Another survey done by Gallup, Management Journal has shown that only 29% of employees are actively engaged in their jobs. Those "engaged" employees work with passion and feel a strong connection to their company. About T! of the business units scoring above the median on employee engagement also scored above the median on performance.

Moreover, 54% of employees are not engaged meaning that they go through each workday putting time but no passion into their work. Only about S! of companies below the median on employee engagement Melcrum, a research and information company recently surveyed 1,000 corporate communications and HR professionals and conducted 40 case studies and found that many respondents credit offering employee engagement programs with the following benefits:

As we all know the universal truth i.e. "survival of the fittest", which is the rule of the game in today's corporate. So in order to survive companies have to go for uniqueness. The organization may have same resource, technology, investment structure etc but what makes them unique and different is the manpower they have. In such situation where global market has already faced economic crisis, and this pressured the companies to give birth employee engagement strategies in order to retain employee and to gain uniqueness. The field of employee engagement has certainly come to an evolutionary crossroads. It has evolved quite rapidly during the past few years. Employee engagement, also called work engagement or worker engagement, is a *business management* concept. An "engaged employee" is one who is fully involved in, and enthusiastic about, his or her *work*, and thus will act in a way that furthers their *organization*'s interests. According to Scarlett Surveys, "Employee Engagement is a measureable degree of an employee's positive or negative emotional attachment to their job, colleagues and organization which profoundly influences their willingness to learn & perform at work". Thus engagement is distinctively different from satisfaction, motivation, culture, climate and opinion and very difficult to measure.

The quest to find out the best practices to retain and engage employees has forced HR gurus to carry out surveys on it.

One of the important survey done regarding employee engagement by Blessing White (global consulting firm) and HR Anexi (HR consulting firm in Mumbai) on January- march 2008. The survey defines 'employee engagement' as an alignment of maximum job satisfaction with maximum job contribution.

Another survey done by Gallup, Management Journal has shown that only 29% of employees are actively engaged in their jobs. Those "engaged" employees work with passion and feel a strong connection to their company. About T! of the business units scoring above the median on employee engagement also scored above the median on performance.

Moreover, 54% of employees are not engaged meaning that they go through each workday putting time but no passion into their work. Only about S! of companies below the median on employee engagement *Melcrum,* a research and information company recently surveyed 1,000 corporate communications and HR professionals and conducted 40 case studies and found that many respondents credit offering employee engagement programs with the following benefits:

- More than 50% report improvements in employee retention and customer satisfaction
- 33% report higher productivity

- 28% report improvements in employee advocacy
- 27% improved status as a "great place to work"
- 27% report increased profitability
- 25% report improved absenteeism

By creating greater involvement, satisfaction and motivation to the employees in the organization, employee engagement can be cultivated. Sudhalini Madhusudan, Asst. Vice President, Talent Enhancement Group, speaks that it is not possible to retain professionals only by paying high salaries and offering attractive benefits. "We need to create enthusiasm for their roles, their work and the organization, and ensure they are well integrated. Employee engagement relates to employee's commitment to the organization's success. Engaged employees who are inspired and guided by the leadership, equipped with the right tools managed by the right systems and processes delivers superior performance." Therefore organizations Goes, Grows and Glows with the engaged employees who builds passion, commitment, alignment with the organizational objectives, strategies and attracts more people, increase employee's trust, creates a sense of loyality in a competitive environment , lowers attrition rate, increases productivity, improves overall organizational effectiveness and the business.

CONCLUSION

With the paradigm shifts in the business environment, future growth prospects, economic and social networking, organizations need to think out of the box to bring about change in the employees. We however feel and believe that stabilizing with building and growing the talent pool and the human capital in this competitive environment should be the winning mantra. Engaged employees are the builders. Organizations and employees share a symbiotic relation, where both are dependent on each other to satisfy their needs and goal. They want to know the desired expectation for their role so they can meet and exceed them with involvement, job satisfaction and motivations. Thus employee retention is a barometer that determines the associations of employee involvement, satisfaction, motivation and engagement for organizational excellence.

Reference

1. Bhattacharya D.K. (2004*), 'Human Resource Development'* Himalaya Publishing House.
2. Tiwari Shashi, November (2010), *"Employee Engagement"*, Vol. X, Issue-XI, pp. 42-45.
3. www.hrsite.com
4. www.iupindia.in
5. www.wiekipedia.com

14

A Sucess Story on Employee Engagement : A Case Study at Tata AIG General Insurance Company

Dr. (Mrs.) Pratima Sarangi
Mr. Sanat Kumar Patnaik

ABSTRACT

Today HR is playing a great role as competitive advantage for Organisational success. HR is a combination of Knowledge, Skills and Abilities (KSAs) which differentiate one organization from other. Commitment of HR not only depends on motivation but on a sense of oneness among them through. The ability KSAs to influence employees to succeed with Organisational vision can be possible if HR efforts are converted into commitment for successful employee engagement.

Here the authors describe the same through case analysis collected through secondary data collected from different sources.

INTRODUCTION

Today, Business is witnessing unprecedented change in an increasingly global marketplace.

To gain a competitive edge, organisations are turning to effective HR practices for employee commitment. Organisations are moving forward to attract, develop and retain talent for success. It is important for them to satisfy HR needs and to secure HR commitment that foster a culture of employee engagement for organisational growth and sustainability.

"The challenge today is not just retaining talented people, but fully engaging them, capturing their minds and hearts at each stage of their work lives".

WHAT IS EMPLOYEE ENGAGEMENT?

Employee engagement is a step ahead than employee satisfaction: It is belief in the organization, desire to work to make things better understanding of business context and the 'bigger picture' respectful of, and helpful to, colleagues willingness to 'go the extra mile' keeping up to date with developments in the field.

Definition

Employee engagement involves commitment, loyalty, pride in the organization, a willingness to advocate for the organization, and a sense of personal responsibility. Like satisfaction, employee engagement is changęable. It is capable of being greatly influenced and thus can vary considerably among organizational units, among companies, and over time.

Employee engagement is the willingness of employee to 'go the extra mile' to achieve the organisational vision. According to IES (Institute for Employment Studies) "Employee engagement is a positive attitude held by the employee towards the organisation and its values". An engaged employee is aware of business context, work with colleagues to improve performance within the job for the benefit of the organisation. The organisation must work to development and nurture engagement which requires a two-way relationship between employer and employee".

An engaged employee has:

- Belief in the organization,
- Desire to work to make things better,
- Understanding of business context,
- Respectful, helpful to others,
- Willings to go the extra mile,

According to Scarlett Survey " Employee Engagement is a measurable degree of an employee's positive negative emotional attachment to their job, colleagues and organisation which profoundly influences their willingness to learn and perform at work". So it is total different from satisfaction, motivation, culture, climate, opinion and very difficult to measure.

Employee-employer relationship evolving/changeing partnerships.
Increased demand for work/life balance.
HR's greater role in promoting the link b etween employee performance and its impact on business goals.
Increasing focus on selective retention for keeping mission-critical talent.
Work intensification as employers increase productivity with fewer employees and resources.
Acquiring and keeping key talent reemerging as top issues of concern.
Decline in traditional communication methods and increase in cyber communication.
Needs, wants and behaviours of the talent pool driving changes in attraction, selection and retention practices.

Source: Adapted from society for Human Resource Management (2006). SHRM special experience panels 2006 trends report. Alexandria, VA; Author.

Fig. 14.1: Top Trends Lead to Focus on Employee Engagement

The ten C's of Employee Engagement by George Ambler on Tuesday, February 27, 2007

So, "*How can leaders engage employees' heads, hearts, and hands?* by starting to apply the following 10 C's of employee engagement:

1. **Connect:** Leaders must show that they value employees. Employee engagement is a direct reflection of how employees feel about their relationship with the boss.
2. **Career:** Leaders should provide challenging and meaningful work with opportunities for career advancement. Most people want to do new things in their job. For example, do organizations provide job rotation for their top talent? Are people assigned stretch goals?
3. **Clarity:** *Le*aders must communicate a clear vision. Success in life and organizations is, to a great extent, determined by how clear individuals are about their goals and what they really want to achieve. In sum, employees need to understand what the organization's goals are, why they are important, and how the goals can best be attained.
4. **Convey:** Leaders clarify their expectations about employees and provide feedback on their functioning in the organization.
5. **Congratulate:** Exceptional leaders give recognition, and they do so a lot; they coach and convey.
6. **Contribute:** People want to know that their input matters and that they are contributing to the organization's success in a meaningful way. In sum, good leaders help people see and feel how they are contributing to the organization's success and future.
7. **Control:** Employees value control over the flow and pace of their jobs and leaders can create opportunities for employees to exercise this control. A feeling of "being in on things," and of being given opportunities to participate in decision making often reduces stress; it also creates trust and a culture where people want to take ownership of problems and their solutions.
8. **Collaborate:** Studies show that, when employees work in teams and have the trust and cooperation of their team members, they outperform individuals and teams which lack good relationships. Great leaders are team builders; they create an environment that fosters trust and collaboration.
9. **Credibility:** Leaders should strive to maintain a company's reputation and demonstrate high ethical standards.
10. **Confidence:** Good leaders help create confidence in a company by being exemplars of high ethical and performance standards.

The employee survey is a diagnostic tool of choice in the battle for the hearts of employees. Studies of Gallup, Mercer, Hewitt and Watson Wyatt (consulting companies) asked workers number of questions relating to their job satisfaction. Gallup being one of oldest consulting organisation {in conducting engagement survey} creates a feedback system for employers that would identify and measure elements of worker engagement most tide to the bottom line. Things such as sales, growth, productivity and customer loyalty are all accessed. After Hundreds of focus group and thousands of interviews with employees in a variety of industries, Gallup came up with Q. 12, a twelve-question survey that identifies strong feelings of employee engagement. They have identified 12 questions that most effectively measure the links (the Gallup Q12).

Twelve question of the studies of Gallup:

1. Do you know what is expected of you at work?
2. Do you have the materials and equipment you need to do your work right?
3. At work, do you have the opportunity to do what you do best every day?
4. In the last seven days, have you received recognition or praise for doing good work?
5. Does your supervisor, or someone at work, seems to care about you as a person?
6. Is there someone at work who encourages your development?
7. At work, do your opinions seem to count?
8. Does the mission/purpose of your company make you feel your job is important?
9. Are your associates (fellow employees) committed to doing quality work?
10. Do you have a best friend at work?
11. In the last six months, has someone at work talked to you about your progress?
12. In the last year, have you had opportunities at work to learn and grow?

EMPLOYEE ENGAGEMENT AS A KEY FOR ORGANIZATIONAL SUCCESS

Engaged employees are work hard workers, more loyal and more likely to go the 'extra mile' for the organisation. There are different levels of engagement and understanding the types of engagement provides perspective into employee behaviors that can either positively or negatively affect organizational success. Employee engagement can be considered as: cognitive, emotional and behavioral.

Cognitive engagement refers to employees' beliefs about the company, its leaders and the workplace culture. The emotional engagement is how employees feel about the company, the leaders and their colleagues. The behavioral engagement is the value-added component reflected in the amount of effort employees put into their work (e.g., brainpower, extra time and energy).[7]

Employees who are highly involved in their work processes—such as conceiving, designing and implementing workplace and process changes — are more engaged.

For example, a recent study analyzed 132 U.S. manufacturing firms and found that companies utilizing high-performance work systems had significantly higher labor productivity than their competitors. When employees have the power to make decisions related to their performance, can access information about company costs and revenues, and have the necessary knowledge, training and development to do their jobs — *and* are rewarded for their efforts — they are more productive. (source SHRM Foundation)

In a recent report by the SHRM Foundation, it was stated that employee engagement can be measured in dollars and can yield significant savings.

For example, at the beverage company of MolsonCoors, it was found that engaged employees were five times less likely than nonengaged employees to have a safety incident and seven times less likely to have a lost-time safety incident. In fact, the average cost of a safety incident for an engaged employee was $63, compared with an average of $392 for a nonengaged employee. Consequently, through strengthening employee engagement, the company saved $1,721,760 in safety costs in 2002. In addition, savings were found in sales performance teams through engagement. In 2005, for example, low-engagement teams were seen falling behind engaged teams, with a difference in performance-related costs of low- versus high-engagement teams totaling 2,104,823.[9]

Related to productivity, employee health is a critical factor in employee engagement. Conditions that support health and psychological well-being are open communication, respect, trust, teamwork and positive work relationships. The Gallup Organization, a leader in employee engagement research, found that employee physical health and psychological well-being affect the quality and quantity of work. For example, 62% of engaged employees feel their work positively affects their physical health. Yet that number drops to 39% among non engaged employees and to 22% among employees who are actively disengaged.

The employee's emotional commitment to the job and company is a key lever for engagement. The degree and quality of performance depend on heart over mind. The level of emotional commitment — the extent to which the employee derives enjoyment, meaning, pride or inspiration from something or someone in the organization — is a significant variable in engagement and thus in performance. Emotional commitment to the job, organization, team and manager has been found to determine stronger performance than rational commitment (the extent to which an employee feels that someone or something within the company provides developmental, financial or professional rewards in employee's best interests).[14]

Key Elements of Effective Employee Engagement Program

There are a large number of companies across the globe which continue to invest in employee engagement programs despite the economic downswing.

HR professionals and HR Consultants define employee engagement differently. Some HR professionals confuse employee engagement with welfare activities like staff dinners, family get-togethers, picnics etc. These are small elements and employee engagement is a much more complex beast. According to mittal about employee engagement in two ways: commitment and emotional attachment with the company or with the workgroup / manager. In different organizational contexts, different definitions may be suitable.

- **Communicate:** The key to a successful employee engagement initiative is top management commitment and communication. The leadership needs to demonstrate its commitment to the initiative and drive its importance in all forums. Another essential aspect of communication is the emphasis on confidentiality of responses. This should ideally come from the head of the organization.

- **Key Drivers:** While slicing and dicing the data by employee demographics like departments, business units, job levels etc. is important to understand the variance in engagement levels, it is extremely important to be able to prioritize from the mountain of data generated by the survey. One could rely on techniques like regressions to understand the drivers of the intermediate outcome – employee engagement. **Benchmarking:** Try and work with consulting firms which have robust benchmarking data for employee engagement and other workplace quality indicators. Firms offering comprehensive benchmarking will help you to further distill the data and arrive at action items. In most cases, organizations should look at industry benchmarks and country-level benchmarks (local labor market comparisons). Other benchmarks may be suitable depending on the context.
- **Feedback:** Employees give feedback in a survey and anticipate a flow of information back. So, inform employees about how you fared and what you plan to do about it. It's easy to lose momentum after the survey because most organizations focus too much energy on the survey and too little on post-survey activities. Remember – surveys are just the starting point of any organizational development program.
- **Act:** This is the most crucial step and the area where most organizations fail to live upto the expectations. While the HR should play the role of the facilitator and provide operational support, the "act' phase has to be driven by the leadership. They need to take the survey to the next level by acting on it. Define ideal state. Draw transformational and transactional change plans. Fix accountabilities. Fix timelines. Monitor and review progress. Improvise. All the time! 'Change' is a constant and your change program needs to run continuously.
- **Involve:** And while you are implementing solutions, do not forget to involve your middle management and front line managers. Educate them about **why employee engagement matters and how it impacts business outcomes.** Encourage them to make engagement a part of the business agenda.

The benefits of employee engagement are many. In today's world, "people" are your only unique competitive advantage. It's not an easy ride, but it's really worth it! (Abhishekmittal.com)

EMPLOYEE ENGAGEMENT: A CASE APPROACH IN TATA AIG GENERAL INSURANCE COMPANY

Tata AIG General Insurance Company Limited (Tata AIG General) is a joint venture company, formed by the Tata Group and American International Group, Inc. (AIG). Tata AIG General combines the Tata Group's pre-eminent leadership position in India and AIG's global presence as the world's leading international insurance and financial services organization. The Tata Group holds 74 per cent stake in the insurance venture with AIG holding the balance 26 percent. Tata AIG General Insurance Company, which started its operations in India on January 22, 2001, provides insurance solutions to individuals and corporates. It offers a complete range of general insurance products including insurance for automobile, home, personal accident, travel, energy, marine, property and casualty as well as several specialized financial lines. The Company believes in offering innovative and relevant insurance solutions in the retail and commercial space. Each product offering is backed by expertise and an unparalleled claims service. The Company's products are available through various channels of distribution like agents, brokers, banks (through banc assurance tie ups) and direct channels like Tele Marketing, Digital Marketing, worksite etc.

Vision

To be India's most preferred General Insurance Company.

Purpose

To create unmatched value for our customers, employees, business partners and shareholders by delivering remarkable service that is consistent, fair and transparent

Values

Tata AIG'sOur values represent the core, shared beliefs that guide how we act and work together to achieve our goals. They share a set of 6 core values: Customer First, People, Passion, Performance, Integrity and Empathy.

- **Customer First:** Anticipate their priorities. Exceed their expectations.
- **Integrity:** Conduct the business fairly, with honesty and transparency. Everything we do must stand the test of public scrutiny.
- **People:** Work cohesively with colleagues across the Group and with customers and partners around the world, building strong relationships based on tolerance, understanding and mutual cooperation. Strive to develop diverse talent and reward excellence.
- **Performance:** Constantly strive to achieve the highest possible standards in day-to-day work and in the quality of the goods and services we provide.
- **Passion:** To be excited about what to do. Must have a strong internalized drive to meet goals. Relentless determination to solve customer problems.
- **Respect:** Must be caring, show respect, compassion and humanity for our colleagues and customers around the world, and always work for the benefit of the communities.

Tata AIG Insurance Company

Tata AIG Insurance Solutions is one of the leading insurance companies that provide both life insurance as well as general insurance. Joint collaboration between the American International Group, Inc. (AIG) and Tata Group. They own the company in the ratio of 26:74. It is a leading financial institution that has carved a niche for itself all over the world.

Tata AIG General Insurance Company

Tata AIG General Insurance Company started its operations in India on January 22, 2001, Gaurav D. Garg is the Managing Director & CEO, Tata AIG General Insurance Co. Ltd.

Tata AIG Life LIFE Insurance Company

- Tata AIG Life Insurance Company was licensed to operate in India on February 12, 2001 and started operations on April 1, 2001. Mr. Suresh Mahalingam, (M. Suresh), MD, Tata AIG Life Insurance Company.

Human Resource Policies in TATA AIG company

Human resource policies are systems of codified decisions, established by an organization, to support administrative personnel functions, performance management, employee relations and resource planning.

Organizational Structure of TATA AIG

CEO 4 Zonal Heads(East West, North, South)

Regional Head,

Area or Cluster Manager,

Branch Managers,

Unit Manager Financial Advisors,

Functions of the HR Department of TATA AIG

Recruitment and Selection Induction Competence Development Providing compensation and other employee benefits • Performance Management • Talent and Career Management.

Sources of Recruitment

Placement Agencies and Consultants Campus Recruitments Off-campus Recruitments Internal Job Postings Promotions (existing employees) Moving across verticals (existing employees)

Selection Process

There is a screening process based on the resumes of applicants followed by group discussion and personal interview.

Types of Employees -TATA AIG has both permanent employees as well employees on contract basis

Culture

Tata AIG have a performance based culture. Your career progression is determined by your experiences, your interests and the results you deliver. They believe in driving a culture that gives you room to achieve, to grow and to seek new opportunities. Company also seek to be the most innovative, the most tenacious in opening new markets and the most creative in developing new products and offering state-of-the-art services to clients, brokers and agents around the world. Indeed, our pace and result-orientation defines us in the marketplace.

Culture at Tata AIG enables its employees to collaborate with people and draw from experience around the country. Tata AIG not only enables you to work with dynamic people, but also enables you to keep a healthy work-life balance. People will find the time and the organizational encouragement to enhance interests and share them with others. Surrounded by smart, resourceful people, you will notice positive-ness in the atmosphere. Tata AIG employees actively contribute to various community-based initiatives and you can be a socially responsible citizen through our Corporate Social Responsibility Programme.

Over just 9 years in India, a young and fun loving Tata AIG has invested in people, culture, values, training and systems & processes to chart a pioneering course for success. It makes us the ideal organization to grow a career with.

Continuous Learning

People at Tata AIG are committed to "Continuous Learning". It believes that the best way to stay competitive is to share intelligence across the organisation, and to foster learning around the changing demands of the marketplace.

Company give our employees the ability to take responsibility of their development, providing them with the tools to chart their own career path. They help our employee's to enhance their knowledge and skills and further acquire expertise in the General Insurance Services. Here learning begins as soon as an employee comes onboard. The new-hire experience is a 2 day program called, "WIN" - Welcome & Induction of new employees, followed by a Buddy Program to ensure smooth handholding.

Tata AIG also offers a variety of programs ranging from Functional Programs to make them experts in their respective domain to Talent Acceleration Programs to improve their soft skills and leadership skills to help you grow as 'Leader of People' of tomorrow. The Leadership Academy helps to accelerate careers of high performers allowing them to advance their career rapidly while working on important projects and building leadership skills for their future. With the help of the Academy our people are able to access clearly defined competencies for their level, gain an understanding of their own skill gaps, and create an individual development plan in collaboration with the Learning & Development team.

Through our programs we commit to bring future value to your job. At the heart of our dynamic culture is an investment in learning. Our employees are both expected and encouraged to fulfill training that helps them navigate a more competitive marketplace, learn domain expertise, develop skills and comply with the Company's integrity and citizenship initiatives.

Insurance Co. Ltd. as an organization truly believes in inculcating a vibrant culture that looks beyond work and engages its employees in various activities. To undertake these activities, our approach is to follow a systematic sustainable & participative model by actively involving employees, soliciting ideas and encouraging employee involvement.

We create and sustain this through our Employee Engagement Activities where we touch the employees and their family in the various forms. Some of them are listed below:

- **Annual Celebration** – Commemorate individual and team victories and a fun filled evening for the employees.
- **Employee Town-Hall** is an event where the head of the organization addresses and interacts with all employees giving them an insight about the company's progress and unfolding the way forward.

- **The Success Matrix** is our Rewards & Recognition Programme where we recognize the performance and contribution of our employees through timely measures. The recipients are acknowledged for their contribution though Awards and citations displayed on the "Wall of Fame" at all the branches.
- **Sports Tournaments** – Inter-departmental cricket & football matches organized every year for sports enthusiasts helps foster a spirit of teamwork
- **World of Work (WOW)** invites the employees' children to come and spend time in their parents' workplace. A theme is designed especially for the children and the décor and games are planned accordingly. This promotes family involvement at the office premises where family members bond with each other and get to understand the culture of the organization.
- **Celebrations of Festivals** – We at Tata AIG believe in celebrating all festivals and ensure that we enjoy as a family. Around these festivities we create avenues for giving expression to employee's creative talent and encourage them to showcase their skills through competitions such as Song & Dance, Rangoli, Painting, Traditional attire.
- **Recharge Zone** – A bright and lively break-away area where employees can brain-storm ideas or flip through books/magazines on business topics.
- **Online Library Service** – This library solution will enables employees to review, choose and borrow their favourite books across a wide spectrum of genres simply at the click of the mouse. Management, Self Help, Fiction, Non-Fiction.

Employee Engagement at Tata AIG is an active process which nourishes a healthy environment within the entity and where contribution of 'Every Employee Counts'.

CONCLUSION

In recent years, a number of studies have focused on employee engagement and its link to company performance and sustainability. Studies highlight the role of employee engagement in today's business environment. HR professionals who seek proactive practices that positively affect employee productivity will find this research pertinent to their work Employee Engagement is the buzz word for employee communication. It is a positive attitude held by the employees towards the organization and its values. It is rapidly gaining popularity, use and importance in the workplace and impacts organizations in many ways. Employee engagement emphasizes the importance of employee communication on the success of a business. An organization should thus recognize employees, more than any other variable, as powerful contributors to a company's competitive position. Therefore employee engagement should be a continuous process of learning, improvement, measurement and action. We would hence conclude that raising and maintaining employee engagement lies in the hands of an organization and requires a perfect blend of time, effort, commitment and investment to craft a successful endeavor.

References

1. Kaye, B., & Jordan-Evans, S. (2003, August). Engaging talent. Executive Excellence, 20, 8, 11.
2. Corporate Leadership Council. (2004). Driving performance and retention through employee engagement. Washington, DC: Corporate Executive Board.
3. (SHRM Glossary of HR Terms, www.shrm.org) website

4. Society for Human Resource Management. (2006). SHRM Special Expertise Panels 2006 trends report. Alexandria, VA: Author.
5. Casner-Lotto, J., & Barrington, L. (2006). Are they really ready to work? Unites States: The Conference Board, Corporate Voices for Working Families, Partnership for 21st Century Skills and Society for Human Resource Management.
6. Konrad, A. M. (2006, March/April). Engaging employees through high-involvement work practices. Ivey Business JournalOnline, 1-6, www.iveybusinessjournal.com.
7. Vance, R. J. (2006). Effective practice guidelines: Employee engage-ment and commitment. Alexandria, VA: SHRM Foundation.
8. Crabtree, S. (2005, January 13). Engagement keeps the doctor away. Gallup Management Journal, http://gmj.gallup.com.
9. Salanova, M., Agut, S., & María Peiró, J. (2005). Linking organizational resources and work engagement to employee and customer loyalty: The mediation of service climate. Journal of Applied Psychology, 90, 6, 1217-1227.
10. Shaufeli, W., Salanova, M., González-Romá, V., & Bakkers, A. B. (2002). The measurement of engagement and burnout: A two sample confirmatory factor analytic approach. Journal of Happiness Studies, 3, 71-92.
11. Glen, C. (2006). Key skills retention and motivation: The war for talent still rages and retention is the high ground. Industrial and Commercial Training, 38, 1, 37-46.
12. May, D. R., Gilson, R. L., & Harter, L. M. (2004). The psychological conditions of meaningfulness, safety and availability and the engagement of the human spirit at work. Journal of Occupational and Organizational Psychology, 77, 11-37.
13. Ramarajan, L., & Barsade, S. G. (2006, November). What makes the job tough? The influence of organizational respect on burnout in the human services. Philadelphia, PA: University of Pennsylvania.
14. Kress, N. (2005, May). Engaging your employees through the power of communication. Workspan, 48, 5, 26-32.
15. BlessingWhite. (2006). Employee engagement report. Princeton, NJ: Author.
16. Wright, P. M., Gardner, T. M., & Moynihan, L. M. (2003). The impact of HR practices on the performance of business units. Human Resource Management Journal, 13, 3, 21-36.
17. Rieger, T., & Kamins, C. (2006, November 9). Are you failing to engage? Gallup Management Journal. Retrieved November 14, 2006, from http://gmj.gallup.com.
18. Thackray, J. (2001, March 15). Feedback for real. Gallup Management Journal. Retrieved November 15, 2006, from http:// gmj.gallup.com.
19. Galinksy, E., Bond, J. T., Kim, S. S., Backon, L., Brownfield, E., & Sakai, K. (2005). Over work in America: When the way we work becomes too much. New York: Families and Work Institute.
20. Vance, R. J. (2006). Effective practice guidelines: Employee engage-ment and commitment. Alexandria, VA: SHRM Foundation.
21. Glen, C. (2006). Key skills retention and motivation: The war for talent still rages and retention is the high ground. Industrial and Commercial Training, 38, 1, 37-46.
22. Gil Saura, I., Berenquer Contrí, G., Cervera Taulet, A., & Moliner Velázquez, B. (2005). Relationships among customer orientation, service orientation and job satisfaction in financial services. International Journal of Service Industry Management, 16, 5, 497
23. Branham, L. (2005). Planning to become an employer of choice. Journal of Organizational Excellence, 24, 3, 57-68.
24. Society for Human Resource Management. (2006). SHRM Special Expertise Panels 2006 trends report. Alexandria, VA: Author.

25. Mercer HR Consulting. (2006, July). Managing attraction and reten-tion in China. Retrieved October 26, 2006, from www.mercer.com.
26. Towers Perrin. (2006, February). Winning strategies for a global work-force. Retrieved October 25, 2006, from www.towersperrin.com.
27. Galinksy, E., Salmond, K., Bond, J. T., Brumit Kropf, M., Moore, M., & Harrington, B. (2003). Leaders in a global economy: A study of execu-tive women and men. New York: Families and Work Institute, Catalyst and the Center for Work & Family.
28. Feeling good matters in the workplace. (2006, January 12). Gallup Management Journal.
29. BlessingWhite
30. Ashok Mukherjee – Engagement for the mind body, and soul – Human Capital, Aug. 2005.
31. Barbara Palframan Smith – Employee connection – Technology to built culture and community – Communication World – Mar / Apr 2004.
32. Charles Woodruffe – Employee Engagement – The Real Secret of Winning a Crucial Edge over your rivals – Manager Motivation – Dec. / Jan. 2006.
33. Christoffer Ellehuus,Piers Hudson-Driving Performance and Retention Through Employee Engagement –Corporate leadership Council 2004,Employee Enagegement Survey
34. Charlotte Garvey – Connecting the organizational pulse into the bottom line – HR Magazine society for Human Resource Management, June 2004.
35. Cifton, D.O. & Hartor, J.K. (2011) – Investing in strength – positive organizational scholarship. Foundation of a new discipline (pp 111-121)
36. Douglas R. May, Richard L Gilson – The Psychological conditions of meaningfulness safety and availability and the engagement of the human spirit at work – Journal of Occupational and Organisational Psychology (2004) 7, 11-37.
37. Ellen Lanser May – Are people your priority? How to engage your work force – Healthcare Executive, July/Aug. 2009.
38. Fox, S, & Spector, P.E.. – Emotions in the work place – the neglected side of organizational life introduction. Human Resource Management Review, 12, 167 –
39. 171. Gretcher Hoover – Maintaining employee engagement when communicating difficult issues – Communication World, Nov / Dec 2009.
40. Heskett, Jame L – Putting the service profit chain to work – Harvard Business Review, Mar / Apr 94 Vol. 72 Issue 2.
41. Jerry Krueger and Emily Killham-At work, feeling good matters-Gallup Management Journal, Dec 2011
42. Remus, Ilies – An experienced sampling measure of job satisfaction and its relationships with affectivity, mood at work, job beliefs and general job satisfaction – European Journal of work and organizational psychology, 2004, 13 (3), 367 – 389.
43. Shamir, B. – Meaning – self and motivation in organization. Organisation studies, 12 (3) 405 – 424.
44. Steve Batts – Getting engaged – HR Magazine society for Human Resource Management, Feb 2010
45. Steve Crabtree – (2009) Getting personnel in the work place – Are negative relationships squelching productivity in your company? – Gallup Management Journal, June 10, 2004.

Website Address

1. www.wiziq.com
2. Tata AIG General www.tataaiginsurance.in/taig/taig/tat
3. www.citehr.com
4. www.hrmguide.com
5. www.wikipedia.org

❖❖❖

15 Employee Engagement as Retention Tool in Indian IT Sector

Subhasree Kar

ABSTRACT

"Employee Engagement" as a business management concept is relatively new but having great significance in the recent time where recruiting and retaining employees is the trend impacting the business. In the present business scenario promising opportunities are there for talented employees and the key issue is "Retention of the Talent" in all the sectors especially in Indian IT sector where the nature of the workforce is dynamic. At this point of time the organizations that truly engage and inspire their employees produce world class levels of innovation, productivity and performance. This paper is an attempt to explore Employee Engagement as a retention tool and the interventions used by the Indian IT organisations for Employee Engagement.

Keywords: Employee engagement, Retention.

INTRODUCTION

Employee engagement has been a leading edge management practice in the private sector in modern times largely in response to the need to recruit, reward and retain critical business talent. Employees who are engaged in their work and committed to their organizations give companies crucial competitive advantages—including higher productivity and lower employee turnover. Thus, it is not surprising that organizations of all sizes and types have invested substantially in policies and practices that foster engagement and commitment in their workforces' .Human resource professionals, on the front line in the fight for talent, know this battle will not be won until their companies view employees as profit centers rather than cost centers. At the top level senior executives cannot ignore the impending labor shortage and the growing research that illustrates satisfied and engaged employees brings success for the organization.

CONCEPTUAL FRAMEWORK OF EMPLOYEE ENGAGEMENT

'Employee engagement' is a relatively new term in HR literature and really started to come to prominence from 2000 onwards. Melcrum Publishing (2005) found that from a global survey of over 1,000 communication and HR practitioners 74% began to formally focus on the issue between 2000 and 2004. As pointed out in Rafferty *et al* (2005), the concept of employee engagement has as its foundation in two well-researched precursors – employee commitment and organizational citizenship behavior.

Though the concept is relatively new ,the underlying concepts have been around for many years. There is confusion in the literature about employee engagement and when engagement is talked about it refers to multidimensional concepts that involve some kind of two-way interaction between the employee and the organization. There is overlapping constructs of organizational commitment, intrinsic motivation, and employee involvement, passion and dedication to work. According to Kahn (1990) employee engagement is different from other role constructs such as job involvement (Lawler and Hall, 1970; Lodahl and Kejner, 1965), commitment to organizations (Mowday *et al.*, 1982) or intrinsic motivation (Deci, 1975). Employee engagement is a multidimensional construct. Employees can be emotionally, cognitively or physically engaged. Luthans and Peterson (2002) proposed Kahn's (1990, 1992) work on personal engagement, which provides a convergent theory for Gallup's empirically derived employee engagement. To be emotionally engaged is to form meaningful connections to others (peers, co-workers) and to experience empathy and concern for others' feelings. In contrast, being cognitively engaged refers to those who are acutely aware of their mission and role in their work environment. According to Kahn (1990) employees can be engaged on one dimension and not the other. Another related construct to engagement is the notion of flow advanced by Csikszentmihalyi (1975,1990) where he defined flow as the 'holistic Sensation' that people feel when they act with total involvement. Flow is the state in which there is little distinction between the self and the environment .When individuals are in the flow state ,little conscious control is necessary for their action. Employee Engagement is thus the level of commitment and involvement an employee has towards their organization and its values it can be a parameter that determines the association of a person with the organization.

Employee engagement was described in the academic literature by Schmidt *et al.* (1993). A modernized version of job satisfaction, Schmidt *et al.*'s influential definition of engagement was "an employee's involvement with, commitment to, and satisfaction with work." This integrates the classic constructs of job satisfaction (Smith *et al.*, 1969), and organizational commitment (Meyer & Allen, 1991).

In this context Schaufeli *et al.* (2002) define engagement "as a positive, fulfilling, work-related state of mind that is characterized by vigor, dedication, and absorption". They further state that engagement is not a momentary and specific state, but rather it is "a more persistent and pervasive affective-cognitive state that is not focused on any particular object, event, individual, or behavior" Schaufeli *et al.* (2002) .Yet engagement is different from satisfaction as Gubman (2004) states that engagement means "a heightened emotional connection to a job and organization that goes beyond satisfaction" that enables people to perform well, and makes want to stay with their employers and say good things about them. In short, there is a psychic income at work that makes people feel socially accepted and respected.

According to Scarlett Surveys, "Employee Engagement is a measureable degree of an employee's positive or negative emotional attachment to their job, colleagues and organization which profoundly influences their willingness to learn & perform at work". Thus engagement is distinctively different from satisfaction, motivation, culture, climate and opinion and very difficult to measure.

CIPD (2007a) defines employee engagement as a combination of commitment to the organisation and its values plus a willingness to help out colleagues. According to this view, engagement is about more than job satisfaction and is a more complex concept than motivation. Similarly, Schmidt (2004) defines engagement as bringing satisfaction and commitment together. Whilst satisfaction addresses more of an emotional or attitudinal element, commitment brings in the motivational and physical elements. Schmidt (2004) contends that while satisfaction and commitment are the two key elements of engagement, neither on their own is enough to guarantee engagement.

Engagement is the state of emotional and intellectual commitment to an organization or group. An engaged employee is a person who is fully involved in, and enthusiastic about, his or her work (Falcone, 2006). It is hearts passion – a person's intrinsic motivation that are the essence of employee engagement.

Unique Features of Engaged Employees

Engaged employees thrive when they are working in a positive, supportive corporate culture. Their inspiration, energy and enthusiasm in turn enhance the corporate culture Engaged employees exhibit many of the following characteristics, enabling them to achieve significantly higher personal performance levels than their disengaged peers:

- Achieve consistently high levels of performance
- High energy and enthusiasm
- Committed to customers and exceeding customer expectations
- Understand the desired outcomes of their job/role
- Professionally and emotionally committed to their job and whatever they do
- Expect and perceive a direct connection between their effort and reward received
- Initiate problem-solving, challenge things that need to be changed
- Innovate and strive for process and product excellence and efficiency
- Focused on achieving goals, committed to completing tasks and assignments
- Expect and enjoy autonomy and the ability to make decisions when needed to do their job
- Initiate and participate in special projects and positive things to act on
- Expand what they do and build on it
- Committed to the company, their group and role
- Proactive building of supportive relationships
- Would recommend their company, products and services
- Attention to details
- Typically prefer complex, challenging work (as they perceive complexity and job challenge)
- Communicate willingly and effectively with employees at all levels
- More likely to identify risks and take appropriate risks
- Committed to and demonstrate personal and professional improvement
- Proactive conflict resolution

Benefits to the Organization

An organization's employees are engaged when they are fully committed, involved and enthusiastic about their jobs and their organizations. This is crucial at all levels of the organization. Engaged employees are willing, able and actually do contribute to company success. Engaged employees regularly go the extra mile, putting effort into their work above and beyond what is expected of them. They willingly and eagerly work extra hours and focus their inspiration, energy, intelligence, skills and experience to achieve success for themselves and their organization.

- Employee engagement builds passion, commitment and alignment with the organisation's strategies and goals
- Attracts more people like existing employees Increases employees' trust in the organisation
- Creates a sense of loyalty in a competitive environment
- Lowers attrition rate
- Increases productivity and improves morale
- Provides a high-energy working environment
- Improves overall organizational effectiveness
- Boosts business growth
- Makes the employees effective brand ambassadors for the company.

Linkage research (e.g., Tracy) received significant attention in the business community because of correlations between employee engagement and desirable business outcomes such as retention of talent, customer service, individual performance, team performance, business unit productivity, and even enterprise-level financial performance .

Factors of Engagement

Many organizational factors influence employee engagement and retention such as: A culture of respect where outstanding work is valued ,availability of constructive feedback and mentoring opportunity for advancement and professional development ,fair and appropriate reward, recognition and incentive systems, availability of effective leadership, clear job expectations, adequate tools to complete work responsibilities, high levels of motivation.

Employee engagement today encompasses training, Career Development, work environment, leadership, Respectful treatment of employees, performance management, work/life balance, communication, compensation, benefits, Health and Safety, commitment, family friendliness, fun and social activities. This enhances the bonding between employees and commitment to the company.

Employee Engagement as a Retention Tool

Employee engagement as a key to the retention of talent (one-of-a-kind hire in 100 employees; Glen, (2006) is an area in which the lead has been taken by practitioners (Parsley, 2006; Baumruk *et al.*, 2006; Woodruffe, 2005; Gallup Management Journal, 2006; Bennett and Bell, 2004; Hay Group, 2002). Research by Gallup and others shows that engaged employees are more productive. They are more profitable, more customer-focused, safer, and more likely to withstand temptations to leave. The best-performing companies know that an employee engagement improvement strategy linked to the achievement of corporate goals will help them win in the marketplace.

Mercer's 2010 Attraction and Retention Survey found that more than one-quarter (27%) of participating organizations are expanding their overall workforce, while only 3% have instituted broad-based reductions. By comparison, Mercer's Leading through Unprecedented Times Survey conducted in May 2009 showed fewer firms (12%) indicated they were hiring/expanding overall, while more firms (15%) instituted broad-based reductions. Cautious optimism prevails, however, as almost half (45%) of organizations are hiring to replacement levels only, while another 25% are hiring just for critical areas among select staff reductions.

According to the survey findings, almost half (47%) of organizations that assessed employee engagement over the past 12 to 18 months report that levels of employee engagement have increased. Despite efforts to engage employees during a difficult year, organizations have growing concerns about whether their valued employees will stay once the economy recovers. Almost two-thirds (62%) of companies believe that voluntary turnover will increase as the economy and job market continue to improve. Moreover, the survey shows that certain positions are more sought-after than others because of skill shortage or market demand. These roles include R&D/scientific engineering and sales, followed by information technology and executives/top management.

"Typically, engaged employees are less likely to seek job opportunities outside the company and therefore, have a more positive impact on both individual and business performance," said Griffith. "By identifying talent needs necessary for future growth, employers can implement the appropriate steps for developing employees internally or hiring staff externally."

Strategies Adopted by IT Organizations on Employee Engagement

Khan (2008) in her paper viewed that most organizations today realize that a satisfied employee is not necessarily the best employee in terms of loyality and productivity. It is only one engaged employee who is intellectually and emotionally bound with the organization and feels passionately about goals and committed towards its values. The person goes the extra mile beyond the basic job responsibility and is associated with the actions that drive the business. Moreover in times of diminishing loyalty, employee engagement is a powerful retention strategy. The fact that it has a strong impact on the bottom-line adds to its significance. An engaged employee gives his company his 100 percent. This is what makes the difference in an industry where the most valuable resource of a company walks out of the door every evening. "This is of particular importance in a knowledge industry particularly in IT industry.

The Indian IT-ITES industry is on a high momentum path with rampant growth and a set of challenges . Chief among them relates to skilled manpower resources. Not only does India need to sustain its vast pool of specialised IT-ITES talent, but it also has to ensure that it remains "industry-relevant" and "rightly skilled" (Simhan, 2006).

Retention of the employees would be possible if organizations provide them with a passion to work, and an engrossing environment which maximizes their performance and gives a continuous work experience that is difficult for competitors to replicate. Effective talent management policies and practices demonstrate commitment to human capital, resulting in more engaged employees and lower turnover. Consequently, employee engagement has a substantial impact on employee productivity and talent retention.

Studies by Luthans and Peterson (2002) state that Gallup has empirically determined employee engagement to be a significant predictor of desirable organizational outcomes such as customer satisfaction, retention; productivity and profitability .

The Hay Group and FORTUNE magazine completed their 13th annual World's Most Admired Company **WMAC** survey. They have done a wonderful job of offering elaboration and insight into top companies and employee engagement. Among them IBM, ORACLE ,HP are there for there best engagement practices .

Employee well-being is incorporated in every aspect of IBM's global business .IBM believes in driving employee engagement through employee benefits and adopted the following strategies –

- IBM's Well-being Management System
- Global Workplace Safety
- IBM's Culture of Health
- Global Wellness Initiatives
- Healthcare Reform & IBM
- Work/Life Balance

Oracle Provides its employees the following facilities to bring employee engagement.

- Flexibility to grow and try new things
- Knowledge Management
- Realistic Schedules
- work flexibility
- Excellent access to bleeding edge technology and training.
- Good Work Culture.
- Flexible Timings.
- Feel good factor - working with Software giant .
- Family friendly Environment.
- Senior management focussed and in touch.

HP rewards its employees and brings engagement in the following ways by providing-

- Work Life opportunity
- Trust and Respect towards Employees
- Flexible culture
- Approachable Management
- Lots of training opportunities
- Fun products

Most organisations have a range of programmes to improve the engagement level of their employees. HCL Infosystems, lists the initiatives made by the organisation, which start right at the selection stage:

- Choosing the right fit and giving a realistic job preview
- Strong induction and orientation programme
- Rigorous training and development, from technical to soft skills to leadership development programmes. Apart from this, there are other forums like enable@HCL which has regular technical/soft-skill updates. HCL also has a certification programme for freshers which empowers young engineers
- To keep up the morale of people and drive them towards excellent performance, HCL has various incentives such as recognition letters, profit sharing schemes, long performance awards, ESOPS, building assets like own home
- Regular feedback to all people
- Communication forums like the in-house magazine Intouch, innovate@HCL (an e-forum to develop entrepreneurship), and regular surveys and conferences
- To maintain the quality of work-life and a balance between personal/professional lives, there are recreational activities like festivities@HCL, get-togethers@HCL, sports@HCL, etc
- An open and transparent culture to empower its people and develop entrepreneurs.

"The result of these practices is evident through the regular feedback from the employees collected through conferences and surveys, apart from the employee engagement survey conducted every second year. The proof is the latest increase in employee engagement from 54 percent to 64 percent," in the organization.

CONCLUSION

Employee engagement is a partnership between a company and its employees where everyone works together to achieve the business objectives of the company and the personal aspirations of the employees. It is therefore largely the organization's responsibility to create an environment and culture conducive to this partnership, and a win-win equation. Employee engagement is a barometer that determines the association of a person with the organization. An associated or engaged employee is, after all, a productive employee. However, in practice, engagement transcends this. It is about creating the passion among associates to do things beyond what is expected of them. A highly engaged employee will consistently deliver beyond expectations. A productive employee who has a sense of belonging and a strong bond with the company and its brand will create a ripple effect that results in a positively charged atmosphere in the organization Some of the approaches aimed at improving employee engagement can significantly increase employee engagement and, in turn, this can have a measurable impact on HR variables such as retention and staff sickness. The links to wider impacts in areas such as client service, satisfaction levels and for private sector business – turnover and profitability - tend to be more tenuous; and Increasing employee engagement is highly dependent on leadership and establishing two-way communication where people's work and views are valued and respected. There are thus ways in which any organisation can work towards better employee engagement without incurring high costs as long as there is the organizational determination to focus on this issue. Even in the absence of robust impact data, the principle of employee engagement is to be endorsed in terms of good practice in people management and the softer benefits this confers to organizations.

References:

1. Baumruk, R., Gorman, B. Jr, Gorman, R.E. and Ingham, J. (2006), "Why managers are crucial to increasing engagement", Strategic HR Review, Vol. 5 No. 2, pp. 24-7.
2. Bennett, M. and Bell, A. (2004), Leadership & Talent in Asia, Wiley, Singapore.
3. Falcone, P. (2006), "Preserving restless top performers: keep your top performers engaged so they don't jump ship once job opportunities arise", HR Magazine, March.
4. Gubman, E. (2004), "From engagement to passion for work: the search for the missing person", Human Resource Planning, Vol. 27 No. 3, pp. 42-6.
5. Glen, C. (2006), "Key skills retention and motivation: the war for talent still rages and retention is the high ground", Industrial and Commercial Training, Vol. 38 No. 1, pp. 37-45.Kahn, W.A. (1990), "An exercise of authority", Organizational Behavior Teaching Review, Vol. 14 No. 2, pp. 28-42.
6. Kahn, W.A. (1992), "Psychological conditions of personal engagement and disengagement at work", Academy of Management Journal, Vol. 33 No. 4, pp. 692-724.
7. Kahn, W. A. (1990). Psychological Conditions of Personal Engagement and Disengagement at Work. Academy of Management Journal, 33, 692-724.
8. Lawler, E.E. and Hall, D.T. (1970), "Relationships of job characteristics to job involvement, satisfaction, and intrinsic motivation", Journal of Applied Psychology, Vol. 54, pp. 305-1
9. Lodahl, T. and Kejner, M. (1965), "The definition and measurement of job involvement", Journal of Applied Psychology, Vol. 49, pp. 24-33.
10. Luthans, F. and Peterson, S.J. (2002), "Employee engagement and manager self efficacy: implications for managerial effectiveness and development", Journal of Management Development, Vol. 21 No. 5, pp. 376-87.
11. Mowday, R.T., Porter, L.W. and Steers, R.M. (1982), Employee-Organization Linkages: The Psychology of Commitment, Absenteeism, and Turnover, Academic Press, New York, NY.
12. McKay, Avery, & Morris (2008). Mean racial and ethnic differences in sales performance: The moderating role of diversity climate. Personnel Psychology, 61, 349-374.
13. Smith, Kendall, & Hulin (1969). The measurement of satisfaction in work and retirement: A strategy for the study of attitudes.
14. Schaufeli, W.B. and Bakker, A.B. (2004), "Job demands, job resources, and their relationship with burnout and engagement: a multi-sample study", Journal of Organizational Behavior, Vol. 25, pp. 293-315.
15. Woodruffe, C. (2005), "Employee engagement", British Journal of Administrative Management, Vol. 50, pp. 28-9.

Websites:

http://www.cipd.co.uk/subjects/empreltns/general/empengmt.htm?IsSrchRes=1

http://www.icn.ch/global/Issue3employer.pdf

http://www.humansynergistics.com/news/EmployeeEngagement.aspx

http://www.gallup.com/consulting/52/employee-engagement.aspx

http://www.davidzinger.com/employee-engagement-50-companies-to-admire-and-imitate-6603/

http://www.hrmreport.com/article/Employee-engagement-is-good-for-the-bottom-line/

http://www.industryweek.com/articles_companies_using_employee_ engagement_to_attract_retain_top_talent_22170.aspx

http://gmj.gallup.com

16 Employee Engagement Practices in Service Sectors

Dr. Rayaguru Kumar, Shri Mangesh Dash & Dr. B.N. Mishra

ABSTRACT

Employee engagement has been a sincere practice of the recent years. Organisations opt for more than commitment from the employees, so that they get physically, emotionally and cognitively connected with the organization. Such connection makes the employees to be identified with the basic objectives of the organization. Therefore this article attempts to understand the perspectives of employee engagement from different perspectives as well as the related practices being practiced in the service sectors. This is a conceptual paper. Some of the key words include, employee engagement, commitment, organizational citizenship behavior etc.

INTRODUCTION

Industries to day opt for workforces who are talented and can contribute voluntarily to the efficiency of the organizations. The tight economy has refocused attention on maximizing employee output and making the most of organizational resources. The attempts in the shape of organizational change management have been taken by several organizations to improve the engagement score of the talent workforce. This is a move in the right direction because when an organization focuses attention on its people, it's making an investment in its most important resource. A company can cut all the costs it wants, but if it neglects its people, the reduced expenses won't make much of a difference. This reflects the organizational thinking that the employees they employ should be able to take up responsibilities, find out new areas of expertise, should give optimum result, maximum value additions, should bear intrapreneurial capabilities and be a part of the organization. They should contribute to the profit, development and growth of the organization. Although with proper compensation and other benefits it is easier to acquaintance the talent workforce (otherwise known as knowledge workforce) but their committed effort with the organization has always been in question. Holding on to talent, especially the top-notch ones, is always easier said than done in industries. According to Rosemary Cisholm, CEO of Kapient, a recruitment consultancy firm, the push for employees to upgrade and become managers has created a job-hopping culture. "Employers are partly to blame," [1]. Sam Lam, senior consultant at E L Consult, echoed Cisholm's view that developed markets have a higher turnover rate, but believed there are other factors shaping the situation hence in Markets where there are large clusters of multinationals and domestic operations, the competition for similar talents are high [2]. Some of the hurdles faced by organizations today are over stress on power and property than honour; not having regular vigilance on employment; failure to solicit input from employees before making changes that affect their responsibilities; creativity versus punctuality; non-recognition of the relation between control, self-esteem and productivity; Non-alignment of desire and effort with talent and methods; organisational politics, work-life imbalance. In case of the less developed markets, organisations tend to have a more close-knit family culture where management has a higher sense of social responsibility to their staff. In their attempts to retain talent professionals, companies often make the mistakes of focusing only on remuneration and promoting employees to managerial positions before they are ready[3]. The need for employees to be in the state of "beyond satisfaction" with their jobs has been felt by the organization. Organizations believe that such employees should influence business success, higher productivity, sales, customer satisfaction and have employee retention. Such is the concept Employee Engagement. Although Hewitt first defined employee engagement and its measurement approach in 1944, but it is of highest importance to organizations today. Employee engagement includes trust, loyalty, pride, and cooperative spirit. This also includes critical intangible assets such as trust, teamwork, and communication. Hence **Engagement** can be **defined** as a measure of the emotional and intellectual commitment that employees have to their organization[5]. Hence, employees feel engaged when they find per-sonal meaning and motivation in their work, receive positive interpersonal support, and operate in an efficient work environment[6]. Although some studies on employee engagement are conducted in international level, but significant studies in India are still to be registered. The impact of talent engagement is highly recognized in organizations like Infosys Technologies Limited, Satyam Computer Services Limited, Tata Consultancy Services, Wipro Technologies, GAIL India Limited etc.

Fig. 16.1: Interface amongst Employee Commitment, Accountability & Ownership and Organization Climate; giving rise to Engaged Employee.

Engagement is considered as the cumulative effects of the employee's commitment to the organization, which embarks sense of ownership and accountability, entailing a productive workforce.

Of course employee engagement requires a supportive organizational climate. Hence there exists a definite interface amongst employee commitment, organizational climate and accountability and ownership, which can stand for engaged employee. Employee engagement figures in the concept of making the employees enthusiastic about the work. Hence can be inter-twined in the threads of passion, commitment, energy or burning desire for achievement.

The views of ISR Surveys reflect that engagement is the interface of the three components such as the Cognitive component or the think component, which relates to the employees logical evaluation, of company's goals and values; the second is the emotional component or the feel component or the affective component, which taps into whether employees have a sense of belonging and pride in the company, and the third one is the behavioural component or the act component, which captures the out comes that employees desire such as retention and willingness to "go the extra distance" for the company when necessary. Engagement it self is actually a measure of these three components.

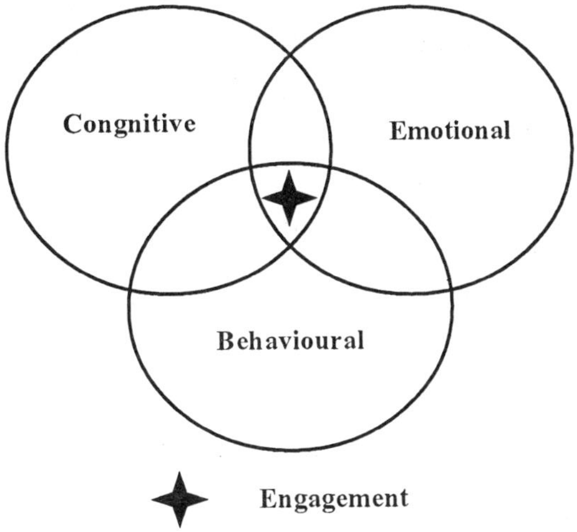

Fig. 16.2: Engagement as interface amongst Cognitive, Emotional and Behavioural Components

WHAT IS ENGAGEMENT?

Passion. Commitment. Extra effort. These terms describe employee engagement-the illusive force that motivates employees to higher (or lower) levels of performance. A scan of studies and other current literature related to employee engagement shows similar descriptors for this coveted energy[7]:

- Commitment to the organization.
- Job ownership and pride.
- More discretionary effort (time and energy).
- Passion and excitement.
- Commitment to execution and the bottom line.

Positive outcomes are directly related to high levels of employee engagement. Engaged employees are those who work longer hours, try harder, accomplish more and speak positively about their organizations. Engagement is an amalgamation of commitment, loyalty, productivity and ownership. It's also a critical element of competitive advantage for most organizations[8].

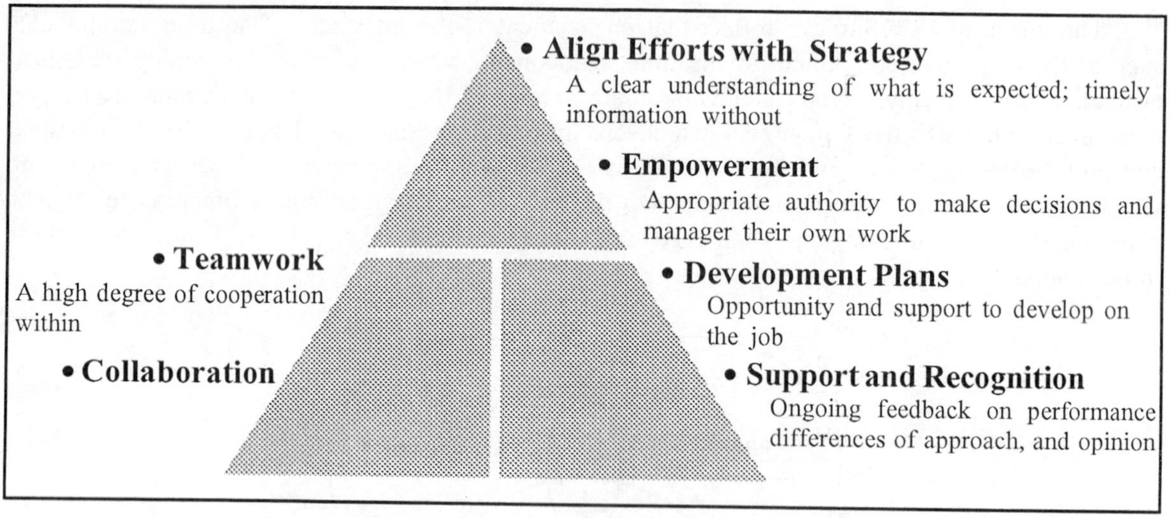

Fig. 16.3: Model of Engagement

Engagement is a complex contract that can best be presented by breaking it down into a number of individual elements. The basic idea is to make sure each of the practices is present to a "high degree" in your workplace. In turn, your employees will respond positively to employee engagement survey items. High scores correlate with better company performance. The first component is focused work, which includes the aligning efforts with strategy i.e. the employees have a clear understanding of what is expected and timely information about changes that affect their work; and empowerment i.e. the employees are given appropriate authority to make decisions and manage their own work. The second component is interpersonal support, which includes teamwork i.e. there is a high degree of cooperation within a workgroup, and an environment of trusting and trustworthy actions that foster rapid and satisfying resolution of conflicts and collaboration i.e. there is a high degree of cooperation between workgroups that fosters common goals, rapid conflict resolution and increased trust. The third component is individual value, which includes the development plans i.e. the employees have the opportunity and support to develop on the job; support and recognition i.e. employees get ongoing feedback on performance and acceptance of individual differences of approach, ideas and opinion.

The feelings or attitudes employees have toward their jobs and organizations can be measured through a set of employee survey items that correlate with multiple business outcomes. Fortunately, more and more organizations are taking this critical measurement step, and the availability of survey tools makes measuring employee engagement easier than ever before.

Slowly the transformation in the paradigm takes place where the employees contribute efforts above the level of prediction. Some assessments such as based on Lev and Schwartz Model highlight the value of employees. It is found that employees contribute to the business by leveraging its growth both financially and non-financially. The business-per-employee is magnifying at a limitless productivity. There was a situation when the performance of the organization were restricted by the limited capability and output of the employees. But now situations witness that the performance of the organization is limited by the capability of the organization to provide supportive climate to the employees. Hence the supportive climate can produce leveraged outputs. The 3S model which further corroborates employee engagement is represented as the interface amongst stay, speak and strive.

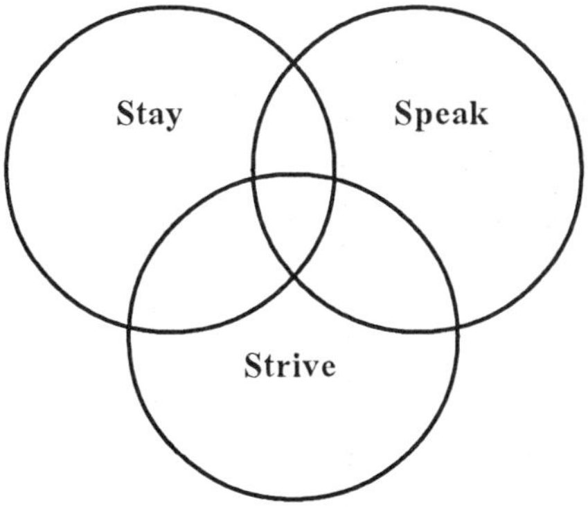

'Stay'
Desire to be wiht the Organisation.
'Speak'
Diffuse positively about the Organisation.
'Strive'
Do best to thte Organisation.

Fig. 16.4: 3S Model of Employee Engagement

Jack Welch opined that today enterprises seek raises in productivity not incrementally but in multiples[9]. Hence the ever-considered difficulty i.e. high level output within the quickest time frame is planned through challenged, empowered, excited and rewarded teams of people. Hence the level of engagement may be taken up, i.e. the engagement of every single mind in the organization, which can make every one the part of the action, and allowing everyone to have a constructive voice and a contributing role in the success of the enterprise.

THE TYPES OF ENGAGEMENT

Employee engagement can be categorized as Actively Engaged Partially Engaged and Passively Engaged. The actively engaged employees are fully engaged who share the vision of the organization and grows with it. The partially engaged employees are committed to the objectives but tempted to leave upon luring. The passively engaged employees are disengaged who are not committed.

An employee is said to be engaged, when the person has the passion and drive to carry out the tasks in a complementing and supporting milieu. The engaged employee shares the organisation vision and experiences the entrepreneurial feeling looking at the bigger picture. Emotionally speaking the "delaying gratification and family focused on goals-aligned to the organization makes the person engaged"[10].

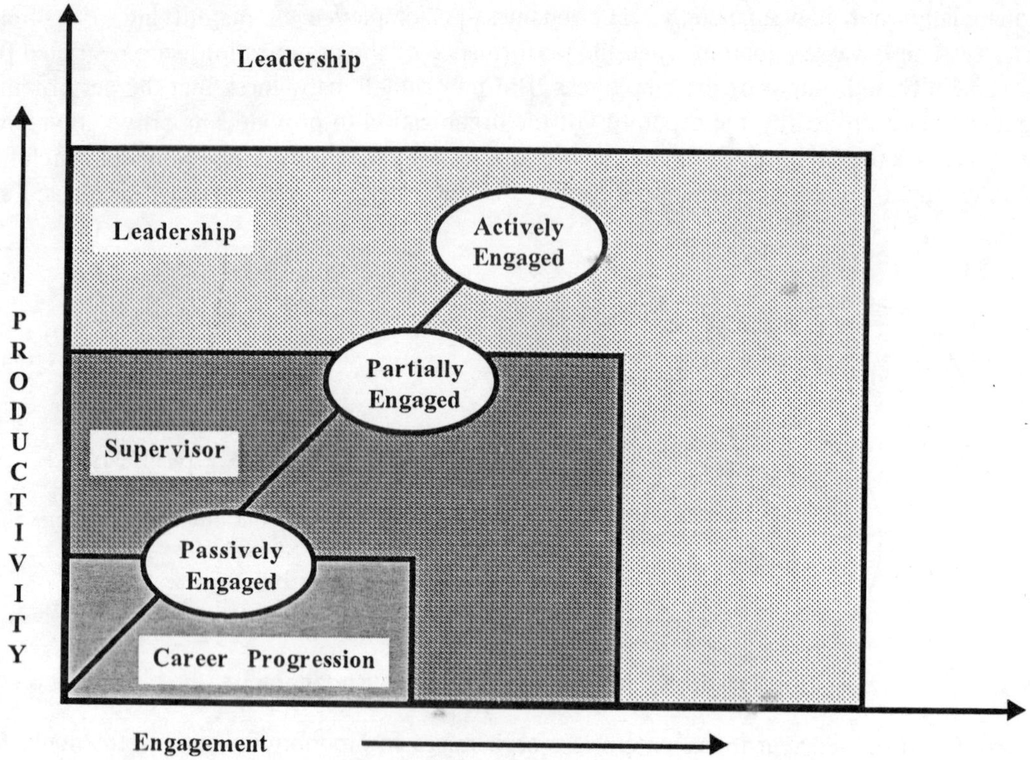

Fig. 16.5: Interface Amongst Engagement and Productivity

The key drivers to employee engagement comprises of leadership, supervisor and career progression as depicted in figure 16.5. Mostly in service sector organizations such as Insurance, Banking, Finance, Electricity Supply, Share & Stock Brokers, Advertising, Marketing Research, Consultancy, Accountancy, Legal, Medical, Educational, Research, Information Technology and IT Enabled Services, Leasing, Employment Agencies, Tours and Travels, Retail Organizations, Transport & Communication, Courier Services, Telephone & Telecommunications, Broadcasting and Telecasting etc.; the employees engaged efforts are considered as dependent variable and the organizational dynamics mostly which contributes to organizational climate are considered as independent variables.

WHAT DRIVES ENGAGEMENT?

Research shows that committed employees perform better. As is accepted that engagement, as many believe, is 'one step up' from commitment, it is clearly in the organisation's interests to understand the drivers of engagement. The strongest driver of all is a sense of feeling valued and involved. This has several key components:

- involvement in decision making
- the extent to which employees feel able to voice their ideas, and managers listen to these views, and value employees' contributions

- the opportunities employees have to develop their jobs
- the extent to which the organisation is concerned for employees' health and wellbeing.

The line manager clearly has a very important role in fostering employees' sense of involvement and value.

THE CHALLENGES OF EMPLOYEE ENGAGEMENT

The engagement levels can vary, in association with a variety of personal and job characteristics and with experiences at work. Some of these are [11]:

- engagement levels decline as employees get older – until they reach the oldest group, where levels suddenly rise, and show this oldest group to be the most engaged of all.
- managers and professionals tend to have higher engagement levels than their colleagues in supporting roles, although people in the latter group appear to owe greater loyalty to their profession than the organisation in which they practice their craft.
- engagement levels decline as length of service increases
- having an accident or an injury at work, or experiencing harassment (particularly if the manager is the source of the harassment) both have a big negative impact on engagement
- employees who have a personal development plan, and who have received a formal performance appraisal within the past year, have significantly higher engagement levels than those who have not.

Mostly in the service sector enterprises, the employees have little flexibility to make things right for the customer. Because of the circumstances, rules, policies, practices, and structure of their organizations, these workers were either compelled to do the wrong thing, or, in the case of the customer service representatives, sometimes even they are punished for doing the right thing, if it over suits the company budgets.

As service sector enterprises realize that emotional connections are vital for business because they drive organic growth, hence if the desired engaged behaviours considered as dependable factors are commitment, accountability, sense of ownership, being focused, achievement orientation, entrepreneurship and strategic thinking etc., then the independent variables which are the dynamics of organizational culture and climate could be supportive organizational climate, employee empowerment, progressiveness of the career, work-life balance, trusted leadership, vision and future growth, transparency and communication as well as objectives and expectations.

Strategies for Employers to Keep Employees Involved and Engaged:

Some of the strategies, which works for employee engagement are[12]:

- The employees must realize that the organisation cares them. It gets them the resources they need to get their jobs done.
- The organisation must be able to connect the work they do as individuals to the big picture. Research shows that employees who are motivated will rally behind their employers, through good times and bad.

- The management must demonstrate fairness when dealing with employees. It must be ensured that all employees are given an equal voice.
- Employees must be given challenging work. People to be put in roles that use their strengths.
- Employees to be given training and opportunity for advancement. Projects may be assigned that let them grow. They may be given more authority over how their job gets done along with clear measures of accountability.
- Responsibility may be shared for decisions and outcomes with employees. Their ideas to be encouraged and to be taken seriously. Employees are more likely to accept and carry out decisions if they're involved in the process.

Employee engagement affects the bottom line because engaged employees deliver high-quality, committed service and they form work teams that produce high-quality results. And when engaged employees come into contact with the public, their commitment comes across and the people they're serving respond by becoming engaged in kind. If you take care of your employees, they'll take care of you and your members.

Employees want to be engaged. Several research studies conducted by the Harvard Business Review (HBR) found that employees rank "the opportunity to do important work that gives a feeling of accomplishment" higher than pay as a prime motivator. But there's one downside to engaging employees—once they're engaged, they expect to be involved and given the chance to deliver. HBR studies also concluded that "those who cared most about their work were the most demoralized when they were thwarted from doing their best" by factors beyond their control such as role ambiguity, inadequate resources, and overwork[13].

Corporate culture is an important component of employee engagement. A company's culture is made evident by its leaders' behavior. Communication styles, internally distributed messages, company celebrations, and how you recognize employees' efforts all define corporate culture. Make sure the culture at your credit union is one you want[14].

On should direct your employee-engagement efforts at managers and non-managers alike. If managers aren't engaged, it's unlikely that employees will be responsive to any efforts to engage them. Leaders who make their employees feel cared for, valued, and heard invoke a culture of trust and credibility. Treating employees as allies and creating a sense of teamwork and emotional commitment increases morale and productivity. Invite feedback from staff instead of laying down the law. And instead of communicating via memos, explain policies and programs in person along with the reasons for why they were developed and implemented. Employees want to be informed about everything that affects them, good and bad[15].

Hence organisations need to work hard to prevent, and minimise the impact of, bad experiences. They also need to ensure that employees' development needs (including the special needs of professionals) are taken seriously; pay attention to, and value the roles of, support staff; and to maintain the interest of longer-serving employees. The relatively high levels of engagement of the oldest employees, and of minority ethnic staff, suggest sources of untapped potential within some organisations.

Since even the most outstanding employee have to operate within the constraints of their environment hence employee engagement has to be taken care of all its propositions.

References

1. http://www.expressitpeople.com/20030901/management1.shtml
2. *Ibid*
3. *Ibid*
4. http://was4.hewitt.com/hewitt/services/talent/subtalent/ee_engagement.htm
5. http://was7.hewitt.com/bestemployers/europe/slovakia/
6. Director, Development Dimensions International, Inc., MMIV.
7. http://www.wpsmag.com/content/templates/wps_article.asp?articleid=138&zoneid=11
8. *Ibid*
9. Nitya Naidu Tupili (2006): "HR of HR (High Rhythm of Human Resources)" HRD News Letter, Vol: 22, Issue: 9, P-29.
10. Article by Mr. Rajesh Balasubramanian, of Value Lanes
11. http://www.employment-studies.co.uk/summary/summary.php?id=408
12. http://www.cunahrcouncil.org/news/422.html
13. *Ibid*
14. *Ibid*
15. *Ibid*

17 Work Culture & Employee Engagement

Tripti Jha

ABSTRACT

Employee engagement is the level of commitment and involvement an employee has towards his organization and its values. An engaged employee is aware of business context, and works with colleagues to improve performance within the job for the benefit of the organization. It is a positive attitude held by the employees towards the organization and its values. The paper focuses on how employee engagement is an antecedent of job involvement and what different organization does to keep its employees engaged and motivated to contribute towards making of a healthy Work Culture. The paper also includes the Employee Engagement Approaches at Jindal Steel & Power Limited with detailed information about approaches at Angul Unit.

ORIGIN

Employee engagement is described in the academic literature by Schmidt *et al.* (1993). A modernized version of job satisfaction, Schmidt et al.'s influential definition of engagement was "an employee's involvement with, commitment to, and satisfaction with work." This integrates the classic constructs of job satisfaction (Smith et al., 1969), and organizational commitment (Meyer & Allen, 1991). Harter and Schmidt's (2003) most recent meta-analysis can be useful for understanding the impact of engagement.

Employee engagement is derived from studies of morale or a group's willingness to accomplish organizational objectives which began in the 1920s. The value of morale to organizations was matured by US Army researchers during WW II to predict unity of effort and attitudinal battle-readiness before combat. In the postwar mass production society that required unity of effort in execution, (group) morale scores were used as predictors of speed, quality and militancy. With the advent of the knowledge worker and emphasis on individual talent management (stars), a term was needed to describe an individual's emotional attachment to the organization, fellow associates and the job. Thus the birth of the term "Employee Engagement" which is an individual emotional phenomenon whereas "Morale" is a group emotional phenomenon of similar characteristics. In other words, employee engagement is the raw material of morale composed of 15 attitudinal drivers. (e.g. Scarlett 2001).

CATEGORIES OF EMPLOYEE ENGAGEMENT

According to the "Gallup" the Consulting Organization there are three different types of people:-

Engaged - *"Engaged"* employees are builders. They want to know the desired expectations for heir role so they can meet and exceed them. They're naturally curious about their company and their lace in it. They perform at consistently high levels. They want to use their talents and strengths at work every day. They work with passion and they drive innovation and move their organization forward.

Not Engaged - *Not-engaged* employees tend to concentrate on tasks rather than the goals and outcomes they are expected to accomplish. They want to be told what to do just so they can do it and say they have finished. They focus on accomplishing tasks vs. achieving an outcome. Employees who are *not-engaged* tend to feel their contributions are being overlooked, and their potential is not being tapped. They often feel this way because they don't have productive relationships with their managers or with their coworkers.

Actively Disengaged--The *"actively disengaged"* employees are the "cave dwellers." They're "Consistently against Virtually Everything." They're not just unhappy at work; they're busy acting out their unhappiness .They sow seeds of negativity at every opportunity. Every day, actively disengaged workers undermine what their engaged coworkers accomplish. As workers increasingly rely on each other to generate products and services, the problems and tensions that are fostered by *actively disengaged* workers can cause great damage to an organization's functioning.

INFLUENCES

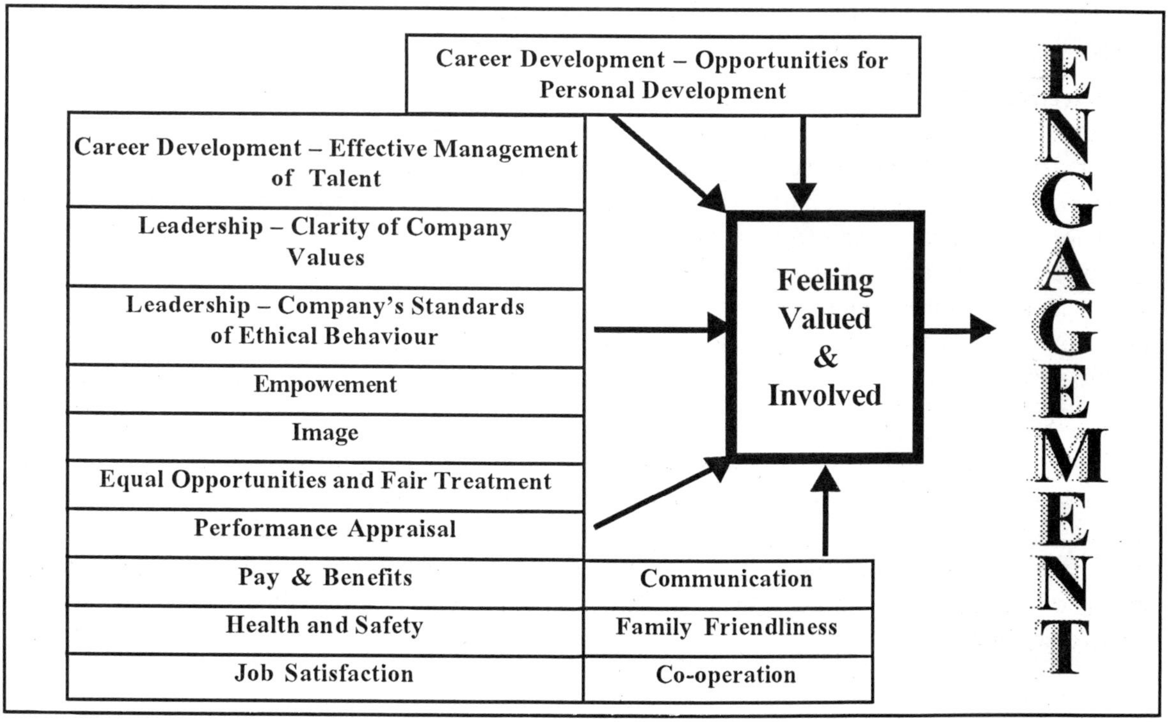

Employer Engagement - A company's "commitment to improving the partnership between employees and Employer." Employers can stay engaged with their employees by actively seeking to understand and act on behalf of the expectations and preferences of their employees.

Employee Perceptions of Job Importance - According to a 2006 study by Gerard Seijts and Dan Crim," an employee's attitude toward the job's importance and the company had the greatest impact on loyalty and customer service then all other employee factors combined."

Employee Clarity of Job Expectations - "If expectations are not clear and basic materials and equipment not provided, negative emotions such as boredom or resentment may result, and the employee may then become focused on surviving more than thinking about how he can help the organization succeed."

Career Advancement/Improvement Opportunities - "Plant supervisors and managers indicated that many plant improvements were being made outside the suggestion system, where employees initiated changes in order to reap the bonuses generated by the subsequent cost savings."

Regular Feedback and Dialogue with Superiors - "Feedback is the key to giving employees a sense of where they're going, but many organizations are remarkably bad at giving it. "'What I really wanted to hear was 'Thanks. You did a good job.' But all my boss did was hand me a check.'"

Quality of Working Relationships with Peers, Superiors, and Subordinates - "if employees' relationship with their managers is fractured, then no amount of perks will persuade the employees to perform at top levels. Employee engagement is a direct reflection of how employees feel about their relationship with the boss."

Perceptions of the Ethos and Values of the Organization - "Inspiration and values" is the most important of the six drivers in our Engaged Performance model. Inspirational leadership is the ultimate perk. In its absence, [it] is unlikely to engage employees."

Effective Internal Employee Communications - which convey a clear description of "what's going on". "'If you accept that employees want to be involved in what they are doing then this trend is clear (from small businesses to large global organisations). The effect of poor internal communications is seen as its most destructive in global organisations which suffer from employee annexation - where the head office in one country is buoyant (since they are closest to the action, know what is going on, and are heavily engaged) but its annexes (who are furthest away from the action and know little about what is happening) are dis-engaged. In the worst case, employee annexation can be very destructive when the head office attributes the annex's low engagement to its poor performance... when its poor performance is really due to its poor communications.

Reward to Engage - Look at employee benefits and acknowledge the role of incentives. "An incentive to reward good work is a tried and tested way of boosting staff morale and enhancing engagement." There are a range of tactics one can employ to ensure one's incentive scheme hits the mark with its workforce such as: Setting realistic targets, selecting the right rewards for your incentive programme, communicating the scheme effectively and frequently, have lots of winners and reward all achievers, encouraging sustained effort, present awards publicly and evaluate the incentive scheme regularly.

APPROACHES TO EMPLOYEE ENGAGEMENT AT JSPL

Rewards & Recognition

JSPL, Angul has initiated 4 genres of Rewards and each one of them encourages employee engagement very tactfully.

(a) Birthday Club

In this scheme, every employee of Jindal Steel & Power Limited is gifted with a customized coffee mug with Jindal Logo and his name printed on it along with a letter from our Executive Director on his birthday. By this, we pass a message, that we all belong to one Jindal Family and thus value each other.

(b) Spot Award

This is a scheme for instantaneous recognition. The process followed is:

Coverage	Frequency	Modalities	Criteria For Selection	Benefit Under the Award	Remarks
CG4* and CG5** except HODs	Monthly	HR dept will purchase small gift items worth Rs.100-Rs.250 and give it to department heads. Gifts will remain in the custody of respective departments. HODs will select one or two winner for the purpose every month. No individual can win the Award for more than three times in a year.	Exceptional operational performance in meeting targets. Outstanding commitment to sustainable development. Shining example of integrity to subordinates. Any other behavior which is exemplary in nature can be awarded but the reason needs to be specific.	Note of thanks by HOD. Awardees will receive one of the monthly budgeted set of awards like utility products or executive products	At the end of month, every Department will have to submit a report containing the reasons for giving these awards to HR department so that the right spirit is maintained and the award is given on fair grounds.

(c) GEM of JSPL

This award is for non executives. The purpose is same as Spot Award.

Scope	Coverage	Process	Periodicity	Details of the Award
Staff up to the level of junior executive and workers	Contribution to productivity Quality and cost Contribution to safety and safety	Every month HODs shall nominate one/ two employees from his department as	Nomination is done every month	First recognition is given by putting up their photographs on display board set

	promotional General conduct/ behavior Exceptional work done Punctuality/Discipline Suggestion given Responsiveness or readiness or willingness to extend help/ support in educating workers about housekeeping green productivity movement.	GEM based on the which encompasses areas like contribution productivity etc.		up at prominent locations in the plant. At the end of the year a program is organized by HR Dept where all the GEMs are felicitated. Gifts may include suite case, dinner set or any other gift as decided by the management.

(d) Smile Scheme

This is the most innovative scheme under Reward & Recognition.

The Process and Guidelines for Smile Scheme are mentioned below:-

- Every employee in the career group CG4 & CG5 (Jr. Manager to Sr. Manager) along with GETs and MTs is given one Smile Pad for the whole year. These smile pads are available with the HODs of respective departments.
- A Smile Note can be written and dropped in the Smile Box anytime an executive goes out of his/her way to help other colleague(s).
- Smile Boxes are fitted near every attendance punch machine.
- Each employee is allowed to make only 10 Smile Notes a year.
- The person giving the smile note would mention the reason for the award on the note itself. The person must then place the same into the Smile Box which is fitted near the punch machine. The smile note should also contain the name and designation of the person writing the Smile Note.
- Every week one of the HODs will read out the entries aloud and draw one among many notes for reward.
- Winner of the draw would be given a book/ any other gift item.
- The very purpose of initializing such scheme is to give instantaneous recognition which is expected to go a long way in motivating executives to demonstrate hard work and excellence.

Following is the process in tabular form for easy reference:

Scope	Coverage	Process	Periodicity	Details of the Award
Every executive CG4 & CG5 GET MT	A **Smile Note** should be written and dropped in the **Smile Box** anytime an executive goes out of his/her to help other colleague.	Every week one of the HODs shall draw one among the many nominations for the winner. The HOD will read all the entries aloud.	Nomination can be done anytime but an executive can use only 10 smile notes in a year.	Winner is awarded with a book/ any other gift item

We also encourage employee engagement by organizing sessions on CORE VALUES of our company known as doing it Jindal Way. An example of such session:

Inculcating "Jindal Way" (Core Values), why they are Important and How to Excel in Our Performance:

Phase	Module	Objective	Description	Duration
Going Through Values	Jindal Song + Jindal Video + Introduction to Jindal Vision-Mission-Vision by JINDAL HR	To Set The Tone of the Workshop	Song + Video + Presentation by Jindal HR	35 Minutes
Going Through Values	Welcome + Intro to Program + Purpose of this Program	To Clarify the Definition + **Meaning** of Values & Core Values + Leadership Competencies	Facilitator Led Questions & Answers + Movie Clipping [Mangal Pandey – on Leadership Competancies]	45 Minutes
Going Through Values	Passion for People	Respect for Others + Care{Development of People} & + Collaboration	Activity on Ignoring & Paying Attention + Broken Square [to make everyone realize how much we really care] + Brick Game for making people acknowledge that collaboration is better than competition	50 Minutes
	Going Through Values	To Focus on Meritocracy	Competition of Knowing More About Others with Prize Activity & Discussion	20 Minutes

	Going Through Values	Crux will be on Process Rigor + Strategic Thinking + Innovation	Handicapped Trekking[every member with handicap cross a difficult terrain] + Discussions on Creative Innovations & Strategic Thinking	40 Minutes
	Going Through Values Going Through Values Going Through Values	Focal Point would be on Integrity, Loyalty & Trust + Pride of being Jindalaite & developing sense of Belongingness	Spider Web/Pipe Game => for Highlighting Integrity + Expanding JINDAL word for pride + Discussions	60 Minutes
		To Highlight How Uplifting Quality of Local Communities Society + Protecting Environment is Important not only for the Organization & the Nation But also for Ourselves	Law of Interdependence Through Law of Cause & Effect + Small Group Discussions	30 Minutes

The Behaviors to be brought out from the application section of Core Values Workshop – for the Supervisors to the Top Management

Phase	**Module**	**Objective**	**Description**	**Duration**
Application of These Competencies/Values	**Verifying** the Understanding of Participants	To Observe **Whether** Under Informal Situation Participants Follow & How Well	Creating Scenario + Discussion	45 Minutes
Why Should We Uphold Our Values	Cascading Them Internally/ Internalization	To Reinforce	Movie Clipping [Saving Private Ryan] + Discussion	20 Minutes
Do's & Don'ts for Appropriate Behavior Needed to Be Excellent	Identifying What	To Come Out With ways to Excel	Facilitator Led + Small Group Discussion	40 Minutes
Action Plan	**My Role**	Creating Action **Plan**	Individual Pen & Paper Exercise	10 Minutes

Area	Values/ Competencies	List of Related Behaviors
People Excellence	Meritocracy	➢ Open to Ideas / Suggestions from others especially Juniors + Invites Ideas / Suggestions from them ➢ Gives freedom to work ➢ Accepts his mistakes ➢ Gives Immediate Feedback ➢ Delegates ➢ Is Fair & Impartial + Has Confidence in Self ➢ Encourages Others to Learn ➢ Develops Second line of Command who can effectively take charge in his absence ➢ Continuously upgrades himself/Learning & Updating Regularly ➢ Tells everyone what He/She needs to do to be FEE & what is their present performance level ➢ Coaches & Mentors to make them grow continuously ➢ Involves everyone in decision making/problem solving/planning how to achieve targets etc. ➢ Sets High Standards ➢ Openly shares information ➢ Develops people horizontally through Job Rotation ➢ Does not tolerates average insists on EXCELLENCE ➢ Give credit to the right person always ➢ Appreciates openly
People Excellence	Care & Respect for Others	Takes responsibility for mistakes of department ➢ Listens Actively ➢ Helps by going out of way in genuine cases ➢ Maintains strict discipline ➢ Coaches & Mentors ➢ Guides ➢ Gives them Constructive Feedback individually ➢ Gives credit to the right persons always ➢ Respects the feelings of everyone right down to workers ➢ Speaks politely
People Excellence	Collaboration	➢ Invites Suggestions/Feedback ➢ Involves people in decision making ➢ Incorporates their decision/tells why it could not be incorporated ➢ Have excellent relationships with other department, customers outside agencies & cooperates with them on proactive basis + encourages others to do so

Business Excellence	Process Excellence Strategic Thinking + Innovation	➢ Always Focus on Continuous Improvement ➢ Launches various ways to bring out the innovative ideas through regular brain storming ➢ Does not compromises with Quality + Safety + Discipline ➢ Always insists & gets Excellence out of people ➢ Recognizes the people who are regular idea gives & motivates others to share ➢ Plans ahead with the team for any exigencies ➢ Sets the Standards high ➢ Promotes Multi Tasking through Job Rotation ➢ Updates Himself & ensures his team members are up to date with the latest in their field continuously ➢ Motivates & Recognizes people on an ongoing way ➢ Learns & Incorporates Best Practices of Other Organizations ➢ Takes complete responsibility of actions of Juniors & Self and DOES not BLAME Others
Sustainable Development	Social Responsibility + Environmental Responsibility	➢ Insist on Saving Water & Electricity at Home + Office ➢ Volunteers for CSR activities ➢ Ensure Good House keeping ➢ Ensures Proper Waste Disposal ➢ Uses Les & Less Papers ➢ Encourages Planting of Trees ➢ Recycles whatever can be ➢ Uses less of Polythene bags ➢ Uses Pool car/Public Transport etc. ➢ Uses Practices which are environmental friendly
Loyalty & Trust	Loyalty + Integrity	➢ Takes Pride in Being Jindalite ➢ Regarded as Fair, Honest & Impartial ➢ Always honors commitments ➢ Courage to accept mistakes ➢ Always gives credit to the right person ➢ Follows Core Values yourself

Every parameter of the above mentioned table encourages employee engagement in its own special way. The core value of our esteemed organization, JSPL caters to the need of every employee's development thirst. Things like regular coaching, mentoring, participation in decision making, problem solving, teaching on group dynamics converts a disengaged employee into a highly engaged one.

Other important activities at JSPL which encourages a harmonious work culture are:

(1) Different Interviews:

(a) Orientation Interview- Conducted after an employee completes first two months in the organization. Aims in knowing about the first impression of the organization and its people. It has questions like were the people friendly? Did u get support from your mentor etc..

(b) Comfort Interview- Conducted after an employee completes 6 months in the organization. Aims in monitoring the comfort level of the employees in the organization. It includes questions like is your boss friendly? Does he discuss various problems with you? Etc.

(c) Stay Interview- Conducted after an employee completes 1 year in the organization. Aims in knowing about the factors which causes the smooth stay of any employee.

(2) Professional Circle:

Here employees from different departments and grade forms various groups to discuss their professional issues related to their growth and career development. The groups meet at least once in a month and discusses about various training and development needs at length.

(3) Performance Appraisal Review:

Unlike many organizations process of delivering appraisal letters as postman, JSPL organizes a small programme where organization's EVC & MD Shri Naveen Jindal addresses every Jindalite and distributes promotion/ increment letter to HODs. These HODs then handovers the letters to their respective subordinate explaining the reason for the given rating. The system is totally transparent which does not leave employees in any doubt of partiality or favoritism creating an open and understanding work culture.

(4) Pulse Survey:

Pulse Survey includes questions regarding the relationship between bosses and subordinates monitoring the avenue of healthy and congenial relationship between two which results in synergy and ultimately aggravates both employee and employer satisfaction. It also checks for any autocratic behavior of people in authority. The survey aims in achieving a healthy workplace where every employee can express himself and gives input for improvement of both, the work culture as well as the employees career development.

(5) OHI Survey Feedback:

An organizational health index was organized for every unit of JSPL. It was a measure to check the organizational health of the organization on the parameters like:

(a) Accommodation

(b) Hospital

(c) Education

(d) Conveyance Service

(e) Entertainment and Sports Facilities

(f) Food and Canteen

Final Words: The Leadership Touch

Every Jindalite understand that his or her leader is behind him, always supportive, always available to hold his/her hand, and lift up whenever he/she falters. The culture of caring for the grass- root employee started with visionary Late Sri O.P. Jindal who founded the organization with great humility and affection for all his employees irrespective of level.

His first concern was always the welfare of employees; if he has had his food on time, if he has proper food, drinking water and decent place to live. Our present leader, EVC & MD Shri Naveen Jindal added his affection and bonding with a clean green environment to the founder's vision of caring for people. Every leader in the Organization is thus expected today to engage with his work alongside caring for people and environment. No wonder steadily our organization is climbing up the stair step by step to acquire the coveted tag of "India's Best Organization to work for". One of our site units at Raigarh has already achieved this laurel. Others are close on its heels.

References:

1. Jindal Portal
2. Policy Manual- JSPL
3. Google Search Engine
4. Archie Thomas, CMA, and Ann MacDi anmid – Encouraging Employee Engagement –
5. CMA Management, Jun/Jul 2004.
6. Ashok Mukherjee – Engagement for the mind body, and soul – Human Capital, Aug. 2005.
7. Barbara Palframan Smith – Employee connection – Technology to built culture and community – Communication World – Mar / Apr 2004.

❖❖❖

18

The Connotations of Employee Engagement for Organisational Bottom Line Results

Prof. Tapati Nandy
Barnishikha Das
Prof. Ramchandra Mahapatra

ABSTRACT

The notion of employee engagement is a relatively new one. One that has been heavily marketed by human resource (HR) consulting firms that offer advice on how it can be created and leveraged. Academic researchers are now slowly joining the fray, and both parties are saddled with competing and inconsistent interpretations of the meaning of the construct. Casual observation suggests that much of the appeal to organizational management is driven by claims that employee engagement drives bottom-line results. Some practitioners view engagement as having evolved from prior research on work attitudes, directly implying that this newer concept adds interpretive value that extends beyond the boundaries of those traditions. Although compelling on the surface, the meaning of the employee engagement concept is unclear. In large part, this can be attributed to the ''bottom-up'' manner in which the engagement notion has quickly evolved within the practitioner community. The relationships among potential antecedents and consequences of engagement as well as the components of engagement have not been rigorously conceptualized, much less studied. Indeed, many HR consultants avoid defining the term, instead referring only to its presumed positive consequences. The academic community has been slow to jump on the practitioner engagement bandwagon, and empirical research that has appeared on the topic in refereed outlets reveals little consideration for rigorously testing the theory underlying the construct. Thus, although research exists demonstrating that some employee attitudes called "engagement" are related to organizational outcomes like turnover and productivity these employee attitudes do not conceptually reflect the notion of engagement. Thus, further development of the construct and its measurement requires attention. Our objective is to present a conceptual framework that will help both researchers and practitioners recognize the variety of meanings the engagement construct subsumes and the research traditions that give rise to or support those meanings. We believe that this is important in itself as it creates a working model for how the research literature can influence practice and vice versa. Thus, as we organize the various literatures relevant to engagement, we establish research agenda that identifies further opportunities for science and improved science– practice linkages.

Keywords: Employee Engagement, Human Resource, Profitability, Bottom Line Results.

INTRODUCTION

Employee Engagement: Getting Oriented: Numerous definitions of engagement can be derived from the practice- and research driven literatures. Additional definitions can be attributed to folk theory: the common intuitive sense that people, and particularly leaders within organizations, have about work motivation. Common to these definitions is the notion that employee engagement is a desirable condition, has an organizational purpose, and connotes involvement, commitment, passion, enthusiasm, focused effort, and energy, so it has both attitudinal and behavioral components. The antecedents of such attitudes and behaviors are located in conditions under which people work, and the consequences are thought to be of value to organizational effectiveness. As a folk theory, engagement is used in a manner that implies the opposite of disengagement. For example, a number of popular views of engagement suggest that engaged employees not only contribute more but also are more loyal and therefore less likely to voluntarily leave the organization. However, for present purposes, we choose to focus on only those aspects of engagement that have positive valence (obviously from low to high). We believe that this is crucial to developing conceptual precision in that it maintains a clear intentional focus on benefits that inure to the organization.

The objectives of the study are:

- To illuminate conceptual research on employee engagement.
- To understand the effect of employee engagement on profitability.

DESIGN & METHOD OF STUDY

The paper is conceptual and review paper in nature. Data collected for this paper is basically from secondary sources. This paper examines an Employee Engagement as a measure for organizational productivity. A range of recently published works, which aim to provide practical advice are examined to aid the research. After reviewing around ninety numbers of research articles it has been thought that employee engagement as a process is a fundamental review which needs to be carried out by employers. Specific cases of organizations in different countries are studied through the published research papers retrieved from secondary sources like books, e-journals, business magazines, etc. for analyzing the importance of employee engagement and its various contributions for organizational growth and success.

LITERATURE REVIEW

Barney, J. (1991). Firm resources and sustained competitive advantage. Journal of Management, 17(1): 99-120. Abstract: In this article exploring the links between firm resources and competitive advantage Barney defines and discusses four qualities a resource must possess — rareness, inimitability, non-substitutability, and value — for it to hold the potential to create a sustained competitive advantage. Drawing a firm distinction between competitive advantage and sustained competitive advantage, which itself is separated by the fact that it cannot be implemented by other firms and cannot be duplicated by rivals, Barney also discusses the implications of the resource-based view for managers and their organizations.

Bates, S. (2004). Getting engaged. *HR Magazine*, 49(2): 44-51. Abstract: Beginning with a discussion of the costs associated with a workforce that is not engaged, this article examines the factors that drive employee engagement as well as the potential benefits to be derived from getting employees engaged. The cases of a California-based specialty mortgage firm and a diagnostic systems manufacturer are used as examples.

Baumruk, R., Gorman, Jr., B., & Gorman, R.E. (2006). Why managers are crucial to increasing engagement: identifying steps managers can take to engage their workforce. *Strategic HR Review*, 5(2): 24-27. Abstract: In this interview with Ray Baumruk, of Hewitt Associates, the antecedents of engagement are discussed as are the steps managers can take on an individual basis to improve engagement among their direct reports. Additionally, key behaviors—say, stay, and strive—indicating an engaged workforce are considered.

Carrig, K. & Wright, P.M. (2006). *Building profit through people: making your workforce the strongest link in the value-profit chain.* Alexandria, Virginia: Society for Human Resource Management. Abstract: This book provides an in-depth examination of how to link your employees with the bottom-line financial goals of profitability and growth. Beginning with the value-profit chain, which provides a model through which satisfied associates can drive business performance, the text describes how making people the firm's strongest asset can turn a failing company around. Special attention is given to how a people-focused strategy affected a turnaround at Continental along with practical information and examples of how that turnaround was achieved.

Cox, D.R. (1992). Causality: some statistical aspects. *Journal of the Royal Statistical Society*, 155 (Part 2): 291-301. Abstract: In this discussion of the conditions necessary to demonstrate statistical causality, causality via association and quasi-experiments is examined as are the subjects of latent variables and hierarchical variation along with their implications for empirical analyses.

DISCUSSION

Unraveling the Concepts behind Engagement Driving Organizational Productivity

To move the discussion of what engagement is to a more concrete level, consider the overall framework for understanding the various components that the engagement construct might subsume. Engagement as a disposition (i.e., trait engagement) can be regarded as an inclination or orientation to experience the world from a particular vantage point (e.g., positive affectivity characterized by feelings of enthusiasm) and that this trait engagement gets reflected in psychological state engagement. We conceptualize psychological state engagement as an antecedent of behavioral engagement, which we define in terms of discretionary effort or a specific form of in-role or extra role effort or behavior. Figure 1 also shows that conditions of the workplace have both direct and indirect effects on state and behavioral engagement. The nature of work (e.g., challenge, variety) and the nature of leadership (especially transformational leadership) are the conditions that most interest us.

Our goal is to illuminate the unique attributes of prior research that most occupy the conceptual space we would call engagement so that future research and practice can more precisely identify the nature of the engagement construct they are pursuing.

Engagement as Psychological State

Engagement as a psychological state has variously embraced one or more of several related ideas, each in turn representing some form of absorption, attachment, and/or enthusiasm. Operationally, the measures of engagement have for the most part been composed of a potpourri of items representing one or more of the four different categories: job satisfaction, organizational commitment, psychological empowerment, and job involvement. We summarize the relevance of each of these to the concept of engagement. This clarity reflects an increasing emphasis on absorption, passion, and affect and a lessening emphasis on satisfaction and perhaps also job involvement and organizational commitment.

Engagement as Satisfaction

Engagement is above and beyond simple satisfaction with the employment arrangement or basic loyalty to the employer—characteristics that most companies have measured for many years. Engagement, in contrast, is about passion and commitment—the willingness to invest oneself and expend one's discretionary effort to help the employer succeed. Satisfaction when assessed as satiation is not in the same conceptual space as engagement. Satisfaction when assessed as feelings of energy, enthusiasm, and similarly positive affective states becomes a facet of engagement.

Engagement as Commitment

Engagement is "the extent to which employees commit to someone or something in their organization, how hard they work, and how long they stay as a result of that commitment." In these and similar definitions, two possible threads of reasoning are implied: organizational and task/goal commitment. Organizational commitment is an important facet of the state of engagement when it is conceptualized as positive attachment to the larger organizational entity and measured as a willingness to exert energy in support of the organization, to feel pride as an organizational member, and to have personal identification with the organization.

Engagement as Job Involvement

Job involvement is defined "as the degree to which an employee psychologically relates to his or her job and the work performed therein". Job involvement is seen in contemporary definitions of engagement as a facet of engagement, a part of engagement but not equivalent to it. Job involvement (including task engagement and job commitment) as traditionally conceptualized and assessed is an important facet of the psychological state of engagement.

Engagement as Psychological Empowerment

Empowerment is the ''experience of authority and responsibility.'' Conceptually, empowerment defined in this manner might be considered an antecedent or a condition of engagement. The state of feeling empowered, as represented in an orientation toward action, would seem to occupy a portion of the conceptual space we would regard as a state of engagement. Feelings of empowerment that connote an inclination to action vis-a`-vis work (feelings of self-efficacy and control and impact from one's action) comprise another facet of state engagement.

Engagement as Positive Affectivity

Engagement is expected to be relatively constant, given the continued presence of specific and recognizable job and organizational factors. In what follows, other models of engagement as an affective state are described, some more and some less relatively persistent and transient psychological states. PA associated with the job and the work setting connoting or explicitly indicating feelings of persistence, vigor, energy, dedication, absorption, enthusiasm, alertness, and pride occupies a central position in the conceptualization and measurement of state engagement. Conversely, measures of psychological states that are devoid of direct and explicit indicants of affective and energetic feeling are not measures of state engagement in whole or part.

Engagement as Involvement of the Self

The experience of personal engagement encompasses elements of both involvement and commitment as psychological states and also a sense of personal identity in role behavior. It is from the experience of being psychologically present in the work — that the work is a part of one's identity — that employee development and productivity follow. Such behavioral engagement follows because when psychologically present, employees are attentive and focused, connected (including the connotation of absorption), and integrated. The ''experience'' of being integrated would entail simultaneously drawing upon all of one's skills, abilities, and other personal resources in order to respond to the demands of a role. State engagement additionally refers to the investment of the self in the person's work and the perceived importance of work outcomes and organization membership to that person's identity.

Measuring Engagement

Probably the most consistent message concerning the concept of employee engagement is that it should be measured through the use of a survey. From there, the similarities seem to end. Many names are used for this survey; engagement surveys, an attitude survey, work climate improvement survey, etc. Even more structures and survey questions are recommended concerning the best way to measure employee engagement. The Gallup study highlights twelve key elements that form the foundation of strong engagement and believes these elements can be accessed through twelve questions. The Institute for Employment Studies (IES) also did a study and found, "twelve attitude statements representing engagement were tested; all were found to 'sit together' reliably, to comprise a single indicator of engagement." But, the IES elements are not a clear match to those of Gallup and IES also state that a subset of five questions is allowed (Robinson *et al*, 2004) if twelve questions are unmanageable. Another measurement example comes from Development Dimensions International (DDI). DDI has their own measure, "E3," which assess three key elements of engagement (individual value, focused work, and interpersonal support) as well as provides a standard measure for employee satisfaction, which they feel is a result or consequence of engaging employees. Kieron Shaw (2005), reviewed employee engagement research and measurement proposals of many entities including Gallup, Towers Perrin, ISR, and Accenture. Concerning *how* to measure, Shaw's study struggles to provide any real clarification. Shaw offers suggestions based on, "sifting through our desk research and interviews and trying to subject the ideas to some reasoned analysis" and breaks engagement questions into three macro categories: climate, driver, and outcome. In the end, Shaw (2005) states, "It's arguably unfeasible to directly measure in the survey all the actions behind engagement," due to the fact that, "there are potentially thousands of different individual actions, attitudes, and processes that affect engagement." A different way to consider the difficulty of measuring employee engagement is to imagine the concept of employee engagement as a large geographical country such as the United States. Survey questions may represent a very specific piece of information about a given city or town in the United States. When you consider all of the subtle and profound differences between cities such as Las Vegas, Nevada and Boston, Massachusetts you begin to understand the complexity of measuring employee engagement.

FINDINGS

Employee Engagement's effects on Business Profitability: As previously mentioned, a relative dearth exists in the academic literature with regard to empirical investigation of the firm-level effects of employee engagement on financial performance. However, the direct studies of engagement that are available do provide considerable insight to how engagement operates, especially when considered within the value-profit chain. Despite this, the nature of the data collected, as well as the design of these studies, fails to allow for causal conclusions to be made. Put more simply, various engagement measures can be determined to relate to various other measures of organizational and individual performance, but the idea that engagement actually causes any of these outcomes is, in this context, unable to be proven. Thus, given the lack of empirical study on engagement and the lack, even within this subset, of studies that make use of predictive or longitudinal designs, one is forced to look beyond the strict realm of engagement to its related concepts in order to gain a feel for its potential to exist as a causal force in the determination of firm-level financial outcomes.

Direct Studies of Engagement: Recent work determined that engagement levels are predicted by perceived support granted to employees by the organization and that measures of engagement themselves predict levels of job satisfaction, commitment measures, intentions to quit, and positive behaviors within the organization. Additionally, in a meta-analysis of data collected by The Gallup Organization, Harter, *et al.* (2002) had similar findings, citing the strong effects employee satisfaction and engagement can have on turnover and levels of customer satisfaction and loyalty. A weaker, but practically significant, effect was also found between measures of engagement and satisfaction and business-level outcomes. In another meta-analytic study, there is a correlation between measures of attitudinal organizational commitment — defined as "the relative strength of an individual's identification with and involvement in a particular organization — and job performance. Interestingly, the strength of this correlation was found to be moderated by the type of data collected and was stronger when self ratings were used as compared to objective and supervisor-rated measures. Additionally, the role of managers with regard to employees' levels of engagement and determined that levels of manager self efficacy partially mediated the relationship. Taken as a whole, these studies reveal some key insights into the nature of engagement and its potential effects on the bottom line. Specifically, the antecedents and proximate effects of engagement appear to fall in line with the value-profit chain, lending credence to the extension of that model to employee engagement. From a theoretical standpoint, this provides some conceptual weight to the argument that engagement does have an effect on the bottom line for organizations — i.e., high engagement levels predict employee behaviors and other proximate organizational outcomes that can logically be connected to drivers of business success. However, some methodological considerations, especially those surrounding the issue of causality, also come to light.

Among these conditions is that of temporal precedence; for instance, superior levels of engagement must precede business performance and not the other way around. Indeed, the argument of reverse causality — that business success allows for more organizational slack in resources and more ample distribution of resources to employees, thus spurring greater investment in HR practices, under which policies facilitating employee engagement are subsumed — is one that is apparent with reliable frequency in academic publications. Additionally, some researchers have conjectured about the possibility of a reciprocal relationship — business success breeds investment in HR which breeds more business success, *ad infinitum*. Put more simply, HR systems for maximizing employee engagement do not appear overnight and thus, the antecedents to the existing system are necessarily included in current measures.

One way around this dilemma is to modify the methodology so as to create a study that employs longitudinal data and a predictive design that allows for a greater degree of certainty when making causal inferences. Several studies of concepts closely related to the subject of engagement have done just that and are examined below.

Longitudinal Analyses: While the relationships through which engagement appears to function within the organization are clarified by cross-sectional studies, the question of how engagement *causes* any significant quantifiable impacts when the annual financial statements are prepared remains unanswered. Unfortunately, there is a veritable lack of studies employing longitudinal analysis to examine the effects of engagement in the firm. Luckily, a substantial body of work examining closely related concepts and establishing their impact on financial performance measures is available. It should be noted, however, that these related concepts are not engagement *per se*, and therefore one must tread cautiously when attempting to draw conclusions about what these studies reveal about engagement, at least as it is formally defined in the small body of empirical literature that exists on the subject. Thus, the goal of the immediately following analysis is not to make any hard conclusions about whether engagement works or does not work, but rather to further clarify how engagement may or may not function as a causal factor with respect to a company's overall financial performance.

That said, the conclusions drawn by longitudinal studies regarding whether engagement-related factors predict market and financial performance rather than the other way around represent a mixed bag. For instance, in a study examining employee attitudes and organizational financial and market performance, Schneider and colleagues found that measures of job satisfaction and satisfaction with security were more strongly predicted by return on assets and earnings per share rather than the reverse. Additionally, the relationship between satisfaction with pay and the aforementioned financial measures was found to be reciprocal.

Other studies have also pointed to the ambiguities of determining the causal relationship between human resource management (HRM) practices and firm performance. The work of Guest and colleagues on HRM practices and their relation to turnover, productivity, and profitability indicated "a positive association between HRM and profitability" but with the qualification that the results did "not support the assumption that HRM led to higher profitability" Similarly, the results of Wright *et al.* (2005: 431) who analyzed HR practices and organizational commitment in the context of firm performance indicated "just as much support for the proposition that performance causes commitment and HR practices as it does the reverse."

CONCLUSION

To summarize thus far, the definition of engagement has been examined in order to better understand how it compares to related concepts of employee satisfaction, employee attitudes, affective (or attitudinal) organizational commitment, and OCB. From this point, the value-profit chain has been expanded to propose a means by which engagement generates positive effect for the firm with special attention paid to the potential for complex relationships between engagement and firm-level financial performance to emerge. Last, evidence supporting and detracting from the argument that engagement exhibits a positive causal influence on firm performance has been assessed.

In some sense, the answer to the latter question is yes. The concept of employee engagement, especially in a practical sense, borrows heavily from better defined, more mature ideas and measures of employee attitudes, satisfaction, and commitment. However, when the significant and growing body of anecdotal evidence of the positive effects of engagement is taken into account (e.g., Bates, 2004) along with the fact that "all things being equal, organizations with happy and committed employees outperform those with less happy and less committed employees" the potential for practical significance in terms of financial performance begins to grow.

Unfortunately, much of the literature that extols the virtues engagement holds for firm performance lacks the empirical rigor to actually prove engagement is responsible for them. Cross-sectional designs, however, reveal consistent positive correlations between engagement and positive proximal outcomes, which, according to theory significant potential for an engaged workforce to drive business success. Despite this, the role of engagement in directly causing increased business performance remains unproven even in the face of claims that increases on a scale measuring engagement levels will lead to specific monetary increases in revenues.

In considering the ambiguity of results generated from inquiries into concepts related to engagement and their causal influence on the bottom line, it is important to note that employee engagement as it is operationalized in a given firm is itself an HR practice and, as such, is subject to the same problems encountered when trying to prove that any HR practice causes any firm-level financial result. As the human resource strategies are likely to have their most direct effects on human resource outcomes, next greatest on organizational outcomes," and next, on financial outcomes

Continuing, the researchers note that "this reflects, in part, what strategies are designed to do and, in part, the complexity of factors which affect outcomes such as profitability, not to mention stock prices."

Thus, a picture of engagement as an important, but single, piece in the puzzle that is bottom-lining financial success emerges. Indeed, there appears to be an emerging recognition that engagement is a necessary, but not sufficient, condition for optimal business performance With respect to implications for practitioners, conjectures about what can be immediately done in the context of the issues discussed here are limited. Put more simply, an HR executive is going to have a much better idea of what will and will not work within his or her organization than any meta-analysis or consulting report. That said, any particular finding cannot be expected to grant sufficient basis for dismantling — or starting up — a program aimed at measuring or improving engagement levels within a given firm.

What can be suggested within the context of this discussion, and, to be sure, should be attempted by practitioner members of the HR field whenever and wherever possible, is to make a concerted effort to link engagement metrics with other metrics a given company tracks. By testing for correlations between engagement and other constructs measured within the firm — e.g., turnover/ retention, performance ratings, managerial quality, etc. — practitioners as well as members of the academic realm will finally be able to determine how engagement is operationalized within the firm and, perhaps, even discover a model of how, or if, it has significant causal influence upon bottom-line financial performance.

References

1. Barney, J. (1991), "Firm resources and sustained competitive advantage", *Journal of Management*, Vol.17 (1), pp. 99-120.
2. Bates, S. (2004), "Getting engaged", *HR Magazine*, Vol 49(2), pp. 44-51.
3. Baumruk, R., Gorman, Jr., B., & Gorman, R.E. (2006), "Why managers are crucial to increasing engagement: identifying steps managers can take to engage their workforce", *Strategic HR Review*, Vol. 5(2), pp. 24-27.
4. Carrig, K. & Wright, P.M. (2006), "Building profit through people: making your workforce the strongest link in the value-profit chain", *Alexandria, Virginia: Society for Human Resource Management.*
5. Cox, D.R. (1992), "Causality: some statistical aspects", *Journal of the Royal Statistical Society*, Vol. 155 (Part 2), pp. 291-301.
6. Dutton, G. (2006), "Engagement vs. satisfaction", *Human Resource Executive Online*, June 16, 2006.
7. Dyer, L. & Reeves, T. (1995), "Human resource strategies and firm performance: what do we need to know and where do we need to go?", *The International Journal of Human Resource Management*, Vol. 6(3), pp. 656-670.
8. Fulmer, I.S., Gerhart, B., & Scott, K.S. (2003), "Are the 100 best better? An empirical investigation of the relationship between being a "great place to work" and firm performance", *Personnel Psychology*, Vol. 56, pp. 965-993.

9. Guest, D.E., Michie, J., Conway, N., & Sheehan, M. (2003), "Human resource management and corporate performance in the UK", *British Journal of Industrial Relations*, Vol. 41(2), pp. 291-314.

10. Harter, J.K., Schmidt, F.L., & Hayes, T.L. (2002), "Business-unit-level relationship between employee satisfaction, employee engagement, and business outcomes: a meta-analysis", *Journal of Applied Psychology*, Vol. 87(2), pp. 268-279.

11. Harter, J.K., Schmidt, F.L., & Keyes, C.L. (2002), "Well-being in the workplace and its relationship to business outcomes: a review of the Gallup studies. In Keyes, C.L. & Hait, J. (Eds.), *Flourishing: the positive person and the good life* (pp. 205-224). Washington D.C.: *American Psychological Association.*

12. Heskett, J.L., Jones, T.O., Loveman, G.W., Sasser, Jr., W.E., & Schlesinger, L.A. (1994), "Putting the service-profit chain to work", *Harvard Business Review*, Vol. 72(2), p. 164.

13. Kahn, W.A. (1990), "Psychological conditions of personal engagement and disengagement at work", Academy *of Management Journal*, Vol. 33(4), pp. 692-724.

❖❖❖

19

Retention through Engagement

Sitanshu Sekhar Das

ABSTRACT

Retention is important because turnover is expensive. And loss of potential employees is having disastrous impact on the success and growth of the corporates. For many years there have been lot of hues and cry among the academicians, HR professionals and consultants regarding the issues of retention or turnover. Good numbers of researches have been conducted to find out the reason of turnover. Most of the research report says that lack of satisfaction, dedication; enthusiasm and loyalty among people compel them to quit their job. This kind of situation is technically known as burnout. But, what is the reason of burnout? The answer is, people are not engaged or they are disengaged. What do we mean by this engagement and disengagement? Engagement means involving in the organization showing enthusiasm for work, commitment, dedication and being aligned with organisational goals. Disengagement on the other hand means retreating both body and mind from the organization and the job performances. When people are actively involved in the job, committed to their organization then, they are satisfied. And when they aren't they show withdrawal behaviour, which ultimately leads to employee turnover. If disengagement is the reason of turnover, can this problem be solved through employee engagement? The present paper throws light on how employees can be retained through employee engagement.

Keywords: Employee engagement, Retention, Turnover, Burnout, Job involvement, Organizational commitment.

INTRODUCTION

In today's competitive world of business, corporates are in the war of talent. So, they always try to attract and retain talented manpower. So, retention is of prime concern for almost all the corporates for two reasons, one turnover is very expensive and second, corporates need talented people to grow and succeed. It is the talent of the employees which take the corporate to the greatest heights of success. Today's successful businesses win with innovative new ideas and top-notch products and services-all of which originate in the knowledge and skills of employees. So, no corporate want to lose their talented manpower. They always go on finding way to retain.

CONCEPT OF RETENTION

Retention can literally be defined as keeping something in possession. Here, employee retention simply means hanging on to the employees. Employee retention is a process of maintaining long term relationship with the employees. It is also defined as a process in which employees are encouraged to remain with the organization for the maximum period of time. Today employees have good opportunities in their hand. As soon as they feel dissatisfied with the current employer or the job, they switch over to the next job. Employee retention is more beneficial to the organization than to employees. Therefore, it is the responsibility of the employer to retain their best employees. If they don't, they would be left with no good employees. A good employer should know how to attract and retain its potential employees.

To retain employees and keep their satisfaction high, organizations must provide three Rs: respect, recognition, and rewards. Respect is esteem, special regard, or particular consideration given to people. Respect is the foundation of keeping employees. Recognition and rewards will have little effect if employees do not get respect. Recognition is special notice or attention and the act of perceiving clearly. Rewards are the extra perks offered beyond the basics of respect and recognition that make it worth people's while to work hard, to care, to go beyond the call of duty. While rewards represent the smallest portion of the retention equation, they are still an important one. Amongst the major reasons of employee turnover, the most important are: (a) salary; (b) lack of challenge; (c) lack of growth and promotional opportunities; (d) lack of recognition; (e) lack of trust in management; (f) lack of participation in the work team etc.

WHY RETENTION IS IMPORTANT?

Andrew Carnegie, a famous 19th century entrepreneur once opined: "Take away my people, but leave my factories and soon grass will grow on the factory floors... Take away my factories, but leave my people and soon we will have a new and better factory." This statement of Carnegie is very true and also holds good today. Employees are very valuable and seasoned and experienced employees especially can really bring a lot of value and added benefit to the business.

In this section focus is on importance of employee retention. Few among them are:

1. Retention is important because the organizations spend time and money on the recruitment, selection and training of employees. Organizations make them corporate ready material. When employees leave the organization immediately after recruitment and training, the organizations do not get any benefit out of investment they make. Recruiting employees consumes a great deal of time and effort. Bringing employees up to speed takes even more time. Various estimates suggest that losing a middle manager costs an organization up to 100 percent of his salary. The loss of a senior executive is even more costly. Employee retention also cut costs on recruitment, training, etc.
2. Through retention organizations maintain a knowledgebase. In the current "Knowledge Era," intellectual capital is what defines a company's competitive edge. Intellectual capital is the unique knowledge and skills that a company's work force possesses. Today's successful businesses win with innovative new ideas and top-notch products and services-all of which originate in the knowledge and skills of employees. Employees are now considered as intellectual capital, and they are very important for the organization's survival and growth.

3. Employees are retained either they are satisfied with the job or organization or both. Employees who are satisfied are more likely to create satisfied customers as they speak positively and act positively.
4. Employee retention also leads to higher productivity among the employees, as the employees who are retained are highly satisfied. Again it is well known that happy employees can only give heavy production or there is positive correlation between satisfaction and productivity. As employees stay longer in a particular organization, they tend to develop their skills and knowledge to achieve higher positions during their stay with the organization.
5. Employee retention brings stability to the organization. When a group of employees are retained for a longer period of time, they strongly hold the mission and vision of the organization and act in a sustainable manner and the newer employees are encouraged and build confidence to maintain the healthy working condition.
6. As the retained employees work for longer period of time develops an environment of collaboration, which creates a sense of connection through shared experiences, responsibility which ultimately leads to company's success.
7. Employee retention is critically important for another reason. Over the next few years while Baby Boomers (age 40 to 58) will retire, the upcoming Generation X population numbers 44 million people (ages 25-34), compared to 76 million Baby Boomers available for work. Simply stated, there will be lot fewer people available to work.

CONCEPT OF EMPLOYEE ENGAGEMENT

William A. Kahn is the pioneer who conceptualized engagement and defined personal engagement in his article, "Psychological Conditions of Personal Engagement And Disengagement At Work" (1990) as the harnessing of organization members' selves to their work roles; in engagement, people employ and express themselves physically, cognitively, and emotionally during role performances. Employee engagement is the heightened emotional and intellectual connection that an employee has for his/her job, organization, manager, or co-workers that, in turn, influences him/her to apply additional discretionary effort to his/her work' (Gibbons, 2006). Schaufeli, Salanova, *et al.,* (2002) defined engagement as a persistent and positive affective-motivational state of fulfilment in employees, characterized by vigor, dedication, and absorption. According to Schaufeli, Salanova, *et al.*, (a) vigor is high energy, resilience, a willingness to invest effort on the job, the ability to not be easily fatigued, and persistence when confronted with difficulties; (b) dedication is a strong involvement in work, enthusiasm, and sense of pride and inspiration; and (c) absorption is a pleasant state of being immersed in one's work, experiencing time passing quickly, and being unable to detach from the job. Maslach & Leiter, (2008) identified engagement as the antipode to the negative state of burnout. Employee engagement refers to the individual's involvement and satisfaction with as well as enthusiasm for work" (Harter *et al.*, 2002). "A distinct and unique construct that consists of cognitive, emotional, and behavioural components those are associated with individual role performance" (Saks, 2006).

Employee engagement is the commitment of the employees towards the organization and their involvement in the job and in the organization. It's the employees' willingness and ability to know and to do contribute towards the company success. An engaged employee is aware of business context, and works with others to improve performance within the job for the benefit of the organization. It is a positive attitude held by the employees towards the organization and its goals and values. Engagement has been used to refer to a psychological state (e.g., involvement, commitment, attachment, mood), performance construct (e.g., either effort or observable behaviour, including pro-social and organizational citizenship behaviour), disposition (e.g., positive affect), or some combination of the above. Wellins and Concelman (2005) suggested that engagement is "an amalgamation of commitment, loyalty, productivity and ownership." Personal engagement is the simultaneous employment and expression of a person's "preferred self" in task behaviours that promote connections to work and to others, personal presence (physical, cognitive, and emotional), and active, full role performances. Full engagement occurs at the alignment of maximum job satisfaction (I like my work and do it well) and maximum job contribution (I help achieve the goals of my organization), (Employee Engagement Report, 2011, BlessingWhite).

Engagement is closely associated with the existing construction of job involvement and organizational commitment (Sharma Baldev R. and Raina Anupama, 2010). Job involvement is defined as the degree to which a person identifies with his/her job, actively participates in it and considers his/her performance important to self-worth. Job involvement is a 'Cognitive or belief state of psychological identification. (Kanungo, 1982). Vroom (1964) defines job involvement as the degree to which employee perceives that his/her job performance is consistent with the characteristics that are central to his/her self-concept. Lodahl and Kejner (1965) defined job-involvement as the degree to which a person is identified psychologically with his work, or the importance of work in his total self-image. Organisational commitment is the degree to which an employee identifies with a particular organisation and its goals, and wishes to maintain membership in the organisation. Bateman and Strasser (1984) state that organizational commitment has been operationally defined as "multidimensional in nature, involving an employee's loyalty to the organization, willingness to exert effort on behalf of the organization, degree of goal and value congruency with the organization, and desire to maintain membership. Organizational commitment refers to a strong belief in and acceptance of the organization's goals and values; a willingness to exert considerable effort on behalf of the organization; and a strong desire to maintain membership in the organization' (Mowday, Steers, & Porter, 1979).

The above discussion on the concept of employee engagement describes it as the intellectual and emotional commitment and rational commitment that an employee has to his/her work and organization. Emotional commitment is the extent to which the employee derives enjoyment, meaning, pride or inspiration from something or someone in the organization. Rational commitment is the extent to which an employee feels that someone or something within the company provides developmental, financial or professional rewards in employee's best interests. That is, employee engagement involves both rational and emotional factors- what employees think (the mind) and feel (the heart) about their work and organization. Rational factors involve the relationship that employees have with the broader organization such as having the resources, tools, and support they need to perform their jobs. Rationally engaged employees understand how their work contributes to the success of the organization and have a clear line of sight between their roles and company objectives. In contrast, emotional factors refer to the sense of inspiration and accomplishment that employees get from their work and by being a member of the firm. Emotionally engaged employees feel inspired to do their best, are passionate about their work, and recommend their company as a good place to work. Simply put, engaged employees are intellectually stimulated and emotionally inspired. They have the tools needed to perform their jobs, are advocates of their organizations, have a desire to stay with their employers, and willingly "go the extra mile" for their organizations when needed.

Employee engagement refers to a situation where all the employees are engaged in their own work and take keen interest in the organization's activities.

How Engagement Retains Employees?

An engaged employee is one who is focussed, enjoys his/her work and learns something new each day. Engaged employees are not just committed, passionate or proud, they are enthused and in gear. They use their knowledge, skills and abilities for their self-growth as well as for the growth of the organization. Engaged employees stay with the company, be advocates of the company and its products and services, and contribute to bottom line business success. Engaged employees are satisfied with their work and never think of quitting the job. They willingly accept responsibilities and looks forward towards a long term association with the organization.

Employees leave job because they don't find their job challenging. Unchallenging work is one of the major reasons as to why an employee decides to move on. Employees who are delegated responsibilities as per their specializations and background deliver hundred percent when they do something which interests them. Problems crop up when individuals have nothing creative and challenging to do.

Engaged employees always stay motivated in their current assignments and do not look for opportunities outside. People engaged in their work strive hard to deliver their level best and live up to the expectations of the management every time. They look forward towards achieving the organization's targets and thus making it one of the best places to work. This attitude of the employees compels the management to reward and recognise employees properly which make them stay longer.

As the one of the famous proverbs says "an empty mind is a devil's workshop". In the same way, idle employees are the ones who loiter around and spread negativity all over the workplace. Individuals who do nothing at workplace spoil their time by gossiping around and badmouthing their organization. They always talk negative about the management and encourage others to leave the organization. So, when these people can be engaged in their job, when they find their job interesting they hate to spend unproductively. As they are both emotionally and rationally involved in their job they also encourage others by helping them to see the positive or brighter side of the organization.

As most of the people opine, organizations which are free from politics and having a stress free environment and good organizational climate are the best place to work. Individuals are reluctant to leave when they enjoy a cordial relation with their colleagues. Employees who are busy with their work stays away from nasty politics, backstabbing and thus maintain the decorum of the office. Such employees do not really get time for controversies. Everyone expects a stress free environment at workplace and tends to leave only when there are constant disputes. An engaged employee does not get time to participate in unproductive tasks instead finishes his assignments on time and benefits the organization and thus making the organization the best place to work.

Engagement helps employees enjoy the job by doing it. When they do it, they feel the "pride of workmanship", which the quality advocate W. Edwards Deming referred as intrinsic motivation. This intrinsic motivation binds employees with the organization.

Engagement gives employees autonomy - the freedom and independence the job holder has, including discretion to make decisions, exercise choice, schedule the work and decide on the procedures to carry it out, and the job holder's personal responsibility for outcomes.

Employee engagement results in great deal of teamwork/collaboration and support amongst the employees. One of the major reasons of employee turnover is lack of teamwork and support of the co-workers. But, when people get all these they hate to leave the company of the colleagues for two reasons; one, they enjoy their company; second, they learn a lot for their self-development and growth.

CONCLUSION

Employee Engagement is the buzz word for organizations these days. Every organization aspire to become successful and focus on becoming truly great places to work and on developing & retaining future generations of happy employees. Happy employees are individuals who are genuinely challenged, dedicated, committed as they are engaged. Employee engagement is the positive attitude held by the employees towards the organization and its values. Employee engagement appears to be good for any organization as it enables it to retain its potential employees. Not only, employee engagement leads to employee retention, it may be a key to competitive advantage for the organization.

References:

1. American Society for Training & Development. (2011) "Employee Engagement Correlates to Career Advancement and Training", T+D.
2. Bateman, T. & Strasser, S. (1984), "A longitudinal analysis of the antecedents of organizational commitment". Academy of Management Journal, 21.
3. Bhatnagar, J. (2007), "Talent management strategy of employee engagement in Indian ITES employees: key to retention", Employee Relations, Vol. 29 No. 6.
4. Bhatnagar, Jyotsna & Biswas, Soumendu, (2010), "Predictors & Outcomes of Employee Engagement: Implications for the Resource-based View Perspective", The Indian Journal of Industrial Relations, Vol. 46, No. 2.
5. BlessingWhite (2011), "Employee Engagement Report, 2011" , BlessingWhite Inc., USA.
6. Cook, Sarah (2008), "The essential guide to Employee engagement", Kogan Page, UK.
7. Federman, Brad (2009), "Employee engagement: a roadmap for creating profits, optimizing performance, and increasing loyalty", Jossey-Bass, USA.
8. Gallup Management Journal (2006), 12 January, available at: http://gmj.gallup.com
9. Kahn, W.A. (1992), "Psychological Conditions of Personal Engagement And Disengagement At Work", Academy of Management Journal, 33(4).
10. Kanungo, R. N. (1982), Measurement of job and work involvement. Journal of Applied Psychology, 67.
11. Kelleher, Bob. (2011), "Employee Engagement and Retention", MWorld Spring, American Management Association.
12. Lodahl, T. M., & Kejner, M. (1965), "The definition and measurement of job involvement", Journal of Applied Psychology, 49.
13. Macey, W.H., & Schneider, B. (2008), "The meaning of employee engagement", Industrial and Organizational Psychology, 1.
14. Markos, Solomon & Sandhya Sridevi, M. (2010), "Employee Engagement: The Key to Improving Performance", International Journal of Business and Management Vol. 5, No. 12.

15. May, D. R., Gilson, R. L., & Harter, L. M. (2004), "The psychological conditions of meaningfulness, safety and availability and the engagement of the human spirit at work", Journal of Occupational and Organizational Psychology, Vol.-77.
16. Mowday, R . T, Portr, L W., & Stffers, R . M. (1982), "Employee-organizational linkages: The psychology of commitment, absenteeism and turnover", Academic Press, New York.
17. Schaufeli, W. B., Salanova, M., González-Roma, V., & Bakker, A. B. (2002), "The measurement of engagement and burnout: A two-sample confirmatory factor analytic approach." Journal of Happiness Studies, 3.
18. Schaufeli, W.B. and Bakker, A.B. (2004), "Job demands, job resources, and their relationship with burnout and engagement: a multi-sample study", Journal of Organizational Behavior, Vol. 25, pp. 293-315.
19. Shankar,Tara & Bhatnagar, Jyotsna.(2010), "Work Life Balance, Employee Engagement, Emotional Consonance/Dissonance & Turnover Intention", The Indian Journal of Industrial Relations, Vol. 46, No. 1.
20. SHRM Conference (2006), "Leveraging Employee Engagement for Competitive Advantage", Vol. 15.
21. Sree Lakshmi, M., Srinivas, K. & Krishna,KVR. (2010), "Employee engagement for talent retention with reference to the Academicians", Review Of Business Research, Volume 10.
22. Wellins, R. & Concelman, J. (2005), "Creating a culture for engagement", Workforce Performance Solutions (www.wpsmag.com).

❖ ❖ ❖

20 Employee Engagement : In The Indian Context

Namita Rath
Sujata Rath

ABSTRACT

A successful employee engagement strategy helps create a community at the work place and not just a workforce. When employees are effectively and positively engaged with their organization, they form an emotional connection with the company. This affects their attitude towards both their colleges and the company's clients and improves customer satisfaction and service levels. Employee engagement plays a greater role in the current era where every contribution by the employees counts. Employee engagement programmes are important as they help to align the human activities to the company strategy. Employee engagement also expects the management to nourish a healthy environment within the entity. Employee engagement can be measured using surveys, attrition rates, number of referrals made and growth in the business.

This paper deals with employee engagement issues, steps to be taken for fully engaged employee and benefits of fully engaged employees.

INTRODUCTION

The Wikipedia defines: "Employee engagement also called work engagement or worker engagement, is a business management concept. An engaged employee is one who is fully involved in and enthusiastic about his or her work and thus will out in a way that furthers their organizations interests. According to Scarlett Surveys, "Employee Engagement is a measurable degree of an employee's positive or negative emotional attachment to their job, colleagues and organization which profoundly influences their willingness to learn and perform at work. Thus engagement is distinctively different from satisfaction, motivation, culture, climate and opinion and very difficult to measure."

THE BIRTH OF THE CONCEPT

It began in the 1920s and owes its origins to the US army during World War-II. In the postwar mass production society that required unity of effort in execution (group) morale scores were used as predictors of speed, quality and militancy. With the adment of the knowledge worker and emphasis on individual talent management (stars) a term was needed to describe an individual's emotional attachment to the organization, fellow associates and the job.

A modernized version of job satisfaction, Schmidt et al's influential definition of engagement was "an employee's involvement with, commitment to and satisfaction with work". This integrates the classic constructs of job satisfaction (Smith *et al*; 1969) and organization (Meyer & Allen, 1991).

According to Ron Schmidt. "Engaged employees produce more, make more money for the company, and create emotional engagement and loyal customers. They contribute to good working environments here people are productive, ethical and accountable. They stay with the organization longer and more committed to equality and growth tan non engaged or disengaged workers. Employee who feel disconnected emotionally from their co-workers and supervisors do not feel committed to their work. They hang back and do the minimum because they don't believe anyone cares. These employees lower bar for themselves by doing the least amount of work necessary".

The success of almost every corporate initiative depends on employee engagement the desire and commitment of employees to go extra mile. There are four pillars on which rests a strong foundation for a constructive employee engagement and a successful organization.

First, employees want to know that their company has and their leaders says vision and a strategy. Second, they want to have both a clear idea of their own responsibilities and the tools and authority to achieve them. Third they expect to receive recognition and rewards for their workplace performance. Finally, desire to work for a supervisor who understands and motivates them.

The picture below depicts a good employee engagement model:

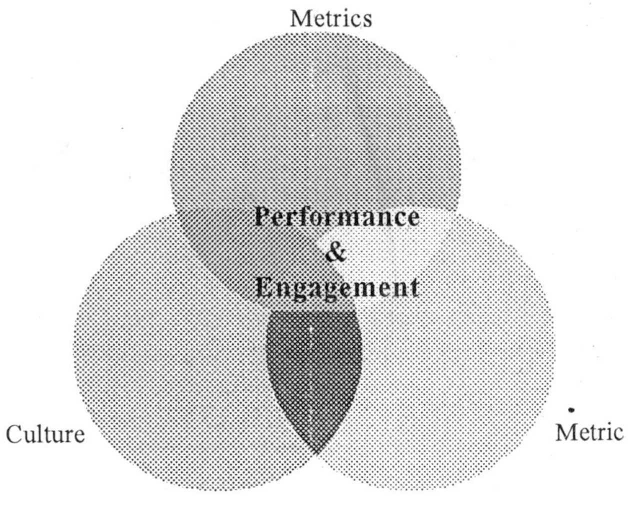

Source: http://retention.naukrichub.com/increaseemployee-engagement.html

The points that will help us understand the concept better.

A Good Culture: It comprises the values, vision, a strong foundation of leadership, effective communication, a strategic plan and an employee focused' HR policy. Providing the required resources for accomplishing their task and empowering them as well. Factors that are essential to the organization's performance are measured. These metrics will encourage people to get the desired result and that is how it ultimately leads to a great level of trust, pride, satisfaction, success and also fun at work.

IMPORTANCE OF EMPLOYEE ENGAGEMENT

It has been proved by research that committed employees always perform better. The strongest driver is of course the feeling of being valued and involved. The factors are:

(i) Involvement in decision making.

(ii) The extent to which employees feel able to voice their ideas better and managers pay attention to them and the employees contribution is also valued.

(iii) The scope employees get to improve their jobs.

(iv) And the organizations concern about the general well being and health of its employees.

The role of recognizing employees has been significantly under rated as an important driver of business success, profitability, and perform in most organizations. According to research, 99.4 per cent of today's employees expect to be recognized when they also good work, while other research has found that only 12 per cent of employees strongly agree that they are consistently recognized in a way that are important to them and nearly three times as may (34 per cent) disagree or strongly disagree that they are recognized in way that are meaningful to them. In addition, employees who do receive recognition where they work are:

5 Times more likely to feel valued

6 times more likely to invest in the company

7 times more likely to stay with the company

11 times more likely to fell completely committed.

According to research conducted by Towers Perrin committed employees have been shown to deliver 57 per cent more effort than uncommitted ones.

The link between employee recognition and employee engagement, satisfaction and loyalty has also become clear in recent year. Recognition is a significant driver of employee engagement, and engaged satisfied employees lead to increased customer satisfaction, greater customer loyalty and profitability, thus enhanced bottom – line success for the organization.

SUCCESS AND CHALLENGES OF EMPLOYEE ENGAGEMENT

Employee engagement depends on the organizations culture, the employees jobs, and the employees themselves (Wildermuth & Wildermuth 2008). It is the combination of how these categories come together that will lead in the end to the greatest level of engagement.

More than half of workers who suffer from stress cite lack of support or employee engagement as a main factor behind their problems according to a survey.

Research from the Mental Health Foundation found that 60 per cent of those who identified work as the source of their stress said that support was not forthcoming from basses. A further 20 percent claimed that they work had become stressed because they felt their work was going unnoticed by employers. The study also highlighted issue over staff retention, with 16 per cent of employees fearing that they would lose their jobs.

IES representative suggests financial reward does not need to be the only motivational technique utilized by managers. Dilys Robinson, principal research fellow at the organization, suggested non financial benefits are capable of going "a long way". She claimed an extra day's holiday or a letter from a senior manager could deliver some degree of motivation for a disgruntled employee when there is no money available for a pay rise.

In her opinion, one of the vital aspects of an employer's relationship with their staff is that communication channels are clear.

"Employees are realistic and know they can't expect large financial rewards. However, they do expect to be valued for their contribution by the organization", said Ms. Robinson.

According to Ferdinand F. Fournies in his book Why Employees Don't Do What They're supposed to do and what to do about it he lists a few reasons :

1. They don't know why they should do it.
2. They don't know how to do it.
3. They don't know what they are supposed to do.
4. They thin your way will not work.
5. They think their way is better.
6. They think something else is more important.
7. There is no positive consequence to them for doing it.
8. They think they are doing it.
9. They are rewarded for not doing it.
10. They are punished for doing what they are supposed to do.
11. They anticipate a negative consequence for doing it.
12. There is no negative consequence to them for poor performance.
13. Obstacles beyond their control.
14. Their personal limits prevent them from performing.
15. Personal problems
16. No one could it.

According to a survey conducted by Akron's Centre for organizational Research, low engaged employees tend to have the following characteristics.

1. **Dissatisfaction:** Low engaged employees tend to be highly dissatisfied with their jobs.
2. **Employee attrition:** One can expect high level of high attrition.
3. **Tolerance:** Employees ability to handle or tolerate economic uncertainty is minimal.
4. **Inconstancy:** Employees are unable to bring a high level of loyalty, creativeness and energy to their jobs.

Impact of Low Engaged Employees on Organization

1. The organization loses its top talent: During economic hardship, investing in employee engagement is best way to retain. Smart, top and talented employees or there will be an exodus of such assets.
2. Negative impact on organizational success: Looking into employee engagement as a strategy is not only essential for organizational success but vital for long term organizational viability. So, if there is low employee engagement it is likely to have a negative impact on organizational success.

Therefore it is important for the leadership in any organization to align the objectives of employees to its corporate objectives.

Steps for Effective Employment Engagement

The team leader should understand his members well and need not assign anything which the employee would not find interesting.

Effective communication enhances employee management if there is transparency in communication at all the levels and everyone is aware of what is happening around him.

The management must constantly motivate his employees through cash prizes, trophies, gift vouchers, certificates which is an effective way to motivate the employees and keep them engaged in their work. If manager give them a target and ask them to achieve that within a particular time frame to earn handsome incentives or lucrative prizes the employees would not waste their time, rather spend their maximum time working and aiming for the rewards.

The team leader or the manager must be friendly with the team. Let them go back on time and enjoy their personal live well. Rejuvenation is essential for an individual to remain happy and stress free. Encourage team members to think out of the box.

In addition, there needs to be a sense of camaraderie and support amongst employees understanding how the organization's culture can influence the level of which one feels engaged is key to creating a work environment that harnesses engaging energy. Understanding individual difference and the different needs of the different individuals is critical for HR professionals to make a successful match. Only when the right people are matched with the right companies and job roles will they experience optimal levels of management. The graph below shows engaged employees are 4 times more likely to have a good understanding of customer needs (70%) than non engaged employees (19%)

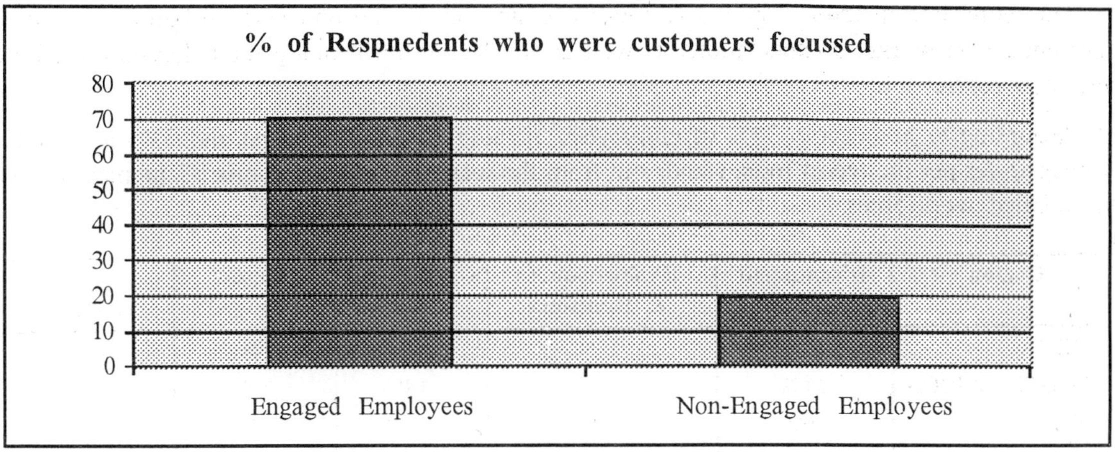

Source: *http://www.righmanagement.com.an*

This reflects customer retention as well. Higher engagement levels has higher customer retention as well.

It leads to a member of success factors such as :

1. Employee performance/efficiency
2. Productivity
3. Safety
4. Attendance & retention
5. Customer service and satisfaction
6. Customer loyalty and retention
7. Profitability.

EMPLOYEE ENGAGEMENT IN INDIA

Employee engagement relies upon aligning the employees interests and goals to that of the organization, which means identifying and satisfying the employees interests as much as the organization while aligning both together. Once they are aligned employee motivation to achieve the organization's goals and objectives becomes stronger.

According to a study done by Blessing white (a global consulting firm, based in Princeton, NJ, USA) in collaboration with HR Anexi (a leading Indian Human Capital Consulting firm in Mumbai) carried out between January 2008 and March 2008. Indian workforce is more focused an helping the organization they work for achieve its goals.

The Study Found That:

In comparison to workers in Asia – Pacific, Europe or North America, Indian, employees enjoy higher levels of job satisfaction and connect more strongly with the objectives of their organization.

The workforce in India also enjoys more buoyant job market and wage inflation. This has a direct impact on worker's expectations as well as the factors influencing their decision to stay or leave their correct job.

According to hranei.com 34% of employees in India are fully engaged and 13% are actually disengaged. As per the report India stands out from the world population as one of the most focused and satisfied workforces.

Region	Disengaged	Honeymooners & Hamsters	Crash & Bum	Almost engaged	Fully engaged
INDIA	13%	13%	11%	29%	34%
SOUTH AFRICA	11%	14%	18%	26%	31%
NA	19%	12%	13%	27%	29%
AUNZ	20%	18%	12%	24%	26%
EUROPE	21%	15%	13%	28%	23%
SEA	21%	9%	18%	31%	22%
CHINA	33%	9%	16%	32%	10%
OTHER	36%	7%	7%	27%	24%
GRAND TOTAL	18%	12%	13%	28%	29%

Source: *http://www.pranexi.com/Employee Engagement_report_2008.pdf*

Segment	Description	General Engagement Strategy
The Engaged High Contribution and High Satisfaction	These employees are at the open. They contribute strongly to the success of the organization and find great satisfaction in their work.	Sustain the level of engagement in the long term.
Almost engaged : Medium to high contribution and satisfaction	These employees are among the high performer and are reasonably satisfied with their current job.	Organizations should invest in item for : (i) They are highly employable. (ii) These employees have the shortest distance to travel to reach full engagement.
Honeymooners and Hamsters : Medium to high satisfaction but low contribution	Honeymooners are new to the organization or their role and are happy to be there. Hamster are more tenured individuals who may perceive themselves as contribution strongly out contribute little to the success of the organization.	Clarify objectives and expectations provide feedback.

Crash and Burn : Medium to high contribution but low satisfaction	Disillusioned and potentially exhausted, these employees are top producers but become bitter due to a lack of personal satisfaction	Provide coaching and support. Recognize efforts
The disengaged Low to Medium contribution and satisfaction	Most skeptical of any organization priorities and are not getting what they need from work.	Spell out expectation and provide opportunity to take on more challenging work. Failing that facilitate exit from the organization.

Source: *http://www.hranexi.com/employee_engagement_report_2008.pdf.*

According to Accenture Research Report : "The High Performance workforce study 2007 – India".

"The key talent management challenge for Indian companies is how to keep workforces highly productive and at the same time satisfied engaged and committed".

One of the reason behind this success is the trust people reposit in their managers and senior leadership. The critical conversations that help in engaging employees must come from a source they trust. In India people higher up in the organization experience higher levels of engagement as they are closer to the centres of decision making, have more say in the direction of the organization. As per the blessing white and hranexi survey – the factors influencing satisfaction are as follows:

	Career development opportunities and training	More challenging work	More opportunities to do what I do best	Greater clarity about my work performs and career goals	Greater clarity about what the organization needs me to do and why	Improved cooperation among my co workers	More say in how may work gets done	A better relationship with my managers
INDIA	30.03%	20.09%	19.33%	10.74%	7.71%	4.47%	4.04%	3.58%
Grand Total	28.22%	12.24%	23.08%	9.80%	8.28%	7.39%	5.43%	4.82%

Source: *http://www.hranexi.com/employee_engagement_report_2008.pdf*

As per the data, the Indian working population lists there items as important to their satisfaction in their work place:

1. Career development opportunities and training 30%.
2. More challenging work 20%
3. More opportunities to do what I do best 19%.

The same survey came out with factors influencing contribution.

	Development and training opportunities	Regular specific feedback about how I am doing	Greater clarity about what the organization needs me to do and why	Better communication with my manager	More resources	A better r relationship with my co-workers	A coarch for a mentor other than my managers
INDIA	26.28%	25.32%	21.74%	7.41%	7.25%	7.25%	4.76%
G.Total	20.35%	20.34%	18.54%	6.77%	17.78%	4.81%	11.41%

Source: *http"//www.hranexi.com/employee_engagement_report_2008.pdf*

Again the top three items for Indian workers match the top three global requests, but the pattern is even more pronounced in India with a clear top 3 :

- Development opportunities and training 26%
- Regular, specific feedback about how I am doing 25%
- Greater clarity about what the organization needs me to do and why 22%

CONCLUSION

The overall work environment in Indian organization seems to be conducive as per this report. Employees are not only extrinsically rewarded but also intrinsically. They trust their leaders as they have a say in matters pertaining to decision making and have opportunities for further career development and growth. It goes on to prove that Indian organization understand the basic needs of their employees recognize their good work and respect individuals and also offer opportunities for further development. Employees get to work in an environment which gives them time, resources and budget and feel safe when they get the cooperation of their seniors and colleagues.

References:

1. www.wikepedia.com
2. http://www.hranexi.com/employee_engagement_report_2008.pdf.
3. ICE SURVEY, 2003
4. http://retention.naukrihub.com/increase_employee_engagement.html.
5. http://www.rightmanagement.com.an
6. http://www.chrmglobal.com
7. http://blog.commlabindia.com. The drawbacks of how Employee Engagement by Asma Zaineb
8. http://www.the britfieldgroup.com/_blog/insight_from_britfield/post/the_importance_of_recongization_and_employee_engagement
9. http://blog.taigacompany.com/blog/increasing_employee_engagement
10. http://www.youatwork.com/128/section.aspx/618lack_of_employee_engagement_causes_setress.
11. http://www.lectrasoft.com/boost_your_confidence/blog/do9

❖❖❖

21

Work Culture and Effective Employee Engagement: The Strategic Initiatives

Prof. Ajit Kumar Sahoo,
Dr. Chandan Kumar Sahoo,
Dr. Santosh Kumar Tripathy,
Mr. Chandrakanta Sahoo

ABSTRACT

The challenge today is not just retaining talented people in the organization, but fully engaging and nurturing them at each stage of their work lives. Now-a-days, in this competitive business environment, a positive work culture leads to employee engagement which has emerged as a critical driver of business success. The concept, employee engagement is influenced by many factors of the organizational work culture, which can be augmented by various employee related factors such as, effective communication, shared decision making, mutual co-operation, employee development, career advancement etc. Employee engagement is indeed a concept which if implemented properly makes a lot of sense. It is a simple idea rationalizing the fact that the engagement and commitment of employees towards their work and organization can make a huge difference. High levels of employee engagement promote employee loyalty, retention of talent, improved organizational performance, increased productivity and organisational success.

Keywords: Work culture, Employee engagement, Principles, Strategy.

INTRODUCTION

In the post globalization scenario, employee engagement (EE) is a pivotal mechanism for nurturing a high performance culture to drive the organization towards success. EE is about building a truly great relationship with the workforce. Any organization that embraces fine management philosophy, recognition of employees' talent, potential and is committed to providing enriching professional experiences is bound to succeed. So EE is directly link with company's growth and development and contribute towards the core competencies of a successful organization. Any employee who is not engaged in their respective jobs strategically, the first thing that affects organizational productivity. The more engaged an employee is, the more is his commitment level towards making a plan more successful in a significant way. So that each of the employee should think like the strategic business partner of the business process. So that success is very important for our own growth and development and that of our organization. Engaged employees do not look for organizational support in each and every step of the way. They are self-starters and believe in supporting the organization in all its endeavours. EE have some merits such as self-starters and believe in supporting the organization, motivates co-workers, work with passion and better performance, gets better aligned to organizational goals and leads to productivity and profitability for sustainability. It is all about giving an employee a bonded eco-system to work in, wherein he shares a common goal, belief and values with the team, with each member having a clear understanding of the goals. Employees should get opportunities to put their knowledge, skills and abilities (KSA) to prove themselves. It's about giving employees a work culture where they are free to take up initiatives.

The challenge today is not just developing and retaining talented people, but fully engaging and nurturing them at each stage of their work lives. In the fast changing business environment the growing global economy has forced many organizations to redefine their ways of operations in order to sustain and survive. They need to get their business wheel move speedily to improve their performance to remain competitive in the market in which they operate. Now-a-days, in this competitive business environment, a positive work culture leads to employee engagement which has emerged as a critical driver of business success.

Theoretical Background

Employee engagement is a relatively recent developed concept in human resource management and a mantra for today's workplace and leading organizations to recognize the vested interest for measuring, monitoring and maximizing the level of engagement amongst the employees and ensuring it is not left to chance. It is defined as the level to which employees are fully involved in their work, committed to their work, care about their organization and colleagues and are willing to extend themselves and go the extra mile for their company to ensure its success. The Conference Board of USA (2006) publication describes employee engagement as a heightened emotional connection that an employee feels for his or her organization that influences him or her to exert greater discretionary effort to his or her work. Employee engagement matters as it impacts on companies' bottom lines, both through human resource (HR) related impacts (such as recruitment and retention) and through wider impacts on productivity, profit and achieving the core values, envisioned future and objectives of the organization. According to the Institute of Employment Studies (IES) has defined engagement as a positive attitude held by employees towards the organization and its values. An 'engaged employee' is aware of the business context, and works with colleagues to improve the performance within the job for the benefit of the organization. The organization must work to develop and nurture engagement, which requires a two-way relationship between employer and employee. EE is a combination of organizational aspects like individual commitment, organizational citizenship behaviour (OCB) and employee motivation. It is a real challenge (Wash, 1999). The argument is that an engaged employee works with passion and is more committed to the organization. In the other words it is the extent to which people enjoy and believe in what they do and feel valued by doing it. It is the degree of commitment towards the hub which an employee performs and till how long the employee remains with the organization as a result of their commitment (Mahendru and Sharma, 2006).

In the changing global market, competition and managing change over a period of time the strategy of an organization has changed from just promoting the knowledge worker to increase EE. Employee engagement and organizational performance are highly interlinked (Concelman, 2005). He further states that engaged employee try harder, contribute more, speak positively about the organization, and stay longer. The trend shows that almost all of the companies explore the possibilities for adopting employee engagement as a strategy for human resource planning (HRP). Harter (2002) examined the relationship at the business unit productivity and employee engagement and noticed that the 'engaged employee' are satisfied employees, which in turn leads to higher productivity. According to Erickson (2004), the best ways to shape the behaviour of an employee towards work is to improve employee engagement. The Corporate Leadership Council (CLC) defines 'engagement' as 'the extent of employees' commitment, work effort, and desire to stay in an organization'. Stockley (2006) defined 'engagement' as the extent that an employee believes in the mission, purpose and values of an organization and demonstrates that commitment through their actions as an employee and their attitude towards the employer and customers. An institution's ability in providing psychological safety such as good support from the supervisors and rewarding system has a positive relationship with employee engagement, job enrichment and work role (May *et al.*, 2004). Value of assessment and taking feedback of employees has been followed as practical strategy for employee engagement according to Glen (2006). He further adds that work environment is a better predictor in this direction. McCashland (1999) defined employee engagement as 'commitment or engagement - an emotional outcome to the employee resulting from the critical components of the workplace. Miles (2001) described it as intensively involving all employees in high-engagement cascades that create understanding, dialogue, feedback and accountability, empower people to creatively align their subunits, teams and individual jobs with the major transformation of the whole enterprise.

Fostering Employee Engagement

Employee engagement has been described as 'a positive, two-way relationship between employees and their organizations where both parties are aware of their own and the other's needs, and support each other to fulfil these needs. Engaged employees and organizations go the extra mile, and both reap mutual benefits (Daniel, 2004). Gibson (2006) has defined employee engagement as "a heightened emotional connection that an employee feels for his or her organization, that influences him or her to exert greater discretionary effort to his or her work". Gallup Consulting (2008) describes employee engagement as "the extent to which employees are psychologically connected to something or someone in the organization". High levels of employee engagement are associated with high levels of organizational performance (Soladati, 2007). A lack of employee engagement can lead to disloyalty and organizational failure (Khan, 2007). In addition, the Involvement and Participation Association (2007) has found that there are five key steps to engagement:

1. Bring employees closer to strategic decisions made by senior management.
2. Creating buy into the strategic decision.
3. The what, the why and the what else? (Dealing with suspicion.)
4. Continued improvement in employee satisfaction and building trust.
5. Create a positive and credible employee voice in a culture where employees want to contribute and get involved.

The key drivers of employee engagement in organizations will help to create a road map for achieving organizational excellence. In order to achieve the organizational effectiveness and drive the organization forward, EE helps to drive value and optimize the resources properly. A work of the Conference Board a major US organization reflected twelve major studies on employee engagement. Each of the study has used different dimensions and, collectively, came up with 26 key drivers of engagement. But out of all the 26 key drivers the Conference Board's synthesis were 8 key drivers of EE (figure 1).

Principles of Employee Engagement

Review of literature confirms that engaged work places compared with least engaged are much more likely to have lower employee turnover, higher than average customer loyalty, above average productivity and earnings. These are all good things that prove that engaging and involving employees make good business sense and building shareholder value. Negative workplace relationships may be a big part of why so many employees are not engaged with their jobs. Employee engagement needs to be measured at regular intervals in order to track its contribution to the success of the organization. But measuring the engagement (feedback through surveys) without planning how to handle the result can lead employees to disengage. The macro-level organizational practices that make up the HR value chain provide the context in which an engaged workforce can develop. However, if these organizational practices are not reinforced at the micro-level, employee engagement may still be lacking. Thus, the micro-level practices may be even more important than the macro practices which are helping to build organizational climate for workforce engagement. The key employee engagement principles based on micro-level practices for organizational effectiveness are given in table 1.

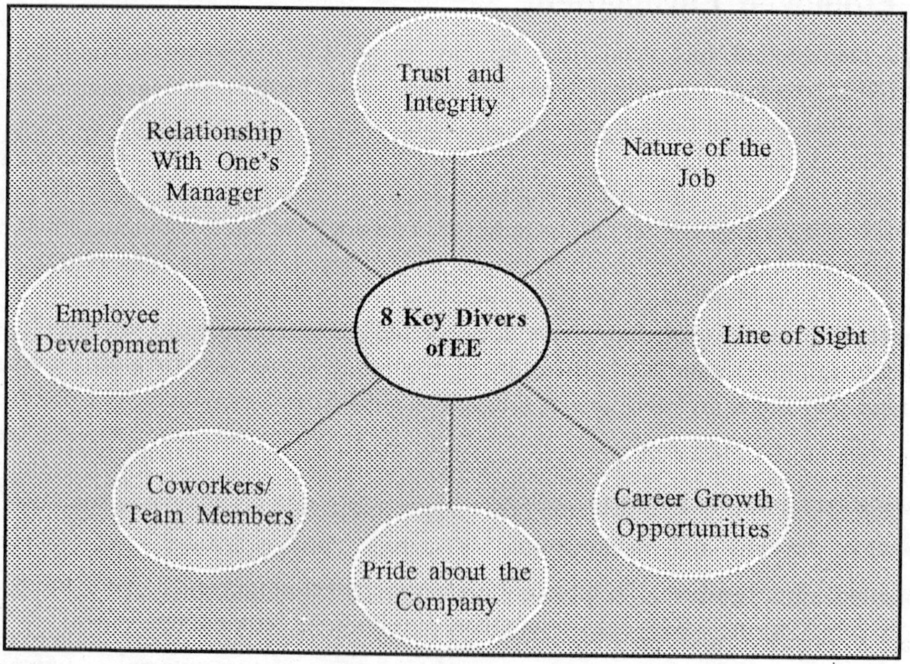

Fig. 21.1: Employee Engagement – Key Drivers

Table 21.1: Key Engagement Principles

Key Engagement Principles	Description
Principle 1	Employee engagement will be positively impacted when the organization has an integrated HR value chain.
Principle 2	When managers engage in a full-range of leader behaviours that incorporate contingent reward and transformational behaviours, employee engagement will be positively impacted.
Principle 3	The level of employee engagement will increase when employees work in jobs that are enriched by providing variety, significance, and task identity.
Principle 4	When employees are working to achieve challenging and specific performance goals, their level of engagement will increase.
Principle 5	Engaged employees are high performers
Principle 6	Engaged employees go beyond the minimum requirements specified in job descriptions and performance evaluations. They are outstanding organizational citizens who engage in a wide variety of extra-role performance behaviours.
Principle 7	When employees have a high level of trust in their leader the amount of engagement increases.

Source: Whittington, J. L. and Galpin, T. J. (2010)

Strategic Employee Engagement

The focus for HR was on improving 'employee engagement', which was about creating an 'emotional connection' with employees so that they are passionate, committed, and long term attachment with the organization (Tomlinson, 2010). The employee engagement strategy consisted of five interventions that were distinct but interconnected for symbiosis and greater impact as reflected in figure 2.

- **Leadership Development**: All members of the management team were sent on a series of training courses to improve their management skills. In order to measure their behavioural change, all managers were tested through a 360-degree assessment tool before and after attending the training. The focus was very much on doing rather than knowing, built around five core behavioural competencies (delivering results, customer focus, communication, managing self or others and teamwork) that are applicable for all employees, each of which has positive and negative indicators.
- **Employee Recognition**: To ensure the awards gained employee support, the nominations came direct from employees, rather than purely from senior management.
- **Internal Communications**: To support the improvement of internal communications, a number of tools to facilitate greater organizational communications were introduced. The content was a combination of key business information, presentations and provision of some more light hearted commentary to build a sense of togetherness across the various departments. Following some focus groups with employees, it was also decided to set up an employee forum that consisted of at least one representative from each department. This

in particular has proven to be a useful tool to support employees in raising items of concern. To further ensure transparency the minutes and agreed conclusions of the meeting are published for all to see.

- **Organizational Development**: This intervention was in many ways the most-wide ranging. HR led the negotiations with the relevant employees, gaining universal support for the implementation of HR policies and programmes.
- **Employee Development**: The organization also ensured that non-management employees received training to support them in both their role and career development. Training needs analysis were collected across the organization and utilized to create a clear training plan for each employee, aligned with their career aspirations as expressed in their annual appraisal.

Work Culture and Employee Engagement

The "work culture" of an organization represents the internal work environment created for operating an organization. Pettigrew (1979) identifies work culture as the system of personally and collectively accepted meanings of work, operating for a given group at a given time. According to Peters and Waterman (1982) work culture is defined as a system of 'shared values', which results in high performance in organizations. Singh (1985) says that the work culture is the prevalent and common patterns of feeling and behaviour in an organization. Sinha (1990) labels work culture as the totality of the various levels of interacting forces around the focal concern of work. Work culture means work related activities in the framework of norms and values regarding work. It includes: work related activities, the cognitions, the affect and the values attached to them. It is concerned with beliefs and values on the basis of which people interpret experience and behave, individually and in groups. Overall the literature indicates that the individual work values may have a lot to contribute to the work culture of the organizations. A model has developed (work culture and employee engagement model) after reviewing a wide range of research studies that lays out the roadmap to increase employee engagement (see figure 3).

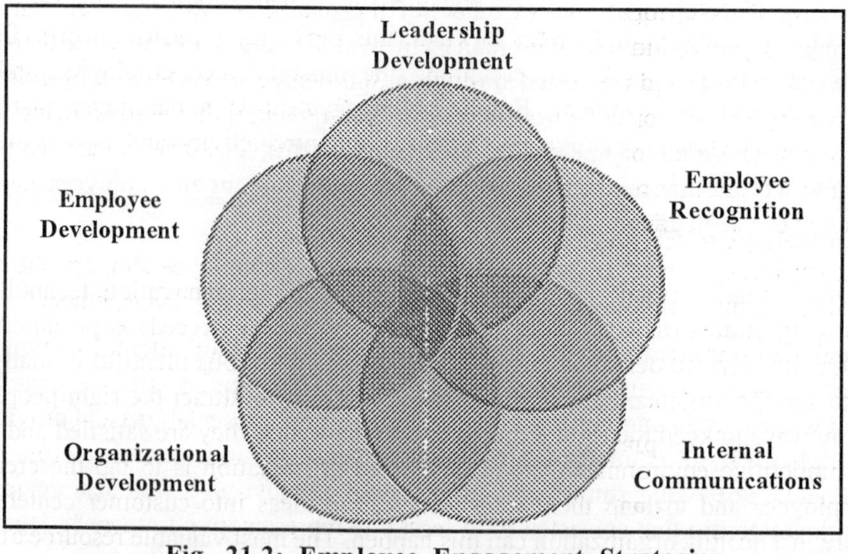

Fig. 21.2: Employee Engagement Strategies

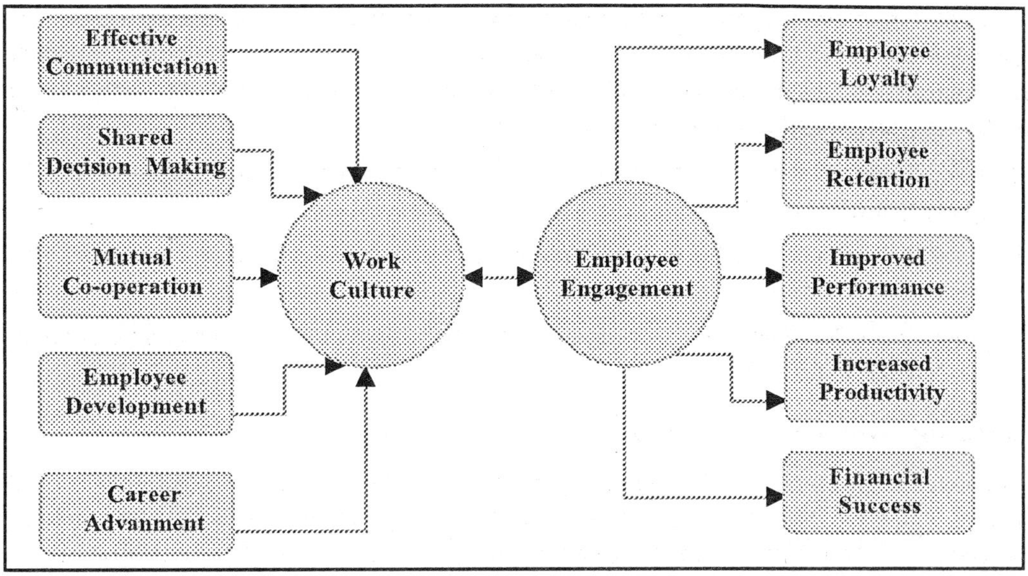

Fig. 21.3: A Model on Work Culture and Employee Engagement

In this model, five work related factors as shown: effective communication, shared decision making, mutual co-operation, employee development and career advancement, are the most important drivers of work culture which foster employee engagement. Effective communication means allowing workers the opportunity to share their views and opinions with management and that when management keeps employees informed about what is going on in the organization, it builds a high level of employee engagement. When employees participate in making decisions, they feel more engaged in the organization. The organization must work to nurture employee engagement, which requires a mutual relationship between employer and employees. Organization that provides employees with opportunities to develop their abilities, learn new skills, acquire new knowledge and realise their potential, fosters a high level of employee engagement. When companies plan for the career advancement of their employees and invest in them, this promotes a positive work culture which influences engagement of employees and retaining the most talented employees and providing opportunities for personal development. Employee engagement is a barometer that determines employee loyalty and retention, improve performance and productivity and also brings financial success in the organization.

Impact of Employee Engagement on Business

Organizations that have created a competitive advantage through innovation, technology, quality products, and pricing strategies, now view "customer service that exceeds expectations" as their key to success. Quality service demands engaged employees. With jobs plentiful in many industries from high tech to service, organizations not only focus on ways to attract the right people; but they must also focus on ways to keep the right employees and make sure they are satisfied and productive. In the today's competitive environment, the ability of an organization is to tap the creative brain-power of its employees and to help them translate creative ideas into customer centered products and services. Only in a healthy organization can this happen. The most valuable resource of a company walks out of the door every evening and sometimes it never come back- this is of particular importance in knowledge and service based industries. The quality of output and competitive advantage of a company depends on the quality of its people, way of thinking, and sharing of knowledge and contacts In general the various outcomes of strategic EE are:

- Employees are able to get 'involved' in the organization and feel that they are genuinely participating and contributing to its performance
- Employees have a pride in their organisation and endorse it as a place to work and for successful business.
- Employees demonstrate real commitment to their job and the organization and are prepared to 'go the extra mile'.

Concluding Remark

Employee engagement can be thought of as a potential outcome to a positive work culture. It is a state in which the employee feels an affinity for the organization, feels that they belong to and are appreciated and are part of something worthwhile. Engagement also implies an alignment with the organization and a level of commitment. Employee engagement is developed when the business values the employees and vice versa.. A culture that facilitates employee engagement, accommodates employee needs, and ensures employee effectiveness and growth, will set the foundation in place for long term success of the organization. Once the culture is created, engagement becomes 'the way we do things around here' and it does not have to be recreated year after year.

Engaged employees create winning organizations that are more profitable, a fun place to work in and offer superb customer services and other solutions for which the organization exists. The concept is thus making headlines and becoming popular among major world class organizations be they in private or public sector. Today, however, there is clear evidence that business leaders are not simply saying this – they are actually experiencing it too with the EE tools. Companies who are able to better engage their people also deliver better business performance and maximize the shareholders value. Now almost all of the organization has investing money towards people (HR-related practices). So that it create value for organizational performance. Increasing EE is highly dependent on leadership and establishes two ways communication where people work and views are valued and respected. EE is about building a truly great relationship with the workforce. EE is the key driver to which employees are fully involved in their work, committed to their work, care about their organization and colleagues and are willing to go the extra mile for their organization to ensure its success.

Managerial Implications

Any organization that embraces fine management philosophy, recognition of employee's talent, potential and is committed to providing enriching professional experiences is bound to succeed. The mantra of effective EE is the highly dependent on the measures taken by the management are:

- Employee engagement starts right at the selection stage by choosing the right fit for the right job and giving a realistic job preview.
- Understanding of corporate goals, mission, and vision.

- Understanding of roles and responsibilities and how it contributes to achieve overall corporate goals.
- Regular feedback on performance to all employees.
- Employee freedom and job satisfaction.
- Employee involvement in decision making process.
- Providing learning and development opportunities.
- Mutual relationship between management and workers.
- Clear communication to the employees through a clear picture of company progress towards targets/goals.
- Keeping up the morale of the employees and driving them towards excellent performance through recognition letters, profit sharing schemes, long performance awards etc.
- Communication forums like in-house magazine, regular surveys and conferences.
- Maintaining the quality of work-life and a balance between personal and professional lives, through recreational activities like festivities, get-togethers, sports etc.

References:

Concelman, James (2005), Referee Bosses give Leaders a Bad Rep", *Employment Relations Today*, Vol. 32, No.1, pp.48-52.

Conference Board (2006), Employee Engagement: A Review of Current Research and Its Implications, Research Report E-0010-06-RR, New York, (Accessed on 1st May 2011), www.conference-board.org.

Corporate Leadership Council (2004), Driving Employee Performance and Retention through Engagement: A Quantitative Analysis of the Effectiveness of Employee Engagement Strategies, CLC, Washington.

Daniel, (2004), Engagement policies boost pre-tax profits at Nationwide, Personnel Today.

Erickson, Bill (2004), Nature Times Nurture, Organisations can Optimize their people's Contribution, Journal of Organisational Excellence, Vol. 24, No. 1, pp.22-30.

Gallup Consulting (2008), Employee engagement survey (Organizational health audit). http://www.police.govt.nz/resources/2007/inquiry-into-police-conduct/new-zealand-police-2007-engagement-survey-results-presentation.pdf.

Gibson, J. (2006), Employee engagement: A review of current research and its implications, The Conference Board.

Glen, Clayton (2006), Key Skills Retention and Motivation, the War for Talent still Range and Retention is the High Ground", Industrial & Commercial Training, Vol. 38, No. 1, pp.37-45.

Harter, James K.; Schmidt, Frank L. and Hayes, Theodore L. (2002), Business-United-Level Relationship between Employees Satisfaction, Journal of Applied Psychology, Vol. 87, No. 2, pp.268-279.

Institute of Employment Studies (2003), (Accessed on 1st May 2011), www.employment-studies.co.uk.

IPA (2007), The five key steps to engagement, Involvement and Participation Association Bulletin, No. 67, July, pp. 1-4.

Khan, A. (2007), Employee engagement: A winning formula for success, American Chronicle, http://www.americanchronicle.com/articles/37656.

Mahendru, Palak, and Sharma, Swati (2006), Engaging the Workforce-Employee Value Proposition and Culture Building, HRM Review, ICFAI, pp.26-29.

May, Douglas R.; Gilson, Richard L; and Harter, Lynn M. (2004), The Psychological Conditions of Meaningfulness, Safety and Availability and the Engagement of the Human Spirit at Work, Journal of Occupational & Organisational Psychology, Vol. 77, No. 1, pp.12-35.

McCashland, C. R. (1999), Core Components of the service climate: Linkages to customer satisfaction and profitability, Dissertation Abstracts International US: Univ Microfilms International, Vol. 60, No. 12-A, pp. 89.

Miles, R. H. (2001), Beyond the age of Dilbert, Accelerating corporate transformations by rapidly engaging all employees, Organizational Dynamics, Vol. *29,* No. 4, pp. 313-321.

Peter T.J. and Waterman, A.A. (1982), In Search of Excellence, Harper & Row, New York.

Pettigrew, A. (1979), On Studying Organizational Culture, Administrative Science Quarterly.

Singh, N.K. and Paul, O. (1985), Corporate Soul: Dynamics of Effective Management, Vikas Publishing House Private Ltd., New Delhi.

Sinha, J.B.P., (1990), Work Culture in Indian Context, Sage, New Delhi.

Soladati, P. (2007), Employee engagement: What exactly is it? Management-Issues. http://www.management-issues.com/2007/3/8/opinion/employee-engagement-what-exactly-is-it.asp.

Stockley, D. (2006), Employee engagement and organizational pride, (Accessed on 1st May 2011), http://derekstockley.com.au/newsletters-05/038-employee-engagement.html

Tomlinson, G. (2010), Building a culture of high employee engagement, Strategic HR Review, Vol. 9, No. 3, pp. 25-31.

Wash, Louisa (1999), Engaging Employees a Big Challenge, Management Review, Vol. 88, No. 9, p. 10.

Whittington, J. L. and Galpin, T. J. (2010), The engagement factor: building a high-commitment organization in a low-commitment world, Journal of business strategy, Vol. 31, No. 5, pp. 14-24.

❖❖❖

22

Employee Engagement and Demographic Characteristics in Orissa Power Transmission Corporation Limited (OPTCL)

Snigdha Mohapatra

ABSTRACT

The study is an attempt to identify the role of demographic characteristics in determining employee engagement at Orissa Power Transmission Corporation Limited (OPTCL). Employee engagement was measured using Utrecht work engagement scale. The sample size consists of 43 respondents working at OPTCL corporate office at Bhubaneswar. The study makes an attempt to investigate whether demographic characteristics like age, sex, marital position, parental position, educational qualification, experience, job tenure and supervisory status has any impact on employee engagement. One-way ANOVA and post-hoc test have been administered to find the significance differences between and among the variables in determining employee engagement level at OPTCL.

INTRODUCTION

The concept of employee engagement is a business management concept (refer to Wikipedia, employee engagement). This is comparatively newer one. Only in 90s researchers had started talking about this concept. But may be due to gravity of this subject it is now a world-wide intense discussion topic. Although there is a great deal of interest in engagement, there is also a good deal of confusion. At present, there is no consistency in definition, with engagement having been operationalised and measured in many disparate ways. Employee engagement refers to positive feelings held by employees about their jobs and also the motivation and effort they put into work. Engagement leads to positive employee behavior that leads to organizational success. According to Macey and Sehneider (1999), engagement should not be confused with satisfaction or commitment. They identified two components of employee engagement:

- Feeling of engagement (Focus and enthusiasm) and
- Engagement behavior (Proactivity and persistence)

Kahn (1990) defines employee engagement as "the harnessing of organization member selves to their work roles; in engagement, people employ and express themselves physically, cognitively, and emotionally during role performances". The cognitive phase of employee engagement recount employees' thinking about the organization, about the employers or the leaders and about the working environment (both physical and social). The emotional aspect takes care of how employees feel about each of those factors. Its basic desire is whether they have positive or negative attitudes toward all these three factors. The physical aspect of employee engagement looks after the physical energies put forth by the employee to accomplish their professional roles. Thus, according to Kahn (1990), engagement means to be psychologically as well as physically present when occupying and performing an organizational role. Employee engagement was described in the academic literature by Schmidt *et al.* (1993) using data from Gallup's Q12 engagement survey (A well known study on employee engagement by Gallup consultancy). Schmidt et al.'s influential definition of engagement was "an employee's involvement with, commitment to, and satisfaction with work." This integrates the classic constructs of job satisfaction (Smith et al., 1969), and organizational commitment (Meyer & Allen, 1991). An employee is expected to be completely involved in all the three aspects cognitively, emotionally and physically. This refer to active thinking about the organization and the work the employee working with, felling happy about the work and putting all the effort to do his/her work effectively. All these three types of involvement should also follow the satisfaction level of the employee to be designated as employee engagement. Most often employee engagement has been defined as the amount of discretionary effort exhibited by employees in their job (Frank *et al* 2004). The effort is categorized as the initiative the employee takes to accomplish the job. Furthermore, it is also argued by the early researchers that the definitions often sound similar to other better known and established constructs such as 'organizational commitment' and 'organizational citizenship behavior' (OCB) (Robinson *et al* 2004). Thus Robinson *et al* (2004) defined engagement as 'one step up from commitment'. Truss *et al* (2006) define employee engagement simply as 'passion for work', a psychological state which is seen to encompass the three dimensions of engagement discussed by Kahn, and captures the common theme running through all these definitions.

Thus it is made clear that employee engagement is a multi-faceted construct, as previously suggested by Kahn (1990).

Role of Employee Engagement in Organizational Performance: Kahn uses terms like 'personal engagement' and 'personal disengagement' to describe the newly developed construct. To decide this two aspects of employee engagement he relies on "behaviors by which employee bring in or leave out their personal selves during work role performances". From his empirical research he concludes that disengaged employees displayed incomplete role performances and were effortless, automatic or robotic and high levels of engagement lead to both positive outcomes for individuals, (e.g. quality of people's work and their own experiences of doing that work), as well as positive organizational-level outcomes (e.g. the growth and productivity of organizations).

Practitioners and academician tend to agree that the consequences of employee engagement are positive (Saks 2006). There is a general belief that there is a connection between employee engagement and business results. A model developed by Harter *et al* (2002) confirms the same. They concluded that, "...employee satisfaction and engagement are related to meaningful business outcomes at a magnitude that is important to many organizations". The Gallup Organization (2004) found critical links between employee engagement, customer loyalty, business growth and profitability. They compared the scores of these variables among a sample of stores scoring in the top 25 per cent on employee engagement and customer loyalty with those in the bottom 25 per cent. Stores in the bottom 25 per cent significantly under-performed across three productivity measures: sales, customer complaints and turnover. Gallup cites numerous similar examples. Further research conducted by Crabtree (2005) reveals that engaged employees are more productive. They stay a comparatively longer tenure at their job and organization. They create stronger customer relationship. They take fewer sick days and so less health care from the organization. Double digit growth companies have more engaged leaders working for the organization and they create a direct impact on their employees' level of engagement. The double digit growth of the company may be because of a higher ratio of engaged employee while lower ratio of disengaged employee.

Personal Demographic Characteristics and Employee Engagement: Gender differences have been found such that men experience enrichment from work to family, while women experience depletion from work to family. While women experience enrichment from family to work, men experience no links from family to work (Rothbard, 1999). Results indicate that older workers (those 55 and older) are significantly more engaged than younger workers (those 54 and younger). However the other studies in 20th century, which studied ageing, accepted the proposition that gradual disengagement from work and community life was expected as people become older.

Exihibit 22.1: Factors that affect Employee Engagement

Personal Factors that Might Affect Employee Engagement	Organizational Factors that Might Affect Employee Engagement
Age	Tenure at Job
Gender	Supervisory Status
Marital status	Number of Work Hours
Parental status	Full-time/Part-time Status
Elder care status	Hourly/Salaried Status
Race/Ethnicity	Satisfaction with Training and Development
Household earning	Access to Flexibility Needed
Education	Culture of Flexibility
Physical health	Whether Access to Benefits Affects One's Decision to Stay with Their Employer
Mental health	Satisfaction with Benefits
Core self evaluation	Supervisor Support
	Inclusion/Exclusion
	Work Overload
	Work-Family Culture
	Job Security

Source: Pitt-Catsouphes. M., Matz-Costa. C., engaging the 21st century multi-generational workforce, this analysis and report was commissioned by the MetLife Mature Market Institute.

The above table finds the different factors that are associated with any employee to lead him/her to employee engagement.

METHODOLOGY

The present paper is an attempt to study the personal characteristics associated with employee engagement among the employees of Orissa Power Transmission Corporation Ltd, corporate office. Data for this paper have been collected through administration of questionnaire.

The questionnaire consists of two parts: first part consists of personal characteristics and the second part ascertains the views by respondents on a five point scale. A total of seventeen questions were asked to measure the state of employee engagement (Utrecht work engagement scale). On the basis of the responses yielded from the respondents employees are categorized into three levels of engagement.

- Disengaged employees are not just the unhappy workers at work; they are also busy in acting out their unhappiness. Every day these employees undermine what their engaged employees accomplish. Respondents having secured less than 50 points fall in this category (Steve Crabtree 2005, www. Garj, gallup.com). On the basis of the personal characteristics category mean score and standard deviation have been calculated. One-way ANOVA and post-hoc test was administered to find out the significance of the differences among the categories.
- Engaged employees work with passion and feel a profound connection to their company. They drive accomplishment of work. They are the task accomplishers of the company. They show interest at their work. These employees are so called as the life line members of the company. Respondents having scored 51-67 points are included in this category.
- Actively engaged employees are interpreted as the essentials of any company. They act as the brain of the company. These employees are not only very happy at their work but also spreads a goodwill of the company among their fellow collogues. In the real sense called as the brand ambassadors of employer branding of the company. These employees accomplish their work and also can bridge the gap of performance resulted because of the disengaged employees. They are the innovators of the company. These masterminds of the company contribute a lot when recognized and handled properly. Respondents securing more than the score of 68 points belong to this category.

The Sample

A total of 70 questionnaires were distributed randomly to the different employees in Orissa Power Transmission Corporation Ltd. Only 43 questionnaires were received back.

Result and Interpretation

On the basis of total scores the results are depicted in the following tables.

Table 22.1: Levels of Employee Engagement

Engagement Level	Frequency	Percentage
Disengaged	14	32.55%
Engaged	22	51.16%
Actively Engaged	7	16.27%

Out of the disengaged employees' category at OPTCL, female and male each constitutes 50%. 6 persons belong to the age group 22-28 contributes 6 and the rest sub-categories contribute two each. With reference to marital status 11 are married and 3 are unmarried. In reference to education diploma category contributes the highest i.e. 6 and other category like degree and master contributes 2 each. In reference to supervisory status categories the contribution of employees with 10 subordinates contributed the highest i.e. 9. Other sub-categories are evenly distributed. This indicates the relevance of supervisory status as a notable factor to determine employee engagement. Apart from these factors other factors don't show a remarkable difference in contribution to disengaged category. Further individual factors are analyzed independently to see the differences they contribute to employee engagement.

Table 22.2: Role of Gender in Employee Engagement

Gender	Frequency	Average	F value	Significance (*P*)	Interpretation
Male	18	51.888	.809	.496	Insignificant
Female	25	57.44			

The present study does not yield any significant difference in reference to gender as a determining factor towards employee engagement.

Table 22.3: Role of Chronological Age in Employee Engagement

Age	Frequency	Average	F value	Significance (*P*)	Interpretation
(22-28)	8	55.25	.809	.496	Insignificant
(29-35)	16	52.25			
(36-50)	12	59			
Above 50	7	54.857			

The above table shows that age is also not a significant factor in determining employee engagement. Though the age group of 36-50 has a slight higher engagement score yet the differences are not found to be significant.

Table 22.4: Role of Marital Status in Employee Engagement

Marital Status	Frequency	Average	F value	Significance (*P*)	Interpretation
Married	31	55.51	.136	.714	Insignificant
Unmarried	12	54.083			

Table 22.4 indicates no significant difference between the two categories of marital status in reference to employee engagement.

Table 22.5: Role of Parental Position in Employee Engagement

Parental Status	Frequency	Average	F value	Significance (*P*)	Interpretation
New born	7	50.1428	.528	.716	Insignificant
Toddler	8	54.375			
School going	11	13.433			
Teenage or Adult	5	55.2			
Not Applicable	12	58			

Table 22.5 shows that the average score of employee engagement for employees with school going kids are very low at 13.43, but these differences are not found in the univariate analysis of variance.

Table 22.6: Role of Education in Employee Engagement

Education	Frequency	Average	F value	Significance (*P*)	Interpretation
Diploma	19	55.21	.081	.922	Insignificant
Degree	17	54.4117			
Master	7	56.571			

The above table shows that there are very minimal differences among the average employee engagement score among the different sub-categories of employees in reference to educational background. This difference is also found to be insignificant in the univariate analysis of variance.

Table 22.7: Role of Experience in Employee Engagement

Experience	Frequency	Average	F value	Significance (*P*)	Interpretation
(0-5)	21	53.857	1.154	.346	Insignificant
(5-10)	10	53.3			
(10-15)	5	**64.4**			
(15-25)	5	57			
Above 25 yrs	2	49.5			

Table 22.7 reflects a higher employee engagement score at the average value for employees with 10-15 years of experience at work. Though this group reflects a higher engagement score but the differences among the sub-categories of experience are found to be insignificant.

Table 22.8: Role of Job Tenure in Employee Engagement

Job Tenure	Frequency	Average	F value	Significance (P)	Interpretation
0-2	14	55	.073	.974	Insignificant
2-5	12	54.333			
5-10	9	55.666			
Above 10	8	56.857			

Table 22.8 reflects the role of job tenure in determining the employee engagement score of employees at OPTCL. This indicates insignificant differences among the sub-categories of job tenure at work in determining employee engagement.

Table 22.9: Role of Supervisory Status in Employee Engagement

Supervisory Status	Frequency	Average	F value	Significance (*P*)	Interpretation
Group of 10	19	51.473	5.136	.002	Significant
Group of 30	10	66.9			
Group of 50	7	54			
Group of above 50	2	49.5			
Not Applicable	5	49.3			

Table 22.9 shows the differences among the sub-categories of supervisory status at employee engagement at OPTCL. It yields a significant difference in this study. The average employee engagement score of each sub-category is found to be highly different from the average value of sub-category having 30 subordinates.

Table 22.10: Post-hoc Test on Role of Supervisory in Employee Engagement

(I) Supervisory Status	(J) Supervisory Status	Mean Difference (I-J)	Std. Error	Sig.
10	30	-15.426*	3.726	.000
	50	-2.526	4.217	.553
	Above 50	1.974	7.090	.782
	NA	2.274	4.794	22.97
30	10	15.426*	3.726	.000
	50	12.900*	4.700	.009
	Above 50	17.400*	7.388	.024
	NA	17.700*	5.224	.002
50	10	2.526	4.217	.553
	30	-12.900*	4.700	.009
	Above 50	4.500	7.647	.560
	NA	4.800	5.585	.395
Above 50	10	-1.974	7.090	.782
	30	-17.400*	7.388	.024
	50	-4.500	7.647	.560
	NA	.300	7.980	.970
NA	10	-2.274	4.794	.638
	30	-17.700*	5.224	.002
	50	-4.800	5.585	.395
	Above 50	-.300	7.980	.970

Table 22.10 describes the post-hoc test conducted for the category of supervisory status to determine the employee engagement level. There is a significant difference between supervisory groups on their employee engagement scores (F = 5.187, p-value 0.002). Importantly, the supervisory group having 30 employees exhibits significant difference on its employee engagement score (p-values of 0.000, 0.009, 0.024 and 0.002 respectively for groups having 10, 50, Above 50 and NA categories).

To sum up it is found that it is only the supervisory status (number of subordinate one lead) that plays a significant role to define level of employee engagement and rest other factors like sex, age, marital status, parental status, education, experience and job tenure did not

CONCLUSION

The employee engagement score reveals the fact that at OPTCL 32.55% employees are disengaged at work. 51.16% employees are engaged and only 16.2% employees are actively engaged at work. This indicates the need of finding out further the reason of low active engagement at work. Hence the study was an attempt to find the role of demographic characteristics to determine the employee engagement level at OPTCL and it found that there is a high significant impact of number of supervisor the employee dealing with i.e. supervisory status. Further the study may be extended to find the basic understanding into how supervisory position plays a role in employee engagement levels in employees. Employee engagement as a construct takes a wide area of concern and this study concludes that mostly demographic characteristics are not the determinant factors. Hence the employers can delve into how to increase employee engagement as this can be a product of the treatment employee is expecting at the work-place.

References

1. Crabtree, S. (2005), http://www.docstoc.com/docs/5294654/Employee-Engagement-The-Key-to-Improving-Performance
2. Cumming, E., & Henry, W.E. (1961). Growing Older: The Process of Disengagement. New York: Basic Books; Streib, G.F. & Scheider, C.J. (1971). Retirement in American Society: Impact and Process. Ithaca, NY: Cornell University Press.
3. *Employee Attitudes and Engagement 2006.* London, CIPD.
4. Frank, F.D., Finnegan, R.P. and Taylor, C.R. (2004) 'The race for talent: retaining and engaging workers in the 21st century', *Human Resource Planning,* Vol 27, No 3, pp12-25.
5. Harter, J.K., Schmidt, F.L. and Hayes, T.L. (2002) 'Business-unit level relationship between employee satisfaction, employee engagement, and business outcomes: a meta- analysis', Journal of Applied Psychology, Vol 87, pp268-79.
6. Harter, J.K., Schmidt, F.L. and Keyes, C.L. (2002) 'Well-being in the workplace and its relationship to business outcomes: A review of the Gallup studies', in Keyes, C.L. and Haidt, J. (Eds) *Flourishing: The Positive Person and the Good Life,* pp205-224. American Psychological Association, Washington D.C.
7. Hewit Associates LIC, www.hewit.co/doubledigitgrowth
8. Jacquelyn B. J., Jennifer E. S., Sharon P. M., Responsive Workplaces for Older Workers: Job Quality, Flexibility and Employee Engagement, Boston college, Issue Brief 11, October, 2007

9. Kahn, W.A. (1990) 'Psychological conditions of personal engagement and disengagement at work', Academy of Management Journal, Vol 33, pp. 692-724.

10. Pitt-Catsouphes. M., Matz-Costa. C., engaging the 21st century multi-generational workforce, This analysis and report was commissioned by the MetLife Mature Market Institute.

11. Robinson, I. (2006) Human Resource Management in Organisations. London, CIPD.

12. Rothbard, N. (1999). Enriching or depleting? The dynamics of engagement in work and family. *Dissertation Abstracts International US: Univ Microfilms International. 59*(10-A).

13. Saks, A.M. (2006) 'Antecedents and consequences of employee engagement', *Journal of Managerial Psychology,* Vol 21, No 6, pp600-619.

14. The Gallup Organisation (2004) [online] Available at: www.gallup.com. Accessed 28th June 2007.

15. The Gallup Organization (2004) [online] Available at: www.gallup.com. Accessed 28th June 2007.

16. Truss, C., Soane, E., Edwards, C., Wisdom, K., Croll, A. and Burnett, J. (2006) *Working Life.*

23

Employee Engagement: A Study at NTPC, Kanhia

Dr. S.C. Parida
Miss Priyadarshini Hota

ABSTRACT

People are a key component of any company's ability to execute its strategies and achieve its goals. Companies who are able to better engage their people also deliver better business performance and return to shareholders .In this context employee engagement, i.e., emotional attachment an employee have for his organization plays very vital role in the attainment of organizational goal.

This study attempts to unravel various dimensions of the employee engagement in organizational context.

It attempts to find out the employee engagement level in NTPC-Kanhia with individual thrust on the various parameters.

It further suggests the efficacy of various initiatives taken towards employee engagement along with suggestions.

This study is a journey from "finding out what is employee engagement" to "How to build an effective and efficient organization entity by incorporating effective employee engagement strategy".

INTRODUCTION

Hewitt Associates pioneered the measurement of employee engagement in the early 1990s. Over the past ten years, Hewitt has conducted significant research with its clients to determine what drives employee and executive engagement, and how companies can sustain and improve it. Engagement is measured through a composite of survey items and is represented by a percentage of employees who are engaged. Engagement levels have consistently been found to highly correlate to business results, including total shareholder return.

Engagement at work was conceptualized by Kahn, (1990) as the '*harnessing of organizational members*' selves to their work roles. In engagement, people employ and express themselves physically, cognitively, and emotionally during role performances. Engagement is most closely associated with the existing construction of job involvement (Brown 1996) and flow (Csikszentmihalyi, 1990). Job involvement is defined as 'the degree to which the job situation is central to the person and his or her identity (Lawler & Hall, 1970). Job involvement is thought to depend on both need saliency and the potential of a job to satisfy these needs. Thus job involvement results from a cognitive judgment about the needs satisfying abilities of the job. Engagement differs from job involvement as it is concerned more with how the individual employs his/her self during the performance of his / her job. Furthermore engagement entails the active use of emotions. Finally engagement may be thought of as an antecedent to job involvement in that individuals who experience deep engagement in their roles should come to identify with their jobs. When Kahn talked about employee engagement he gave importance to all the three aspects -physical, cognitive and emotional. Whereas, in job satisfaction, more importance has been given to cognitive side. HR practitioners believe that the engagement challenge has a lot to do with how employee feels about the work experience and how he or she is treated in the organization. It has a lot to do with emotions which are fundamentally related to drive bottom line success in a company. There will always be people who never give their best efforts no matter how hard HR and line managers try to engage them. "*But for the most part employees want to commit to companies because doing so satisfies a powerful and a basic need in connect with and contribute to something significant*".

DEFINITION

Though various definitions have been put to define "employee engagement" more accurate and blended definition of *employee engagement is "a heightened emotional connection that an employee feels for his or her organization, that influences him or her to exert greater discretionary effort to his or her work*".

People are a key component of any company's ability to execute its strategies and achieve its goals. Companies who are able to better engage their people also deliver better business performance and return to shareholders. An engaged employee is aware of business context, and works with colleagues to improve performance within the job for the benefit of the organization. The primary behaviors of engaged employees are speaking positively about the organization to coworkers, potential employees and customers, having a strong desire to be a member of the organization, and exerting extra effort to contribute to the organization's success. In other words, an engaged employee acts as an ambassador for the organization and a torch-bearer of its values. Many smart organizations work to develop and nurture engagement. This requires a two-way relationship between employer and employee. Thus Employee engagement is the barometer that determines the association of a person with the organization. It is a critical parameter in defining the organizations long-term success and sustainability.

ENGAGEMENT AND THE HUMAN FACTOR

The figure below represents employee engagement as a confluence of three factors- commitment, involvement & motivation.

Engagement is measured by three primary behaviors:

- **Say** – The employee consistently speaks positively about the organization to coworkers and refers potential employees and customers;

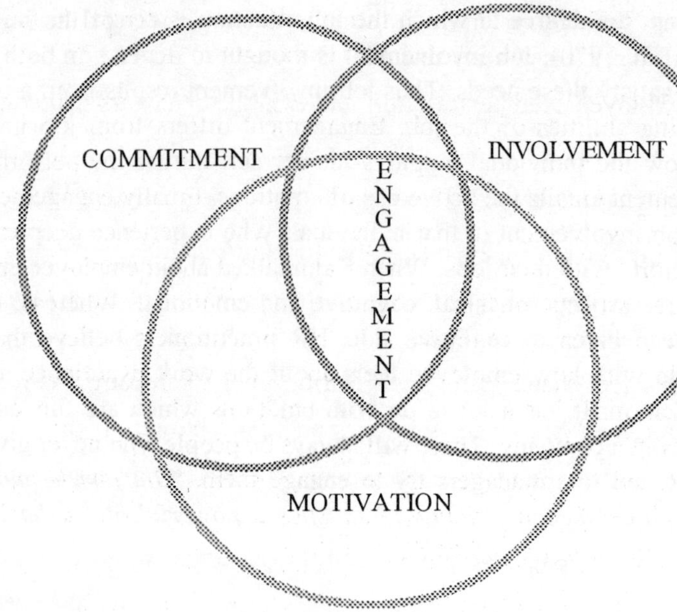

WHAT DOES AN ENGAGED EMPLOYEE THINK, FEEL AND DO?

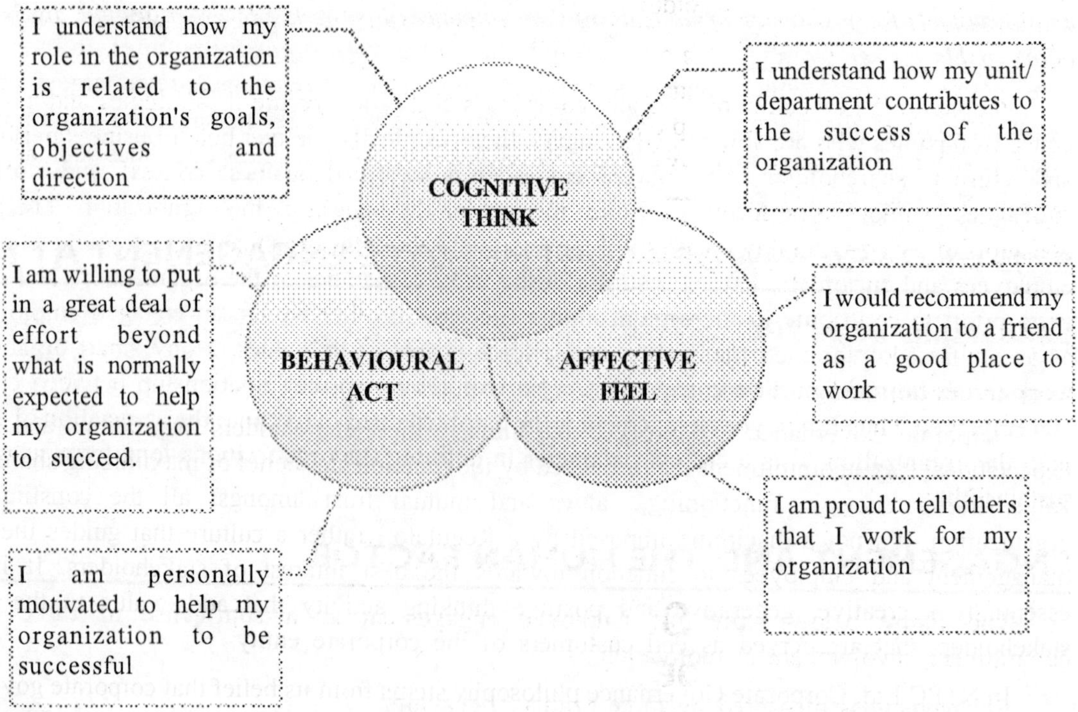

- **Stay** – The employee has an intense desire to be a member of the organization, despite opportunities to work elsewhere; and
- **Strive** – The employee exerts extra effort and exhibits behaviors that contribute to business success.

Key Drivers of Engagement

For High levels of Employee Engagement Organizations should

- Provide employees with opportunities to develop their abilities, learn new skills, acquire new knowledge and realize their potential
- Make employees feel that leaders have clarity on the company's core values
- Show respect for each employee's qualities and contribution –regardless of their job level
- Create a trustful and challenging environment ,wherein employees are empowered to make decisions on their own
- Provide equal opportunities for growth and advancement to all employees

Simply put, fully engaged employees are those who go beyond what their job requires, putting in extra effort to make the company succeed. "Engagement is not about "WHAT" our people do. It is the driver of "HOW" they do it and "WHO" they do it for." Recent research among management consultants has shown links between employee engagement and positive business outcomes such as revenue growth (Towers Perrin Talent Report-2003). Engagement is strongly related to a ***constructive*** culture and negatively related to both aggressive and ***passive*** cultures. In other words, constructive cultures – which promote both high performance expectations (stretch targets) and offer strong support to members (in terms of resources, guidance & top management commitment) – promote more staff engagement, which in turn results to positive business outcomes such as revenue growth & higher market share.

EXISTING FRAMEWORK FOR EMPLOYEE ENGAGEMENT AT NTPC

Leadership at NTPC

Leaders Exhibit High Standards of Corporate Governance

Corporate Governance is a process that aims to meet shareholders' aspirations and societal expectations. It is a commitment that is backed by the fundamental belief of maximizing shareholders value, transparency in functioning, values and mutual trust amongst all the constituents of organization. It's not a discipline imposed by a Regulator, rather a culture that guides the Board, management and employees to function towards the best interest of stakeholders. It involves essentially a creative, generative and positive thinking activity that adds value to the various stakeholders that are served as end customers of the corporate entity.

In NTPC Ltd, Corporate Governance philosophy stems from its belief that corporate governance is a key element in improving efficiency and growth apart from enhancing investor confidence. The Corporate Governance philosophy is quoted below:

> ***"As a good corporate citizen, the Company is committed to sound corporate practices based on conscience, openness, fairness, professionalism and accountability in building confidence of its various stakeholders in it thereby paving the way for its long term success."***

Leaders develop the mission, vision, values and ethics and are role models of a culture of excellence.

The leaders of NTPC have envisioned NTPC as a global integrated power Company with a mission to add capacity in quick succession. The vision mission and value (VMV) statement were revisited in 2005 and again in 2010 to align it with the changing business scenario. These statements were evolved through a process of shared views and employee participation at all the Units of NTPC. Leadership at Kaniha has developed the Kaniha vision aligned with NTPC vision. Leaders take interest in communicating the VMV of the Company to all its stakeholders during important occasions and meetings. Focus is on imbibing a culture of 'walk the talk'.

The vision and core values are well communicated to all employees through various communication channels as mentioned .The core values "BCOMIT", being the guiding principles of employee behavior, all out effort is made by Kaniha leadership to manifest them in day-to-day functioning. There is a system of assessing all executives for demonstration of core values as part of their annual assessment through PACE.

To inculcate mutual trust and respect, Business unit heads along with respective HODs participate in functions to felicitate and bid farewell to transferred/ superannuating employees. Also ED wishes all the employees on his/her birth day by a signed greeting delivered to the employee. Leaders of Kaniha always utilize opportunity for interaction with people by participating in days of national and local importance like Republic Day, Independence Day, NTPC & Kaniha Raising Day, Environment Day, Communal Harmony Day, Sadbhavana Diwas and Prajamandal Diwas, etc. The senior leadership also takes lead role in conceptualizing celebration of festivals and Socio-cultural events like Rath yatra, Kavi Sammelan, Cultural meets etc. ED and HODs encourage employees and section heads to organize picnics and informal family get-togethers frequently by providing infrastructural support.

In order to reinforce culture of excellence within the organization's people, Business Excellence Department (earlier named as TQM) has been established at Kaniha in 2003 with a basic motive to emphasize Quality Concepts.

As part of enabling competency building process, leaders encourage people by deploying them in using learning opportunities. At Kaniha, a new Employee Development Centre with all infrastructural facilities is there to provide technical and managerial inputs to all levels. It is a leadership commitment to ensure 7 man-days training per year to each employee. To sharpen the junior, middle and senior level executives are trained in various management capsules offered by PMI of NTPC, IIM Kolkatta, and ASCI Hyderabad etc. To stimulate learning and competency development, tie ups have been evolved with financial support. Non-executive employees find opportunity in company funded programs tied up with Department of Technical education Orissa, BITS Pilani & Jamia Milia Islamia University to upgrade their professional qualification. It also plays a pivotal role in sharpening the competency of its executives through programmes like Energy Auditor course, Project Management Course, etc. Besides, the leadership encourages its people to strengthen their knowledge & competencies by taking of courses which adds to their capability and qualification. Incentives are provided for acquiring such qualifications.

To update and prepare themselves for future challenges, leaders of Kaniha participate in learning Processes by attending contemporary management and technical modules like LEADS, Strategic & advanced Management Programmes, CEOs retreat, Conferences & Seminars like Knowledge Management workshop at PMI, HOD Meets, Workshop on Internationalization of Business, International O&M Conferences at PMI etc.

PEOPLE CENTRIC INITIATIVES

Recruitment and Training: "We make people before we make product"

NTPC considers human resource to be the greatest asset of the organization. NTPC has a well structured recruitment policy which enables the organization to attract the best talent of the country & make it available at the right time in right number. Executives are recruited centrally as executive trainees at entry level through a rigorous country wide selection test followed by GDs, psychometric tests & interview. The ETs undergo a comprehensive one year training conducted at Power Management Institute & EDC of various stations of NTPC. The training consists of class room & on job training. To meet the growing requirements of HR in line with organizational strategy of capacity addition & diversification into different areas, lateral recruitment of Asst. Engineer E1 level is also being done. Initiative is also taken to attract best post of talent through campus interview in IITs, NITS & reputed Management schools in country. Recruitment of Non-executives is done at station level.

Employee Development Centre

TSTPS Kaniha aligns its with HR Vision "To enable our people to be a family of Committed world class professionals, making NTPC a learning organization". The company believes and uses training as a tool to enhance Human potential, to meet the upcoming challenges and to retain talent. NTPC have a comprehensive Training Module. It is centrally coordinated by Power Management Institute (PMI), Noida and at Plant level the training programs are conducted by Employee Development Center.

Roles of PMI (Power Management Institute)

NTPC being committed to employee development has established a world class training institute at Noida to cater to the training needs of All employees of NTPC. In addition to imparting training to its employees PMI also organizes training programs/Workshops related to Power Industry to forge technological advancements in the field.

The Executive Trainee Training Program, MDI Gurgaon, Foreign Training, MTech Power Generation, Certification Program for Project Management are some of the programs coordinated by PMI. The company has set a policy to impart 7 man days of training per employee per year in various aspects like behavioral, technical and personal growth.

The training calendar is systematically developed by consolidating the training requirements assessed through the Training Need Analysis given by the executives through their reporting officer/ reviewing officer in Performance Management System.

TSTPS Kaniha has been identified as a major EDC and has been grooming the young Executive Trainees through a rigorous and memorable one year training program through Class room/ Workshops/ on the job training. The Evaluation of the Executive trainees is being conducted on a regular basis and their final postings are decided based on the evaluation. In addition to ET training TSTPS EDC formulates its own training calendar to fulfill the local site training requirements. If need be employees are also sent out to PMI and other Prestigious institutions to acquire training in the area of interest of the individual suiting Organizational requirements.

In order to develop the Competencies in executives for succession planning NTPC has devised a system of planned Intervention as given below

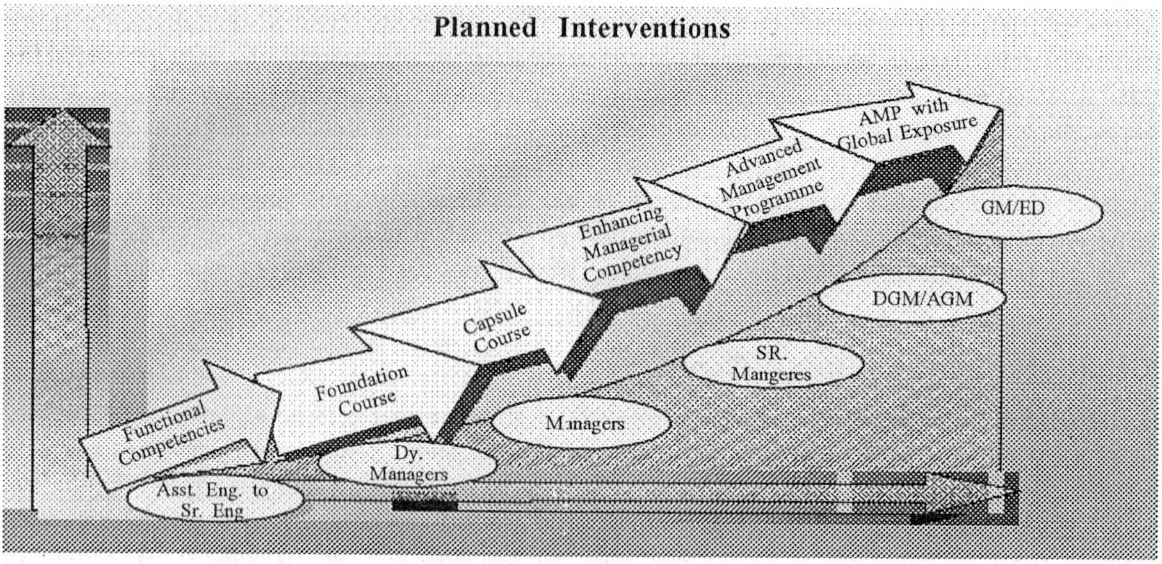

Fig. 23.1

Planning and Management of Human Resource

NTPC People Management policies are formulated at corporate centre on the basis of HR Vision which is evolved to support realization of company's Mission, Vision & core values. The HR policies strategies & plans are formulated keeping in view the employee welfare studying latest trends & benchmarks of the industry & after due deliberations with unions & association at various forums.

People's Knowledge and Competencies are Identified, Developed and Sustained

Human Resource management at Kaniha press a key roll in ensuring that the knowledge and competency profile of employees are aligned with their tasks and rolls. Under the recommendation of **Project Disha,** competency mapping was carried out in the Organization and the directories of KPAs (Key Performance Area) for all levels, roles and departments were made. Further classification

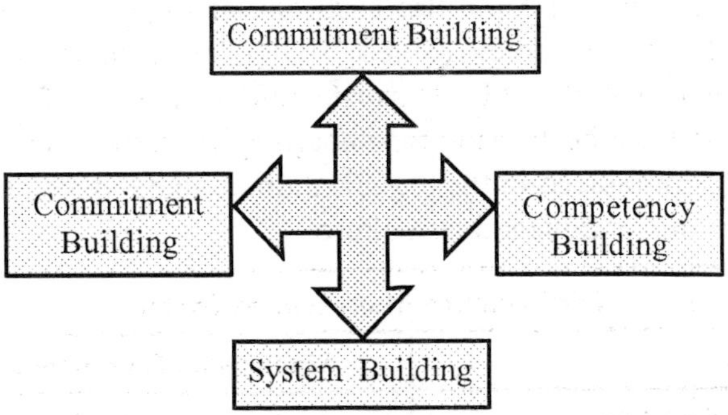

was done on the basis of function and type of plant. These competencies (technical/functional and managerial) have been detailed in the new performance management system. Different weightages have been assigned to these competencies and core values based on the level/grade of the employees.

	Goals	HR Process	Enablers
COMPETENCY BUILDING	Recruitment of best talents	Recruitment	ET test, Campus Recruitment, Open recruitment, Group Discussions, Interviews
	Developing skills & knowledge	Training & development	ET-phased training, Need based planned interventions, Job rotation, Sponsorships to all India institutes
	Creativity and innovation	Learning	Refresher/cross functional/cpsule training/ NOCET/Business minds, Medha pratiyogita
COMMITMENT BUILDING	Satisfaction	Posting, Employee benefits, Welfare	Posting based on past experience/ education/ need based, Salary, perks, benefits, advances, reimbursements, incentives, quarter allotment
	Shouldering social responsibility	Corporate social responsibility	CSR-CD activities for providing basic amenities, livelihood to adjoining villages
	Post employment care	Processing for separation benefits	PF, Gratuity, Leave encashment, Post retirement medical benefits, Engaging retired employees on contract basis for NTPC Assignments
CULTURE BUILDING	Acculturisation	Orientation	aInduction Program, Mentoring, Video magazines, In-house Journal
	Motivation	Performance recognition	Performance Management System, Promotions, Empowerment, Rewards & recognition scheme, Fast track promotions
SYST-EM BUILD-ING	Compliance to statutory obligations	Employee relations	Harmonious relations with unions & associations

Performance Management System forms the basis for employee appraisal and identifying the training and developing needs of individuals. The concept of Development centers is used for executives at E5 level for assessing the managerial competencies of the middle level managers and identifying strength and weakness of individuals so that the gap in competencies can be identified for improvement within a time frame to suit needs of the organization. Continuous learning and developing the competencies of its people has been one of the prime objectives of the leadership at Kaniha. Organizational climate survey named 'BODH' is conducted periodically to access to perception of employees on different employee satisfaction parameters. Tie ups with leading technical and management institution have been made for imparting different types of quality education to its employees. Mentoring was introduced in the organization to guide, develop and groom new entrance and acclimatize them into our organizational culture.

Performance Management System	
Potential Competency	**Managerial Competency**
Leadership, System orientation,	Analytical ability, Learning, Team Player
Resource Management	Communication, Managerial effectiveness
Administrative ability	Decision Making, Inter Personal Skills
Team Building	Innovation/Creativity, Adoptability
	Cost consciousness, Quality consciousness

There are initiatives and programmes for enhancing learning at individual, team, and organization level aimed at improving the performance of organization. To promote learning to teams there are performance improvement project (PIPs), quality circle, and professional circle, NOCET, Medha Pratiyogita etc. At individual level there are training programmes aimed at enhancing the knowledge/ competence of employees in their specific work area. The employees at various levels are also encouraged to visit other power stations in order to learn their practices.

There is a system of job rotation to develop and groom executives by making them work in different area/ departments so that they have a fair level competence in 3 to 4 departments before assuming higher responsibility. To this effect they are also transferred from one station to another. People in HR and finance at station are rotated in different sections within the department.

The corporate goals, objectives and other initiatives cascade down to regions and in turn to station level through annual business plans, MOU targets etc. The station goals and objectives then percolate down to HOD and then to individuals through the chain of hierarchy. Teams like cross-functional team, PIPs, QCs etc. also help to achieve the targets.

Employee performance is monitored and reviewed periodically by the HOD and the reporting officers. A series of workshops on Performance review and Feedback system for all reporting officers at E5 and above were conducted at station EDC for reporting officers along with the introduction of PMS in 2004 so as to equip the reporting officers with skills required to give feedback to the appraisee and on the finer nuances on communication. In line with the PMS procedure, appraisal and appraisee set annual targets mutually. On the same line, performance is reviewed and mutually agreed scores are given at the end of the year. Recently a leadership development initiative has been introduced for developing leadership at all levels starting from E5. Annual Training plans at Corporate Training centre-PMI and station EDC are devised keeping in view the factors contributing to competence and performance gaps.

People are Involved and Empowered

Involvement & empowerment of people at Kaniha is embedded in the system and institutionalized through various cross-functional teams, committees & councils.

People are given opportunities to show and release their innovative and creative potential by suggesting modifications in the plant, participating in **Suggestion Scheme, Quality Circles, Professional circles and PIPs**. People also have opportunity to publish articles, poems, papers in the in-house Magazines/ Newsletters like Horizon, Deepvani, etc. Our CMD has launched an initiative called **IPON (Idea portal of NTPC) on-line suggestion scheme** where employee can directly give suggestion to the highest office of the organization regarding process improvement, restructuring of organization or any innovative idea contributing to enhance the organizational performance. Every year, PMI is organizing an **International O&M Conference** in which Papers are invited in mainly technical areas from all executives.

People and the Organization have a Dialogue

Recognizing the vital need of effective communication for internal harmony, growth & survival, a number of communication means & channels have been put in place at Kaniha to implement various communication policies & plans based on organization & site specific requirements.

People are Rewarded, Recognized and Cared for

Kaniha follows NTPC policy of common remuneration & benefits which is revised at regular intervals after due deliberations with representatives of Unions & Associations at the National Level. The remuneration benefits are aligned to its aim of maximizing employee satisfaction and productivity. The remuneration ,rewards, perks and facilities are as shown in below.

BENEFIT SCHEMES	
SCHEMES	Applause
Allowances	Thank You Slips
Loans & Advances	Appreciation Letter
Facilities	Star of the Month
Reimbursements	Employee of the Year Award
Terminal Benefits	Vidyut Awards
Social Security/ Insurance	Power Excel Award

NTPC Rewards Scheme
Applause
Thank You Slips
Appreciation Letter
Star of the Month
Employee of the Year Award
Vidyut Awards
Power Excel Award
PEARL Award
ACE (Award for Corporate Excellence) Award.
Mentors Samman

CONCLUSION

An organization's productivity is measured not in terms of employee satisfaction but by employee engagement. Employees are said to be engaged when they show a positive attitude toward the organization and express a commitment to remain with the organization.

Thus, we see that employee engagement is critical in ensuring success & sustainability and driving competitive advantage in the challenging times. Employee Engagement must not be treated as yet another management fad but should be given adequate time, attention & resources for driving organizational success and profitability. In a rapidly changing environment, only those organizations with the most engaged employees shall survive and seek newer horizons in the future. In any organization the raising and maintaining employee engagement lies in the hands of an organization and requires a perfect blend of time, effort, commitment and investment to craft a successful endeavor. The Current study at NTPC-Kaniha gives an insight to the existing framework of engagement and the recommendations given can further strengthen the hidden potential of this organization. It should thus recognize employees, more than any other variable, contributors to a company's competitive position. It should not be forgotten that Employee engagement is a continuous process of learning, improvement, measurement and action.

References

1. Archie Thomas, CMA, and Ann MacDi anmid – Encouraging Employee Engagement – CMA Management, Jun/Jul 2004.
2. Ashok Mukherjee – Engagement for the mind body, and soul – Human Capital, Aug.2005.
3. Charles Woodruffe – Employee Engagement – The Real Secret of Winning a Crucial Edge over your rivals – Manager Motivation – Dec. / Jan. 2006.
4. Christoffer Ellehuus,Piers Hudson-Driving Performance and Retention Through Employee Engagement –Corporate leadership Council 2004,Employee Engagement Survey
5. Michael Treacy – Employee Engagement higher at DDG company – Hewitt Research Brief. 2005
6. KAREN WILSON- A SURVEY OF EMPLOYEE ENGAGEMENT, University of Missouri – Columbia, MAY 2009
7. NTPC Corporate Plan 2002-2017
8. Value Survey (2006-07) and E- Darpan -2006 Findings, Corporate HRD,NTPC
9. BODH-II SURVEY REPORT, Corporate HRD, NTPC
10. BODH-III SURVEY REPORT, Corporate HRD, NTPC
11. PROJECT DISHA, Corporate HRD, NTPC

❖❖❖

24

Retention and Engagement: A Descriptive Study

Dr. Sujit Kumar Acharya
Snigdhamayee Choudhury
Siddharth Shankar Kanungo

ABSTRACT

Employee retention is the dependent variable of this study and thus its nuances, such as the importance of retention, retention management, professionals' suggestions, and employee turnover will be reviewed thoroughly.

Institute for Employment Studies defines employee engagement as "a positive attitude held by the employee towards the organization and its values." (Perryman & Hayday, 2004). Employees will feel engaged when they find motivation and personal meaning in their work, get positive interpersonal support and also operate in a work environment that is efficient (Bernthal, 2008; Seijits & Crim, 2006). Employers are highly engaged when they are performing roles that are non-job. Many employees have a sense of fairness even if they are treated unfairly in the work place and therefore many usually do their job role. However, employees' just coming to work and performing their roles does not bring long term competitiveness for the employer. This is because they can be hired by another employer and continues performing what they did for you (Welbourne, 2003).

INTRODUCTION

Human resources are an organization's greatest assets. Without human resources, everyday business functions such as managing cash flow, making business transactions, communicating through all forms of media, and dealing with customers could not be completed. H R and the potential they possess drive an organization. Today's organizations are continuously changing. Organizational change impacts not only the business but also its employees. In order to maximize organizational effectiveness, human potential-individuals' capabilities, time, and talents-must be managed. Human resource management works to ensure that employees are able to meet the organization's goals. "Human resource management is responsible for how people are treated in organizations.

EMPLOYEE RETENTION

Employee retention is the dependent variable of this study and thus its nuances, such as the importance of retention, retention management, professionals' suggestions, and employee turnover will be reviewed thoroughly.

The Importance of Retention

The "Sears Case Study" (Ulrich, 1997) substantiates the close link between the key drivers of business such as employee commitment, customer commitment and bottom line performance, where, for example, even a five per cent rise in employee commitment can generate a three percent rise in customer commitment and consequently, it can raise 0.25 per cent in the shareholder value. This represents a model of "employee value chain", which many global players has recognized besides recognizing the deep links between quality HR practice, employee commitment, and financial performance (Guest, 1997).

However, even back in the 1990s, Allen and Meyer (1990) strongly suggested the deep connection between affective commitment of the employees and organizational performance. These effective commitments are divided into three categories which are (a) Affective, (b) Continuous, and (c) Normative.

Some suggested that employee engagement and employee commitment are all the same but McBain (2006) put that debate to rest by stating that employee commitment is an outcome of employee engagement.

Even a little before that, Towers Perrin (2004, 2005) underpinned the significance of employee engagement by two studies with the following outcomes: (i) Organizations with higher employee engagement enjoy 70 per cent more chance of achieving their targets; (ii) Such organizations also achieve higher operating margins, where a five per cent increase employee engagement can generate 0.7 per cent rise in operating margins; (iii) Such organizations achieve high talent retention rate, as their employees are found to twice as eager as to remain with their employer; (iv) Such organizations outperform industry sector growth by 6 percent.

RETENTION MANAGEMENT

Wildermuth and Cris (2008) also presented a 10-point solution to employee engagement, naming it as "10 Ms of engagement". They stated that nine components out of the ten operate in the three dimensions like organization culture, the job, and personal issues are in a way connected to one another while the final factor, which they named as "match" factor, occupies the spaces between culture, job, and personal issues. According to them, "engagement is built on time, commitment, and consistent monitoring" and "ultimately engagement requires that all employees operate from their own strengths and passions" (p. 51). A brief version of their 10-point suggestion is as follows:

(1) Model: It symbolizes integrity and quality commitment to the ethical part of business that contains both reward and punishment for ethical violations.

(2) Metropolis: Through this M they point at the importance of camaraderie, support, and respect which eventually turn as a package of positive social interactions and bring acceptance and safety to workplace, which are vital for an engaging workplace environment.

(3) Magnate: This M refers to the value of acknowledgement and appreciation, where the company includes all employees in its celebrations of significant achievements to formally inform the employees about the significance of their contributions.

(4) Moderation: This term points at the need to check over enthusiasm to save the energy of the employees and instead focus on a steady, controlled progress interspersed with energy recharging phase to maintain a consistent level of engagement.

(5) Manager: This coinage represents the issue of empowerment of the employees with the view that employees feel more engaged and likes to stay if they too have roles in decision-making.

(6) Moon: This term points at the power of learning to boost employee confidence, where learning provides sense of accomplishment, which in turn enhances employee engagement/retention.

(7) Mirror: A healthy self-esteem of the employees, i.e., a sense of self and pride about their achievements usually gets reflected and this coinage refers to that, highlighting its efficacy in attraction/retention/engagement of employees.

(8) Malleability: This coinage highlights the factors like resilience and flexibility and insists that developing such attitudes among employees generates high engagement in employees as it helps bind employees with the organization.

(9) Microphone: This M focuses on the ability of the employees to speak for themselves and identifying the areas they need help for improving their and company future. This generates a sense of belonging to the company and thus considerably enhances employee engagement and the will to stay on.

(10) Match: This M serves as the pointer to the need of recognizing each employee's personality traits and individual talents, which in turn facilitates the identification of the elements required to keep each individual engaged and willing to stay. For example, if an outgoing person is given outdoor job that would make the person happy and continue with the job.

Professional Suggestions

Duncan Brown (2008), the director of HR services at Price water house Coopers, has suggested that companies need to focus on the following four areas under the current circumstances:

(1) Raising Pay for the Performers: According to Brown (2008), the main question is how to link reward with performance and not whether to link it.

(2) Focusing on Equal Pay: "It is essential to ensure that pay differences are justifiable and nondiscriminatory," argued Brown (p. 22), pointing at the importance of eliminating any discriminatory pay amid this crunch hour.

(3) Ensuring Employee Engagement: To explain its significance, Brown cited references from Sears's research (Haskett *et al.,* 1994), where the research openly suggested that employee engagement is critical to corporate performance.

(4) Effectiveness: Brown (2008) considered it as a tool to reduce the pressure of cost. However, under the present context, it is doubtful how the companies would provide extra money for better performance or to maintain a policy like equal pay. Therefore, if the companies fail to cover the first two conditions, it is obvious that they would not be in a position to retain their employees. As a result, the companies cannot be in a position to raise employee effectiveness and thus, to earn more!

There are also other suggestions to enhance the company performance amid the current downturn like Wellins's (2008) view that "It's now the responsibility of each employee who holds a great job to offer great value to the company in return," though not forgetting to add, "Leaders should provide support for their staff without removing individual responsibility." Such expert suggestions will be explored in the proposed study.

EMPLOYEE TURNOVER

Employee skill factor, employment situation or demographic factors can be instrumental in employee turnover but what is startling is the amount of loss the companies have to incur in that. The recent research by the Conference Board (2005) has further provided a tangible evidence of the significance of employee engagement and retention by utilizing the proposition that with the expansion of knowledge economy, the value of intangible assets grows rapidly and accordingly they have found that the percentage of intangible assets out of the total value of the company has risen from 38 in 1982 to 85 in 2000, along with the startling facts as listed below:

(1) The cost of losing a talented person in 2002/3 was between $200,000 and $250,000. (2) The end result of a bad recruitment was at least $300,000. (3) The operating cost of without a key player (technical person) even at a low level stood around $500,000 per annum.

The above findings establish the significance of employee engagement, retention and attracting quality employees. It also highlights the importance of managing such an important capital of business. It also justifies the rise of HR from the concept of personnel management to Human Resource Management (HRM) and subsequently to Strategic Human Resource Management (SHRM). Thus, the relationship between turnover and retention will be explored in this study.

ROLE OF HRM IN RETENTION

Since, this study wants to explore the possibility of finding a universally applicable retention solution through a concerted effort of the leadership and HRM, it will review the role of HRM in retention in detail.

Human Resource Management Practices

This is another important area that will be explored by this study. One of the few studies that examined the entire human resource system was conducted at Wells Fargo Bank using largely proprietary tools termed tools developed to guide and improve management, newly designed HR policies and procedures and a new performance appraisal process aligned with the Wells PACA (People as a Competitive Advantage). In this study, Lawson and Hepp (2000) reported that PACA tools (competency models used for team member selection, management, and development, a proprietary 360 degree feedback and development process, learning Fargo business system) and PACA management practices (workforce and business planning; competency based interviewing; leader-team member supervisory principles; identifying, developing, implementing development plans; and improving the frequency and quality of team member communication relative to organizational goals, objectives, and work related decisions) had a positive and significant impact on employee commitment, return on expenses (ROE), return on assets (ROA), and on the bank's efficiency ratio (ER). Karami, et al. (2004) too reported a positive relationship between core competencies and firm performance, company performance as well as product and service quality, HR effectiveness and the linkage between HR and business strategy, and HR involvement in the design and implementation of business strategies and organizational effectiveness.

These findings are consistent with other HR practice effects but also offer a direct and independent relationship between human resource practices and organizational outcomes suggesting that effective human resource decisions that drive leadership and management practices can help ensure a unique and sustainable competitive advantage.

ENGAGEMENT

Business process outsourcing is a booming industry in India. With the increase of so many BPO companies in the country, the attrition rate has increased many folds and companies have started loosing some of their treasured employees to their competitors. This situation is just a representation of the ongoing trends in the BPO industry. Such situations are been fueled by many factors, one of them being the lack of employee engagement.

What is Employee Engagement?

Institute for Employment Studies, UK defines employee engagement as "a positive attitude held by the employee towards the organization and its values." (Perryman & Hayday, 2004). Employees will feel engaged when they find motivation and personal meaning in their work, get positive interpersonal support and also operate in a work environment that is efficient (Bernthal, 2008; Seijits & Crim, 2006). Employers are highly engaged when they are performing roles that are non-job. Many employees have a sense of fairness even if they are treated unfairly in the work place and therefore many usually do their job role. However, employees' just coming to work and performing their roles does not bring long term competitiveness for the employer. This is because they can be hired by another employer and continues performing what they did for you (Welbourne, 2003).

Measuring Employment Engagement

To measure employee engagement, organizations need to get the opinions of the employees in different ways. Employees' opinion surveys can then be utilized to derive the standardized engagement metrics. This is in addition to the official and unofficial meetings, workers' focus groups, manager's interviews and finally the performance measures, instrumental in assessing the employees' engagement. As a part of measuring employee engagement, Gallup organization came up with questions directed to the employees. Such questions included what the employees expected in their work and whether their opinions at the work place seem to count (Workforce Management, 2011). By measuring employee engagement, the employer shows his or her employees that he or she needs their feedback and thus they feel more valued and respected. Measuring employee engagement gives the employers the insights into which factors influence employee's performance, satisfaction, loyalty and motivation (Inforsurvey, 2009; Neilly, 2008).

FINDING AND RETAINING TALENTS

Starting a culture in any organization is easy but what is hard is retaining it. One major factor in retaining business culture is by defining the culture that employer wants from the start and then integrate it in the hiring of the employees, treatment of the employees, customer service provision and the organization environment (Leberman, 2009). When talented people who can develop thinking and also challenge the status quo are lacking in a company, the growth ambitions of a company is hindered. If there are no programs to identify talent, strengthen the present leaders' capabilities and also increase the number of people in the leadership, the organization is likely to fail. This has made the recruitment of talents become the first priority for many companies even as competition between different firms continues increasing (Feldman, 2008; Guthridge *Et al*, 2008).

Promoting Employee Engagement

Engaging employees is crucial to satisfying and understanding the organization's customers (Castries, 2009). This has a measurable and direct impact on productivity, talent retention, financial results and customer satisfaction. When employees are listened to communication is enhanced and acting on their feedback improves effectiveness (DecisionWise, 2011). A research conducted by Gallup showed that when employees are engaged in an organization they become profitable, productive, safer, increased customer relationships, and stay longer in the company (Gallup, 2009). Promoting engagement among the employees is done by leveraging the three sources of influence for chance; that is leaders, employees as well as organizational strategies and systems. Organizations must be willing to tap into the workers' commitment, passion and their identification with the company (Wellins, 2009). This can also be done through building trust between the employees and open communication. Some of the factors that are employed to engage and retain employees include; a culture of respect, mentoring and feedback, professional and advancement development, appropriate reward, effective leadership, job expectations, tools to finish work responsibilities and finally, motivation (Greenberg, 2009; Elton 2007).

Factors Fostering Employee Engagement

(1) Team Work: Teamwork has been listed as an important aspect in an organization and should be provided by both the employees and the employer. This is unfortunately one of the aspects that are nearly non existent in the work environment of many companies (Binkley, 2007: Higgins, 2007). A team that is well knit is composed of competent individuals that care about one another deeply. They are committed to the mission of the organization, and also motivated to use their expertise and energy to achieve an objective that is common (Stowell, 2009). When an employer builds team work capacity, he or she will be in a position to get better production for the employees (Londrie, 2009). It is stated in the Centre for Management and Organization Effectiveness' (2011) website that teamwork may experience some difficult challenges. However, it can still be accomplished by having one direction, purpose and defined mission.

(2) Pleasant Working Conditions: A pleasant work environment is very instrumental in the motivation of employees as it influences originality and productivity. When the facilities are poor the employees would be demotivated (Tilley, 1992). Many employees would like working in organizations with pleasant working environment. They would be more productive if the relationship between themselves and also between them and the employer are bettered (Asmed, 2011).

(3) Considerate Treatment of Employees: Employers willing to retain their workers and attract other talented ones as well as improve employees engagement in the companies and their jobs must be ready to treat their workers with respect and dignity and also deal effectively with workers who are poor performers (Sircta Survey, 2006). If an employer engages with his or her employees and be ready to treat them well, then the latter will definitely make a difference for the organization (SAS Institute Inc., 2011).

(4) Growth Opportunities: Employees' anticipation that they would be promoted keeps their morale high and motivates them to work at their best level, as they are sure that opportunities will finally come (Prosales, 2004). A survey that was conducted by Robert Half International showed that talented and good employees quit jobs when advancement opportunities in an organization lacks. If employees who are ambitious do not foresee any growth potential of an organization, they are likely to quit for other organization.

(5) Flexible Working Practices: Flexible working refers to those working practices that are equally agreed between the employer and the employee covering the working hours, work patterns and locations. The benefits of flexible working include better health, less absenteeism, less stress, staff turnover, skill retention and better productivity (Graduate Prospects, 2009: Cooper, 2005). Flexible working practices include; part time working, term-time working, job sharing, flexitime, compressed hours, annual hours, working from home, compressed hours, annual hours, teleworking and career breaks (CIPD, 2011).

(6) Good Leadership and Management Practices: Leaders of an organization can engage their employees by; one, making sure that the latter feel valued. They should also communicate the organization's vision clearly and also provide meaningful and challenging work but with advancement opportunities. They should also be ready to appreciate what their workers do and provide feedback on the employees' functioning (Ambler, 2007; Yvette, 2009). The management should provide unambiguous direction on what constitutes good performance, in terms of character and performances and also promote the culture of accountability (Crawford, 2011).

CONCLUSION

It is clear that employee engagement involves the relationship between the employer and the conditions, teamwork, proper treatment of employees, increasing growth opportunities and flexible working practices. Employee engagement is very vital for the success of any organization as it enables it to find and retain its talented employees who may be an easy target by other similar organizations. This would be catastrophic to the organization because it would reduce its profitability and innovation.

Refernces

1. Ambler, G. (2007). The ten C's of employee engagement. Retrieved May, 2011, from: www.thepracticeofleadership.net/2007/02/27/the-ten-c%e2%80%99s-of-employeeengagement/
2. Asmed. (2011). Motivating by creating a pleasant working environment. Retrieved May, 2011, from: http://www.business.gov.vn/advice.aspx?id=215&LangType=1033
3. Bernthal, P. (2008). How effective are Surveys in Measuring employee engagement. Retrieved May, 2011, from: www.pracademy.co.uk/wp.../Example-assignment-IC-_CC_-extract.pdf

4. Binkley, S. (2007). The importance of teamwork in the work place. Retrieved May, 2011, from:www.associatedcontent.com/article/317564/the_importance_of_teamwork_in_the_workplace.html?cat=31
5. Castries, H. (2011). Promoting equal opportunities. Retrieved May, 2011, from: www.axa.com/en/responsibility/Employees/promoting-equal-opportunities/
6. Centre for Management and Organization Effectiveness. (2011). Teamwork in the workplace. Retrieved May, 2011, from: www.cmoe.com/team-work-in-the-workplace.htm
7. CIPD Website. (2011). Flexible Working. Retrieved May, 2011, from: www.cipd.co.uk/subjects/hrpract/flexibleworkingpractices/flexwkgfst.htm?IsSrchRes=1
8. Cooper, C. (2005). Flexible Working: The business case. Retrieved May, 2011, from: www.flexible working.co.uk/
9. Crawford, D. (2011). Employee engagement research. Retrieved May, 2011, from: www.agenda consulting.co.uk/download_file.php?file=ne_36_1_employee_engagement_research. pdf&cat=news
10. Workforce Management. (2011). 12 Questions to measure employee engagement. Retrieved May, 2011, from: www.workforce.com/section/hr-management/article/12-questions-measure-employee-engagement.html
11. DecisionWise. (2011). Employee Engagement: Engaging the organization. Retrieved May, 2011, from: www.decision-wise.com/employee-engagement/employee-engagement.html
12. Elton, C. (2007). The carrot principle: Engage, retain and drive employees. Retrieved May, 2011, from: www.enewsbuilder.net/chartenews/e_article000929855.cfm?x=b11,0,w
13. Feldman A.E. (2008). Hiring and retaining talent biggest concern for US firms. Retrieved May, 2011, from: www.blog.aefeldman.com/2008/04/18/hiring-and-retaining-talent-biggest-concern-for-us-firms/
14. Gallup Inc. (2009). Gallup study: Engaged employees inspire company innovation. Gallup Management Journal. Retrieved May, 2011, from: www.gmj.gallup.com/content/24880/Gallup-Study-Engaged-Employees-Inspire-Company.aspx
15. Graduate Prospects. (2009). Flexible working: What is it? Retrieved May, 2011, from: www.prospects.ac.uk/cms/ShowPage/Home_page/Flexible_working/What_is_it_/p!eXemkpa
16. Greenberg, J. (2009). Increasing employee retention through employee engagement. Retrieved May, 2011, from: www.ezinearticles.com/?Increasing-Employee-Retention-Through-Employee-Engagement&id=10575
17. Guthridge, M.ET all. (2008). Making talent a strategic priority. Retrieved May, 2011, from: www.managing peoplebook.com/WarForTalentNeverEnded.pdf
18. Higgins, S. (2007). Designing a great workplace. Retrieved May, 2011, from: www.trustedally.com/Designing%20a%20Great%20Workplace.pdf
19. Informsurvey. (2011). Measuring employee engagement. Retrieved May, 2011, from: www.infosurv.com/employee-engagement-survey.html
20. Lieberman, S. 2011. How to create and maintain the culture of your organization as you grow. Retrieved May, 2011, from: www.simmalieberman.com/articles/howtocreatemaintain.htm
21. Londrie, K. (2009). Team building in the work place. Retrieved May, 2011, from: www.ezinearticles.com?Team-Building-in-the-Work-Place&id=251179
22. Neilly, D. (2008). How to measure employ engagement. Retrieved May, 2011, from: www.employee engagement.ning.com/forum/topic/show?id=1986438%3ATopic%3A12847
23. Perryman & Hayday. (2004). The drivers of Employment. Retrieved May, 2011, from: www.employment-studies.co.uk/summary/summary.php?id=408
24. SAS Institute Inc. (2011). Working at SAS: An ideal environment for new ideas. Retrieved May, 2011, from: www.sas.com/jobs/corporate/index.html

25. Seijits, H. & Dan Crim. (2006). "The Ten C's of employee engagement." Ivey Business Journal.
26. Sirota Survey Intelligence. (2006). Two ways to improve employee retention and engagement. Retrieved May, 2011, from: www.sirota.com/pdfs/Two_Ways_To_Improve_Employee_Retention_Engagement.pdf
27. Stowell, C. (2009). Teamwork in the workplace. A definition. Retrieved May, 2011, from: www.ezinearticles.com/?Teamwork-in-the-Workplace:-A-Definition&id=47798
28. Tilley, C. (1992). Working conditions. Dicestar Ltd. Retrieved May, 2011, from: www.faqs.org/abstracts/Travel-industry/Rewards-Work-conditions.html
29. Welbourne, T. (2003). Employee engagement: Doing it vs. measuring. Retrieved May, 2011, from: http://www.eepulse.com/documents/pdfs/HR.com-9-8-03.pdf
30. Wellins, R.ET all. (2009). Employee engagement: The key to realizing competitive advantage. Retrieved May, 2011, from: http://www.ddiworld.com/DDIWorld/media/monographs/employeeengagement_ mg_ddi.pdf?ext=.pdf
31. Vyette, M. (2009). The art appreciating your employees. Retrieved May, 2011, from: hubpages.com/hub/employeeappreciation
32. Cherrington, David J. (1995). The Management of Human Resources. Englewood Cliffs, NJ:Prentice-Hall.
33. Mondy, R. Wayne, and Noe, Robert M. (1996). Human Resource Management. Upper Saddle River, NJ: Prentice-Hall.
34. Nadler, Leonard, and Wiggs, Garland D. (1986). Managing Human Resource Development. San Francisco: Jossey-Bass.

❖❖❖